The Russia File

Russia and the West in an Unordered World

Daniel S. Hamilton and Stefan Meister
Editors

Center for Transatlantic Relations
The Paul H. Nitze School of Advanced International Studies
Johns Hopkins University

German Council on Foreign Relations/
Deutsche Gesellschaft für Auswärtige Politik

Daniel S. Hamilton and Stefan Meister, eds., *The Russia File: Russia and the West in an Unordered World*

Washington, DC: Center for Transatlantic Relations, 2017.
© Center for Transatlantic Relations, 2017

Center for Transatlantic Relations
The Paul H. Nitze School of Advanced International Studies
The Johns Hopkins University
1717 Massachusetts Ave., NW, 8th Floor
Washington, DC 20036
Tel: (202) 663-5880
Fax: (202) 663-5879
Email: transatlantic@jhu.edu
http://transatlantic.sais-jhu.edu

Deutsche Gesellschaft für Auswärtige Politik DGAP
German Council on Foreign Relations
Rauchstraße 17-18, D-10787 Berlin
Tel: +49 (0)30 25 42 31-0
Fax: +49 (0)30 25 42 31-16
Email: info@dgap.org

Funded by the
Robert Bosch **Stiftung**

ISBN: 978-1-947661-03-5

Contents

Preface and Acknowledgements v

Introduction vii
    The Russia File: Russia and the West in an Unordered World
    Daniel S. Hamilton and Stefan Meister

Chapter 1 1
    Russia's Changing Relations with the West:
    Prospects for a New Hybrid System
    Andrey Kortunov

Chapter 2 19
    Fuzzy Alliances, Flexible Relations
    Fyodor Lukyanov

Chapter 3 31
    Can Ukraine Change Russia?
    Vladislav Inozemtsev

Chapter 4 47
    Russia, the West, and Eastern Europe
    Lyubov Shishelina

Chapter 5 63
    Russia and the West: Energy Warfare
    Mikhail Krutikhin

Chapter 6 81
    The Worst Friends: EU-Russian Economic Relations
    at a Time of Hostility
    Andrey Movchan

Chapter 7 101
    Russian Foreign Policy in the Middle East:
    New Challenge for Western Interests?
    Nikolay Kozhanov

Chapter 8 127
    Russian and Western Engagement in the Broader Middle East
    Mark N. Katz

Chapter 9 137
  Sino-Russian Relations and Transatlantic Ties
  Richard Weitz

Chapter 10 149
  Russia-China Relations and the West
  Marcin Kaczmarski

Chapter 11 169
  The Struggle for the Hearts and Minds of Russians
  András Simonyi

About the Authors 179

Preface and Acknowledgements

Dramatic developments across Europe's east are testing fundamental assumptions that have guided Western policies over the past quarter century. At the same time, the United States, western and central Europe have been distracted by a range of home-grown challenges and dangers from other parts of the world, and have been divided over proper approaches to the vast and turbulent space of Europe that is not integrated into the EU and NATO. With this in mind, our two institutions, together with our partner, the Robert Bosch Stiftung, are engaged in an ongoing effort to bring together leading analysts and decision-makers from the United States, Russia, eastern and western Europe to address these new dynamics.

In the first phase of our project we sought to build Western awareness, understanding and, where possible, renewed Western consensus on Eastern policy. We engaged senior officials, regional experts, scholars, foreign policy strategists and other opinion leaders in a Transatlantic Strategy Group as well as in a series of consultations in Kyiv, Moscow, Berlin and Washington, DC. Eminent authors were asked to contribute their perspectives, which resulted in our book *The Eastern Question: Russia, the West, and Europe's Grey Zone*.

In the second phase of our project, we turned to east European scholars and opinion leaders for their perspectives on challenges facing their countries and the region as a whole, including their views on the role of the United States, the EU and NATO, and their expectations of western and central European countries in this part of the world. We featured their views in a second volume, appropriately entitled *Eastern Voices*.

In the third phase of our effort we engaged on the issues with Russian, American and European experts at meetings in Moscow, Berlin and Washington, DC. We asked a diverse range of Russian interlocutors and experts on Russia for their perspectives, which we feature in this companion volume, *The Russia File: Russia and the West in an Unordered World*. We want to thank Andrey Kortunov and his colleagues at the Russian Council on Foreign Relations (RIAC) for their hospitality in Moscow and for our open and frank discussions.

We are particularly grateful to the Robert Bosch Stiftung for its support of our efforts, its continued commitment to transatlantic partnership, and its sustained engagement with eastern Europe and with Russia.

We would also like to thank our colleagues Juulia Barthel, Hans Binnendijk, David Cadier, Britta Gade, Michael Haltzel, Vladislav Inozemtsev, Jason Moyer, Heidi Obermeyer and Andras Simonyi.

The views expressed are those of the authors, and do not necessarily reflect those of any institution or government.

Daniel S. Hamilton
Stefan Meister

Introduction

The Russia File:
Russia and the West in an Unordered World

Daniel S. Hamilton and Stefan Meister

"What to do about Russia" is a matter of almost daily debate among Europeans and Americans. Few of those debates directly include Russian views on contemporary challenges. To offer some perspective, we asked a diverse range of authors from Russia, as well as non-Russian experts on Russia, to present Russian views on relations with Western countries. This volume is the result.

In a nutshell, these essays—written from wide and often contradictory points of view—tell us that Russia and the West are stuck. Experts and officials from each side are talking past each other, their views rooted in different perceptions and oriented to different interests and goals. An initial conclusion we can draw is that for today, and for the foreseeable future, the key question is not how both sides might develop a cooperative relationship or strike a new modus vivendi, but whether, and to what degree, they can peacefully coexist.

Our Russian authors are very clear on this. Despite their different vantage points, they believe the Russian leadership sees the West more as a faltering competitor than as a partner. While it may be crucial to agree on some terms for ongoing relations, a substantial improvement is not to be expected. Andrey Kortunov argues in his chapter that any significant change in current relations is likely to be a long, slow, and gradual process. He argues that the Kremlin currently has little reason to rethink its fundamental approaches to the West. For Moscow, the current status quo is not just acceptable, it is preferable to potentially risky changes that could disrupt the position of Russian President Vladimir Putin, who for the moment feels he is on the "right side of history."

During the quarter century since the end of the Cold War, the paradigm prevailing in the West was of a robust, largely unchallenged, and gradually expanding Western-led order, in which a reformed Russia could potentially find a place. Discordant Russian views were often discounted or ignored. Today, as Russia challenges that order, this post-Cold War framework seems to have become a paradigm lost. What our Russian authors make clear is that Russia has not somehow gotten lost in transition, it is going its own way. Fyodor Lukyanov asserts that Moscow is intent on establishing (or, in the mindset of the Kremlin, re-restablishing) itself as one of the critical poles in a multipolar world, in which great powers determine the rules of the road. Lukyanov posits that on this basis the Kremlin would be ready to negotiate the terms of a new global order, but that the West is still so focused on defending the old, and in his view, crumbling, post-Cold War order that it is unable, or unprepared, to discuss a very different model of relations.

Russia's new assertiveness comes at a moment when the West itself is more fluid and fractured than at any time over the past quarter century. Revisionist powers such as Russia and China have enhanced their critique of the prevailing Western-led order just as Western defenders of that order either seem exhausted or are fighting revisionists within their own ranks who are questioning the elite bargains and social underpinnings that have sustained that order. In fact, the most unpredictable actor in this complicated equation, surprisingly, has turned out to be the ultimate steward and guardian of Western-led order, the United States.

Under Donald Trump, the United States is engaged in a selective burden-shedding exercise of potentially global scope, with uncertain ramifications for Europe and for relations with Russia. Although U.S.-Russian ties are arguably the worst since before the Gorbachev era, president Trump has been reluctant to criticize Moscow and has hinted at possible deals that could put the relationship on an entirely different footing—perhaps at the expense of smaller countries or of U.S. alliance commitments. He has thus far been constrained, however, by the U.S. Congress, including most members of his own Republican party, as well as by ongoing investigations into possible collusion with Russia during the 2016 presidential campaign, and by members of his own cabinet, who have been far more outspoken in voicing U.S. objections to Russia's annexation of Crimea, its military intervention in eastern Ukraine, its activities in Syria and Afghanistan, its interference in U.S. and European elections, and Russian deployments that threaten to undo the 1987 Treaty on Intermediate-Range Nuclear Forces in Europe.

The new political constellation in the United States has unnerved its European allies, who have themselves been challenged by a conflation of crises. The European Union (EU) has been suffering through a decade-long crisis of confidence, generated by a series of shocks, ranging from the financial crisis and disruption within the eurozone to Russia's military interventions in neighboring countries, unprecedented migration flows and the decision of the United Kingdom to leave the EU.

These crises have forced some unpleasant realities. The financial crisis and subsequent eurozone uncertainties have generated considerable economic anxiety and discontent, strained intra-EU solidarity and eroded trust in European elites and EU institutions. The Brexit vote has made it clear that European integration is neither inevitable nor irreversible. Russian aggression, migration inflows, and Trump's demands that Europeans pay a fairer share for their defense signaled that Europe may not be as peaceful and secure as many had thought.

Under the Kremlin's zero-sum logic, troubles within the West not only offer potential gains to Russia, they can be exploited. Yet over the past two years, the Russian leadership has miscalculated in three areas. First, it expected an improvement of relations with Washington under Trump. Second, the Kremlin anticipated—and even sought directly to engineer—political changes via elections in the Netherlands, France and Germany, where right wing populists had the potential to win a considerable number of voters. Third, many Russian elites expected that the Ukrainian state would soon collapse, because for them Ukraine is not really an entity that can survive on its own.

In each of these three areas, Russia deployed assets to facilitate these outcomes. Yet each of these expectations went unfulfilled. Trump is blocked at home. The Front National failed to win French parliamentary or presidential elections. Right wing populists failed to register big successes in the Netherlands. While the right-wing Alternative for Germany (AfD) has emerged as the largest opposition in the German parliament, mainstream parties—and mainstream policies towards Russia—continue to prevail in Germany. Despite Ukraine's many challenges, on balance the country has proven to be more resilient than many Russian observers had come to believe, in part because of its active civil society and in part because of the consolidation of Ukrainian identity as a result of Russian agression. Furthermore, despite the host of irritating issues currently bedeveling transatlantic relations, there is notable continuity in Western approaches to Ukraine, forward deployment of allied forces to eastern NATO allies, and heightened defense spending all across the Alliance.

Andrey Kortunov argues that this new consolidation of the West is still very fragile and not irreversible. The debate about the future of transatlantic relations has only just begun, and the course of U.S. foreign policy under Trump remains an open question. Yet recent European rhetoric about "strategic autonomy" has yet to be given any real substance, despite EU efforts to develop a more robust defense identity. And in terms of ultimate security gurantees, NATO and the United States will remain indispensible for a long time to come.

What is telling about our authors' perspectives is that despite Russian emphasis on a multipolar world, the United States, and the West more broadly, remain the primary reference points by which the Kremlin assesses its own actions and options. In the end, Vladimir Putin reacts first to what the West is doing or, increasingly, not doing. To the extent that Russia can speak of strengths, they appear to be based on Putin's political will and tactical ability to capitalize on Western divisions or diminished engagement than on strong and sustainable Russian resources or bold strategic vision. This influenced Moscow's decision to intervene in Syria, as well as Russia's rapprochement with, and concessions towards, China.

Russia is still more a spoiler than a security provider. But the less active the West is in regional conflicts such as in the Middle East, the more able Russia is to step into the breach. Mark N. Katz argues that Russia and the West are doomed to cooperate on the Middle East; lack of cooperation will only excerbate ongoing problems. Russia has shown with regard to Syria or Iran, for instance, that it is not only a spoiler, but also increasingly a mediator in conflicts. Nikolay Kozhanov argues that Russia can add value because it is among only a few countries that have sustained positive relations with Iran, Turkey, Syria, Saudi Arabia, Egypt and Israel. He argues that more active involvment of Russia in the Middle East should not be considered automatically as a threat to U.S. and EU interests, but also as an opportunity, even if Moscow's resources are limited. According to Kozhanov, there are several areas where Russia's interests converge with those of the West, including ensuring the viability of non-proliferation regimes in the Middle East, stabilization of Iraq and Yemen, and countering the spread of jihadism. He points to Russia's positive role in securing an effective dialogue, and ultimately a nuclear deal, between Iran and the West. In this regard, Donald Trump's questioning of the Iran deal raises alarm bells in Moscow as well as EU capitals. For Russia, abrogation of the deal risks destroying fragile balances of power in the region, because several Middle Eastern regimes could consider joining the nuclear club. This cooperative approach has its limits, however, for instance when Russian authorities believe that they can exercise additional pressure on the United States and the EU via their contacts with Middle East pariah states.

Marcin Kaczmarski asserts that Russia's cooperation with China remains an important element of Moscow's policy towards the West. Moscow's closer ties with Beijing, he argues, prevented the West from isolating Russia, and enabled the Kremlin to compensate in part for economic losses, following its interventions in Ukraine. This weakend Moscow's bargaining position towards China, however, and prompted the Russian leadership to make concessions, for instance, on oil and gas prices.

While Western influence on Russian-Chinese relations is rather limited, Richard Weitz argues that growing ties between Moscow and Beijing have not given either any leverage over Europe or the United States. The West can, howver, exploit differences between Russia and China with regard to economic globalization. Kaczmarski asserts that Beijing is more cooperative than Moscow when it comes to global economic governance. Because Beijing has benefitted more than Moscow from the existing order, it is more inclined to shape it than to challenge it. This might lead the United States and the European Union to conclude that at the margin they could have greater influence over Russo-Chinese ties by leveraging China's interest in international stability and the economic gains it receives from a open economy than by seeking to influence Russian approaches to China.

Can Russia sustain its global activism? In the end, as Kortunov acknowledges, Russia's foreign policy will be defined by its economic and social development trajectory. And the current model is running into serious challenges, including stagnating oil and gas prices.

Despite Western sanctions imposed on Russia following its intervention in Ukraine, both trade and energy exports to the EU grew in 2017. Neither side has an interest in undermining mutually beneficial economic and energy relations. But here again changes under way in global energy markets, and in the energy mix of EU-member states, are likely to have a long-term impact. Andrey Movchan argues that while commercial relations between the EU and Russia will remain stable for many years, their scale will diminish. He expects a gradual decline of Russian oil and most likely gas exports to the EU, due to changes in the nature of EU energy consumption. Russian imports from the EU will also fall, however, simply because a stagnant Russian economy, and perhaps even economic recession, will lead to shrinking exports and limit Russia's ability to buy abroad.

Because Russia is unlikely to diversify its economy and is even less inclined to open itself up to the global economy, Movchan argues that over the next decade or so the EU is likely to become much less energy dependent on Russia and Russia much less reliant on Europe in the financial, industrial and infrastructural spheres. While this decoupling will not lead to complete isolation, it will change the foundations of the relationship.

Schto delat'?

Vladislav Inozemtsev is very pessimistic when it comes to potential changes in Russian politics or any possible impact of Western politics on Russian society. While he argues that the EU should do what it can to help Ukraine transform successfully into a prosperous and democratic European nation, he disagrees with those who believe Ukrainian reforms will ripple into Russia. While successful Ukrainian reforms would inoculate the country from reintegration into the Russian empire, for Russian elites and society integration into Europe means abandoning Russia's imperial past and global ambitions. For these reasons, Inozemtsev asserts, Russia will not follow Ukraine on a path to Europe, and could in fact become even more conservative and aggressive if Kyiv succeeds. Lyubov Shishelina offers a counter narrative. She argues that the only real way to overcome the conflict over the grey zone of eastern Europe is for both sides to return to, and reinvent, the so-called four common spaces between Russia and the EU.[1] Whether, and when, either side might be prepared to reestablish such a framework, given current difficulties, remain open questions.

Mikhail Krutikhin argues against any grand bargains or punish-the-aggressor strategies, and favors instead a wait-and see approach. He suggests that the West should simply monitor the situation in Russia and resist the temptation to interfere. This would minimize any negative Russian reactions that could be damaging to Western interests. The most effective way to punish Putin, he argues, is through indifference. Don't take him very seriously and don't overreact to his statements or actions. This could be an effective approach, he argues, especially if combined with a containment strategy that essentially lets Russia's deteriorating economic

---

[1] In May 2003 the EU and Russia agreed to reinforce cooperation with a view to creating four EU/Russia common spaces covering economic issues and the environment; issues of freedom, security and justice; external security, including crisis management and non-proliferation; and research and education, including cultural aspects. See European Commission, "EU/Russia: The four "common spaces"," MEMO/04/268 Brussels, 23 November 2004.

and social situation worsen until it reaches a tipping point that would provoke internal change. Krutikhin's strategy harkens back to George Kennan's original conception of containment, or in current parlance, "strategic patience." To support his argument, Krutikhin draws on lessons from international energy company negotiations. These cases demonstrate that the Russian leadership does not take compromise or appeasement seriously, but respects firmness that is based on strength and reinforced by strong personal relations.

Nikolay Kozhanov underscores the importance of maintaining communication channels, even at difficult times. Building trust is the foundation of any improvement in relations, he argues. This will take time. Moscow wants to be heard and respected. If it is isolated, it can become an even more unpredictable troublemaker. At the same time, Kozhanov reinforces Krutikhin's point that the West needs to be able to defend its red lines. Putin and his team respect strong counterparts and ignore the weak.

Russia can definitely survive without the West, argues Andrey Kortunov. But given the structure of its economy, it will only prosper if commodity prices rise. The alternative is stagnation. What this might mean for Russia, in turn, depends on how other countries address globalization and economic change. If the international system evolves in the direction of nativism, protectionism and a negotiated balance of interests among great powers, together with an erosion of international institutions and international law, survival would be the main game in town, according to Kortunov, and understanding national survival in terms of security rather than societal development is something Russia and its leadership are good at. If, on the other hand, the United States and the European Union invigorate their economies and civilize their politics, and if China becomes a main driver of development in the world, the trendlines would be different, and the pressures on Russia to reform, correspondingly, would be greater.

Kortunov proposes three horizons for relations between Russia and the West in an uncertain enviroment. The first is de-escalation, which must include a stable cease-fire in Donbas, more moderate rhetoric on both sides, a truce in the information war and the reestablishment of political and military contacts at all levels. The second is stabilization with a more general stettlement of Ukraine, gradual lifting of sanctions and countersanctions, confidence-building measures, and cooperation in areas of mutual concern, including limitations on military deployment. Third is the reinvention of the concept of a Greater Europe that includes Russia and the EU, and that can involve a common economic space. But this is a rather optimistic long-term vision, given the current state of affairs.

Indeed, for the foreseeable future, moving Russia from spoiler to stakeholder seems to be a difficult proposition. This is not a moment for resets or grand bargains. The more relevant analogy is less architecture than art. The structured frameworks of the post-Cold War—and even the Cold War—have given way to a much more fluid landscape, less akin to a grand edifice than a Calder mobile.

Mobiles tend to spin less when their anchors are sturdy and winds are mild. That suggests a return to basics. In this regard, András Simonyi argues for the reinvention of the West. The best way the United States and its European partners can act together vis-a-vis Russia is by getting their respective acts together within their own respective domestic systems. While our Russian authors may disagree with Simonyi's prescriptions, a number do agree that Putin's challenge is as much about the West as it is about Russia.

In that regard, Simonyi also argues for a shift of our communication away from president Putin. He argues that the West must define a more relevant democratic message for the 21st century, and use that message to reconnect and engage fully with the Russian people. The West should not only blame Vladimir Putin for the deterioration in relations, it should look to itself. Western actors have largely ignored what is going on in Russia and disconnected from Russian society. They should engage as robustly as possible with the Russian people, including with alternative elites, civil society, media and opposition figures, as well as opportunities for student and professional exchanges and visa-free travel. Such initiatives will be difficult as Moscow seeks to isolate its people from Western non-governmental organizations. But Russia is not the semi-autarkic Soviet Union. It is integrated in many ways in the global economy, and the digital age offers many points of access to Russian society.

Vladislav Inozemtsev would answer that Russian politics is dominated less by Vladimir Putin than by a long history of antidemocratic and quasi-despotic rule that no leadership and society can reverse within 30 years. But both authors agree that it is crucial to stay firm, defend your credibilty, and stick to your values. This task, whether in Russia or in the West, starts at home.

Chapter 1

Russia's Changing Relations with the West: Prospects for a New Hybrid System

Andrey Kortunov

At the end of 2016, both the political and expert communities in Russia appeared to be very pessimistic about the future of the world order in general, and the about the future of the West in particular. Indeed, the year had turned out to be an *annus horribilis* in many ways; numerous doomsday prophets referred to various harbingers of the looming cataclysms. They mentioned the United Kingdom's decision to leave the European Union and the victory of a non-system candidate in the U.S. presidential election. They highlighted the nearly global rise of right-wing populism and anti-globalism to a level that was unprecedented in recent decades. They talked about the wave of migration that was threatening to consume Europe. They pointed to the impotence of international organizations in the face of multiplying regional conflicts, and they noted a widespread decline in public confidence in practically all institutions of power.[1]

These apocalyptic visions were, of course, somewhat self-serving. Notwithstanding all its problems, in 2016 Moscow demonstrated a lot of political, economic and social stability amidst this global turmoil. Inflation was put under control, devaluation of the national currency was stopped and even reversed, Western economic sanctions failed to bring Russia to its knees, and the parliamentary elections in September resulted in a predictable triumphant victory for the Kremlin's United Russia Party. Political and economic risks in the coming year 2017 appeared to be relatively low and manageable. Technocrats in the government and in the presidential administration had reasons to be proud of their performance: the Russian system turned out to be more adaptive and flexible than its in-house and foreign critics had maintained.

---

[1] As an example, see a Valdai Club Report of February 2017 by Oleg Barabanov, Timofey Bordachev, Fyodor Lukyanov, Andrey Sushentsov, Dmitry Suslov, and Ivan Timofeev "Global revolt and global order: the revolutionary situation in condition of the world and what to do about it," available at http://valdaiclub.com/files/13306/.

The notion of stability as the supreme value was back in circulation and used widely in both domestic and international propaganda. Even if Russia's stability looked more and more like the stagnation of the late Soviet period, stagnation still appeared to be a preferable alternative to the West's disorder and commotion. Not surprisingly, the greatest portion of gloomy and even apocalyptic prophesies of Russian pundits had to do with the fate of the European Union. In 2014–2016, the EU found itself in a perfect storm that revealed the frightening fragility and obvious obsolescence of many of its fundamental political, financial, economic, institutional and even spiritual foundations. Russia's problems appeared much less dramatic against the background of the EU seemingly sinking into chaos, and the apparent hopelessness of the "European project."[2]

Subsequent developments in Europe, however, demonstrated that the European Union had not lost its resilience and its cohesion. In this chapter, I argue that in 2017 Russian foreign policy started a painful process of reassessing its previous assumptions about the EU and its midterm prospects. This reassessment ran parallel to a growing disappointment in the ability of the Trump Administration in the United States to change the negative momentum in the U.S.-Russian relationship or to pursue a consistent foreign policy in general. One can foresee these changes in the Russian approach to the West continuing in 2018 and beyond.

Engagement Can Wait

The expectation (and, for some, the eager anticipation) of the inevitable collapse of the current world order influenced Russia's foreign policy and relevant discussions, particularly in late 2016 and early 2017. Indeed, what sense did it make to invest effort, energy and political capital in difficult negotiations with leaders whose days were numbered anyway? Would it be reasonable to keep following rules of the game that had been accepted way back when if these same rules would be rewritten very soon? Was it worth agreeing to concessions and uncomfortable compromises if a new post-Western world was about to arrive? Would it not be wiser to wait it out and observe from a safe distance the epic demise of the old era, which had formed at the turn of the century?

---

[2] Стратегия для России. Российская внешняя политика: конец 2010-х—начало 2020-х годов. Совет по внешней и оборонной политике, Москва, 2016 (http://svop.ru/wp-content/uploads/2016/05/тезисы_23мая_sm.pdf).

Russian foreign policy at that juncture seemed to follow a wait-and-see approach, abstaining from any far-reaching proposals, not to mention potential concessions to Western partners or recondition of Russia's past mistakes. The last visible attempt to set Russia-EU relations into motion was the occasion of EU Commission President Jean-Claude Juncker's visit to Russia for the St. Petersburg International Economic Forum on June 16, 2016. President Vladimir Putin handed to his guest a list of specific proposals on restoring Moscow's relations with Brussels. The EU, however, never reacted to the Russian list. Instead, the Kremlin had to live with the five principles of Federica Mogherini, only one of which (selective engagement with Russia on foreign policy issues vital to the EU) could be interpreted as a promise of limited cooperation in the future, but even this principle was deliberately vague and ambiguous.

A similar last-minute pitch failed in relations with the Obama Administration. On September 10th, 2016 in Geneva, after long and exhausting talks, John Kerry and Sergey Lavrov announced a tentative ceasefire deal for Syria. They also stated that this deal was to lead the way to a joint U.S.-Russian air campaign against ISIS and other extremist groups and new negotiations on the country's political future.

This hope—to use Syria as an opportunity to limit the damage in Russian-American relations caused by the Ukrainian crisis—did not last very long. The painfully negotiated Kerry-Lavrov peace plan collapsed just a few weeks after signing. The Russian side accused the United States of failing to exercise the needed pressure on the select groups of the anti-Assad opposition to make them abide by the terms of the ceasefire agreement—a task that was arguably too big for Washington to handle successfully. Russians also complained that the United States had not been able to separate the moderate Syrian opposition from more radical factions gravitating to ISIS and al-Qaeda. Again, it remains unclear whether the United States was in a position to arrange such a separation. However, the main source of the Kremlin's frustrations was the perceived unwillingness of the U.S. military to work in any substantive way with its Russian counterparts. In the fall of 2016 in Moscow, it became popular to argue that the Pentagon had managed to overrule the State Department, and that the hawkish views or Ash Carter had prevailed over the more moderate positions of John Kerry.

It seems that these failures to engage Europe and the United States, as well as the perception that the West was entering a long-term period of disarray and decline, led to a serious reassessment of Russian foreign policy priorities. Syria serves as an example of this reassessment. After the unsuccessful attempt to create a Russian-U.S. alliance, the Kremlin focused its energy and diplomatic skills on building a coalition of regional players through the Astana de-escalation process. Bringing Turkey and Iran to the negotiating table was an unquestionable diplomatic victory for Vladimir Putin, and the Kremlin worked hard to get major Arab countries interested in this new arrangement. The invitation was also extended to the United States, but U.S. participation was no longer considered critical for the success of Russia's Syrian strategy.

Taking all of Russia's internal problems and restraints into account, in 2016 Moscow appeared to have one undeniable advantage over the West: a more considerable reserve of time. Russia's ailments, extremely serious as they are, are chronic and sometimes even dormant in nature: they have matured over years if not decades. The problems of the West, meanwhile, went from dormant to acute within a single year in 2016, and international experts started talking about the possibility of a fatal outcome. At any rate, the Kremlin had reasons to believe that in any possible confrontation scenario, Moscow would be able to outperform Western capitals, precisely because it had more time on its hands. The nature of the Russian political system, the high level of political mobilization and social consensus reached after the crisis of 2014, the marginalization of the domestic opposition and the relatively stable performance of the Russian economy—all these factors made the Russian leadership confident that it would not encounter major problems during, or following, the presidential elections of 2018.

Finally, the election of Donald Trump as the 45th President of the United States raised hopes in Moscow that Russia would be in a position to cut a deal with Washington above the heads of European capitals. Some of the election campaign statements by the new President sounded very encouraging; they apparently reflected a worldview and a set of foreign policy principles not very different from these of President Vladimir Putin. Though some Russian experts on the United States cautioned against too high expectations about possible change in U.S. foreign policy, the mood in Moscow on the eve of 2017 was largely optimistic. Only the pro-Western liberal minority was looking to the future with concerns and fear. This cohort of Russian intellectuals suspected that any further deepening of the crisis in the West would become a significant boost to authoritarian political trends inside Russia; the crisis and the growing impotency of the West could also create temptations for a more adventurist and risk-taking Kremlin foreign policy.

No Revolution This Week

Looking back to the "Trumpomania" of late 2016—early 2017, today many in Russia have turned from enthusiasm to fatalism. The common view in Moscow is that Trump had been overrated, that U.S.-Russian relations did not have a chance, that the Deep State is simply too powerful for any President to turn around, and that the U.S. establishment is genetically Russo-phobic. The logical conclusion is that in 2017, Russia could have done nothing and can do nothing today to change the momentum of the relationship. We now have to sit on our hands waiting for some shifts in U.S. politics. This is not a very optimistic view. However, was it really the case? Could we speculate about an alternative track of the relationship if Moscow had taken a different, more proactive approach, beginning in January 2017?

The inertia of negative trends in Russian-U.S. relations in early 2017 was very powerful and hard to stop. Policies toward Moscow became an important component of U.S. domestic politics and President Trump was significantly constrained in what he could offer his counterpart in the Kremlin. However, in my view, Russian policy made a few tactical mistakes that closed the door to even limited progress in the bilateral relationship during the first few months of the new Administration.

First, the political fallout of the alleged Russia's interference into the U.S. presidential election of 2016 was grossly underestimated in Moscow. Instead of demonstrating its understanding of American concerns—no matter how grounded and justified these concerns looked from the Russian side—and offering full cooperation in investigating the hackers' case, the Russian leadership took a very condescending and dismissive position in this matter. "This isn't for us to get into; these are your domestic political squabbles. Therefore, you deal with them. Nothing to talk about,"[3] was how President Putin responded to Megyn Kelly's question about hackers at the St. Petersburg International Economic Forum in early June. This dismissive attitude played a significant role in consolidating the anti-Russian consensus in America. Two month later the U.S. Congress almost unanimously approved a new far-reaching sanctions package against Russia.

Second, it its attempts to reach out to the United States, the Russian leadership targeted exclusively the new Administration, instead of sending

---

[3] http://en.kremlin.ru/events/president/news/54688.

meaningful signals to the U.S. public at large, including its representatives in the U.S. Congress. For instance, Moscow could have announced the abolition of the notorious Dima Yakovlev Law that banned adoption of Russian orphans by U.S. citizens. It could have demonstrated its good will by reconsidering the list of U.S. undesirable organizations that had been kicked out of Russia during the last years of the Obama Administration. It could have restarted a number of frozen U.S.-Russian exchange programs in education and civil society (the FLEX program being one of the most evident options). Unfortunately, none of these evident steps was made—probably because the Kremlin did not consider U.S. public opinion to be an important factor in shaping the Trump Administration's foreign policy.

Finally, to the extent we can judge the initial Russian proposals to the new U.S. Administration, which allegedly were submitted to the White House in late March-early April 2017, they were limited primarily to restoring communications in three areas. Moscow offered to resume political dialogue, contacts between top U.S. and Russian military officials and information exchange between intelligence agencies of the two countries. Nothing suggests that these proposals contained any substantive ideas or demonstrated any new flexibility in Kremlin positions on matters like Syria or Ukraine. There was nothing in the proposals that would give the Trump Administration the prospect of an early and spectacular foreign policy success.

In 2017 it became evident that not only had the Trump Administration inherited the U.S.-Russian crisis from its predecessors, this coincided with what was arguably the most profound political crisis in the United States since Watergate. What was more, America had also entered a social crisis that went way beyond the Washington, DC Beltway and had the potential to affect the whole of American society. The hope that Donald Trump could be a strong president capable of restoring the shaken unity of the American people did not pan out, while the polarization of different political and social groups increased throughout most of 2017. The White House became significantly restricted in its ability to conduct a consistent foreign policy, not to mention implement any long-term strategy.

At the same time, the developments of 2017 suggest that the decline of the old era in Europe has been postponed, if not cancelled outright. The populist Eurosceptics failed in the Dutch and French elections, and the German election reaffirmed the continuity of Berlin's European strategy. Notwithstanding all of Brexit's negative implications, it actually resulted in the European idea gaining more popular support within the EU's 27 remaining member states, and it became unlikely that any would follow suit any time soon. The migration crisis was not completely resolved, but in 2017 it no longer appeared as dramatic as it did in 2016 and especially in 2015. The euro did not crash, and no eurozone nations were thrown out.

It seems that Moscow was late to accept the important change of the curve in European developments and to change its tactics, if not strategy, towards Europe. Otherwise, it is hard to understand, for example, why Vladimir Putin chose to greet personally French far-right presidential candidate Marine Le Pen at the Kremlin in March and why the Russian mainstream media were so critical, if not hostile, to Emmanuel Macron literally until the day of the second round of the French presidential elections. To be fair to the Kremlin, it demonstrated a much more prudent approach to the parliamentary elections in Germany in September. On the other hand, one can argue that there was a fundamental difference between the French and German election cycles of 2017: in France, three of four presidential candidate argued for a more accommodative EU policy toward Russia, including possible change to the regime of sanctions; in Germany no mainstream political party contemplated such a change.

The Resilience of the West

It would appear that the United States and Europe followed opposite courses in 2017: while Brussels was beginning to react to its systemic problems, albeit slowly and falteringly, Washington only watched its problems grow. On the other hand, these processes in Europe and North America, which might seem incompatible through the prism of global politics, essentially reflected in different ways the same fundamental meaning of 2017. The Western world as a whole demonstrated more ability to adjust, more resistance to destabilizing factors, and more resilience than anyone could have credited it with in late 2016. It would probably be an overstatement to label 2017 as *annus mirabilis*, but it was definitely not as bad as 2016, and it countered some of the most pessimistic views on the inevitability of Western decline.

It is true that after Trump became president, disputes intensified within NATO as to how the burden of defense expenses should be distributed within the Alliance. However, the May 2017 NATO summit in Brussels did not prove catastrophic, and any attempts to write NATO off appear to be very much premature. It is also true that the Transatlantic Trade and Investment Partnership project is no more, but this has not resulted in heated trade wars between Europe and North America, nor will such conflicts break out in the future. Washington has left the Paris climate accord, but the major part of American business and society continue to observe the letter and spirit of that agreement.

This does not mean that 2017 resolved the postmodernist crisis in international relations: the fundamental problems of the modern global political system did not disappear in 2017, and the system will still have to change one way or another. However, we can now see that postmodernism is characterized by a good share of momentum and will continue to fight against advancing traditionalist forces for years to come. Therefore, current changes will most likely be characterized by a protracted evolution rather than a swift revolution; they will take years and even decades to complete. This process will have its ups and downs, speedups and slowdowns. However, it is unlikely that historians of the future, let alone contemporaries, will be able to pinpoint the moment when global politics transitioned from one qualitative state to the next. Speaking specifically of 2017, one can conclude that this period was dominated by restorative trends rather than by revolutionary ones.

What does this all mean for Russia? First and foremost, in 2017 decision-makers in the Kremlin should have cast away all illusions that Russia's problems with the West would disappear on the back of the radical changes taking place within the West itself. The assumption that Moscow's main task was to wait out this period in global politics, which, although extremely unpleasant for Russia, might appear to be short-lived, turned out to be highly questionable. In 2017, it became apparent that the Kremlin had no guaranteed advantage in short- and mid-term planning over the West. The Russian leadership had to plan for a marathon, not a sprint, and it was by no means a given that Moscow was better equipped to last out this contest than its Western opponents.

The upheavals of the past few years might not have completely cut down the snobbish, overconfident and not entirely perspicacious European bureaucrats and strategists, but they may at least have forced them to come down to earth. For the sake of the future of the European project, Brussels and other European capital cities were actively looking for new EU development paths, discussing possible solutions to key issues of political and economic reforms and plans to reform the key European institutions. Can we say in earnest that in 2017 Russia was discussing the future of the Russian project with the same zealousness, breadth and intensity?

It is of course possible that skeptics will soon mount another attack on the European Union, and that pro-Russian leaders will come to power in one or two European countries. It is also possible that Trump will manage to win a tactical victory over the Deep State, minimizing the practical implementation of new anti-Russian sanctions. A new major armed conflict in the Middle East could distract the West from its confrontation with Russia, or global political instability could lead to a steep oil price hike. However, building a strategy on such premises is akin to planning a family budget in hope of a hefty lottery win. The unpredictability of international developments should not justify the absence of a cohesive strategy, especially when one has to deal with an opponent who is far superior in terms of overall economic, social and military attributes of power.

In addition, it is now becoming clear that Russia will not be able to engage in strategic interaction with the Trump administration while leaving the disintegrating EU by the wayside. So far, the opposite has been true.

It appears that in the foreseeable future, Russia cannot hope for much more than tactical interaction with the United States on a limited set of issues, such as Syria, North Korea, the Arctic and nuclear non-proliferation. If Moscow is particularly lucky, it might expand this list to add strategic stability, the fight against global terrorism and certain other problems. However, cooperation with the Americans on the creation of a new world order is no longer possible. The firmness of the anti-Russian consensus in Washington is indisputable; splitting this consensus will take a very long time, if it happens at all. Very few people in Moscow today believe that the decisions on anti-Russian sanctions made in Washington in 2017 are likely to be reconsidered anytime soon. What is currently happening in U.S.–Russia relations is more than a worsening of the weather; it is a fundamental climatic shift, the coming of a new Ice Age.

The EU, on the other hand, appears to be more promising for Russia. In order to overcome its numerous problems and ailments, the European Union will inevitably have to revise many of its existing mechanisms, procedures and priorities, and even, to an extent, its rules and principles. Russia could assist with the European Union's transformation for its own benefit by supporting a stronger Europe and abstaining from patronizing anti-European parties and movements across the continent. In this case, it could hope to gradually expand cooperation with Europe, on the condition that at least some minimal progress is achieved on Ukraine, which is central to Russia–EU relations.

This does not imply that fundamental disagreements between Moscow and Brussels will cease to exist. The worldview of the current political leadership in the Kremlin is not going to change; an ideological revolution in the European Union is no more likely. In the observable future Russia will not become a part of the European project. Nevertheless, this division does not preclude various forms of cooperation similar to these during the 1970s or 1980s.

Back to the Cold War

Since no revolution took place in global politics in 2017, practical solutions need to be sought in the framework of the existing system of political coordinates; more grandiose plans have to wait. The old model of geopolitical confrontation between East and West, i.e., the Cold War model, should be revisited as an interim solution for the Russia-West adversarial relationship. This model is certainly far from ideal, it is expensive and to a great extent outdated. Nevertheless, notwithstanding all its shortcomings, the Cold War model used to ensure a satisfactory level of stability and predictability, both in Europe and in the world as a whole.

This model included numerous channels of political interaction, contacts among militaries, risk mitigation measures and arms control treaties. Furthermore, the Cold War model was based on mutual respect and even a degree of mutual trust. So why not fall back on this time-tested confrontation management practice, using such mechanisms as the NATO–Russia Council, the Organization for Security and Co-operation in Europe (OSCE) and the Council of Europe, or new ad-hoc formats like the Russia-NATO Crisis Management Group, which has been repeatedly proposed?

At this stage the name of the game in Russia's relations with the West is not mutual trust, but rather mutual predictability. Since it is very difficult to make predictions about the Trump Administration, major European counties and the European Union at large become more important for Russia than was the case earlier. For example, both Russia and the EU have strategic interests to secure the multilateral agreement of the Iranian nuclear dossier. Likewise, the Russian and the EU positions are close on the North Korean problem.

In some areas, there is actually no need to return to the old model because it is still in place. This goes for Russia's nuclear interaction with the United States, for example. The two remaining pillars of this interaction, the Intermediate-Range Nuclear Forces Treaty (INF) and New START Treaty, while certainly offering some positive aspects, are nevertheless fully compliant with the logic of controlled confrontation and are fully within the Cold War paradigm. Retaining and reinforcing these accords would not require any historic political breakthrough, unilateral concessions, or switching to a fundamentally new format of Moscow's relations with Washington.

The goal to preserve INF and New START is definitely worth fighting for. Nevertheless, even if this hard battle is won, this will not signal the end of the fight to secure and to strengthen strategic arms control in the 21st century. Neither INF nor New START prevents the United States from spending $1 trillion in the next 30 years on modernizing its nuclear bombs, bombers, missiles and submarines. Russia will also continue its large-scale strategic modernization program, even if the two agreements remain in place.

The crisis of strategic arms control is more complex and fundamental than the uncertain future of the two agreements, as important as they are. In the 21st century, strategic arms control is no longer about arithmetic; it requires applications of higher mathematics. These days, mobility dominates location, precision beats throw-weight; and the line between nuclear and conventional weapons has become almost invisible. The old arms control paradigm has entered into its own perfect storm. While preservation of its Cold War heritage is indispensable, preservation in itself is clearly not sufficient to provide for strategic stability in a completely new global environment.

One can argue that traditional distinctions between strategic, intermediate-range and tactical systems are becoming antiquated. The reality is that the United States and Russia have and will continue to have strikingly different geopolitical and geostrategic positions in the world; their threat perceptions and their respective strategic doctrines will never be identical to each other. If so, the United States and Russia could merge New START and INF into one umbrella agreement that would set overall ceilings for nuclear warheads and launchers on both sides. Within these overall ceilings both Washington and Moscow would be in a position to blend individual cocktails of strategic, intermediate range and tactical systems to their liking. For a better taste, they could even add the missile defense component to the mix. The only sub-ceiling that they might need to preserve is the sub-ceiling for deployed warheads, which are of particular concern to the other side. This sub-ceiling can amount to a half or one third of the total number.

This approach will not address all the contemporary challenges to strategic arms control. For example, the time has come move away from a bilateral U.S.-Russian format to a multilateral one, but this approach will not do that. Still, an innovative approach would be a loud and clear signal to third nuclear powers that there is political will in both the White House and in the Kremlin not only to preserve, but also to enhance and to modernize global strategic security.

Skeptics can argue that today is not the best time to experiment with new approaches to strategic arms control. U.S.-Russian relations have hit historical lows, trust between the two countries is non-existent, political opposition to any new deals will be too strong to generate domestic support for any new agreements. These are exactly the arguments used back in the 1950s against a possible U.S.—Soviet collaboration to write a set of rules for the new nuclear world. It took the Cuban missile crisis of October 1962 to start moving away from this perception, and another ten years to sign the first U.S.-Soviet Strategic Arms Limitation Talks Agreement (SALT 1). Are we ready to wait for another missile crisis—in North Korea or elsewhere? Can we afford another ten years for a new détente between Washington and Moscow?

The Second Layer of the Pie

Overhauling and restarting the old Cold War model is a necessary but insufficient factor for the future stabilization of Russia's relations with the West. With all its comparative advantages, this model has at least four key structural limitations. First, the Cold War model is inherently static. It is aimed at preserving the status quo and precludes any evolution. Such a model is extremely difficult to reform; it was no accident that the Cold War ended not in an orderly transformation of the controlled confrontation model, but in a dramatic and chaotic collapse in the late 1980s. Given the dynamics of the international system today, any attempt to codify Russia-West relations for an extended period of time is unlikely to be successful. There are simple too many independent variables that might affect these relations, from rising China to the fourth industrial revolution to global climate change.

Second, the Cold War was primarily fought by two vertically structured politico-military blocs, which split Europe into the Soviet and U.S. spheres of influence. It would be absolutely impossible to divide today's Europe into distinct spheres of influence; the very idea of spheres of influence is considered to be hopelessly antiquated and unacceptable, at least in the Western world. Besides, contemporary Russia is not comparable to the former USSR at the peak of its might; a geopolitical parity between Moscow and the combined West is only possible if Russia creates a political and military alliance with China, but it is highly unlikely that Russia would be the leading partner in such an alliance.

Third, Soviet and U.S. leaders built the Cold War model in order to counter the most dangerous threats of the 20th century. Even though many of these threats still exist, the 21st century has brought up new challenges, including those posed by non-governmental actors. The Cold War model cannot offer much in terms of counteracting the new generation of threats to international security. In many ways, the Cold War model was the last incarnation of the traditional Westphalian world, which is no longer the world in which we live.

Fourth, the Cold War model was relatively effective in a situation when the two confronting systems remained virtually isolated from one another and separated by incompatible ideologies. No such economic, political or humanitarian confrontation between Russia and the West exists anymore, nor could it be reinstated, despite certain attempts being made on both sides. The current media war between Russia and the West looks like a caricature of the ideological struggle between communism and liberal democracy in the middle of the 20th century. Nor can Russia be isolated from the West in an age of unprecedented human mobility, porous borders, global information and communications technologies. Despite all of Russia's efforts aimed at self-reliance, import substitution and higher protectionism, the country's dependence on the outside word is likely to increase, not decrease.

The old model's considerable limitations necessitate the introduction of a new complementary dimension to Russia-West relations. The role of such a dimension could be played out through a system of global, regional and sub-regional regimes that would preserve and expand the common space between Russia and Europe, between Eurasia and the Euro-Atlantic area.

In the initial phase, such regimes would be easier to preserve and develop in less politically sensitive fields, such as education, science and culture. However, it may be possible to apply the regimes model to non-traditional security challenges, including international terrorism, drug trafficking, cross-border crime, energy security and even cyber security. The regimes model can also work on the sub-regional level: for example, it has long been applied effectively in the Arctic.

In the current situation, the regimes model could efficiently complement the old Cold War model in Russia's relations with the West. As distinct from the inherently rigid Cold War model, which requires strict codification of agreements reached, the regimes model is flexible, often making it possible to do without burdensome negotiations over technicalities and avoid complex and protracted ratification procedures.

While the Cold War model requires a universally recognized hierarchy of parties in international relations, the regimes model is based on horizontal interactions between the parties involved, which may include not only large and small states, but also non-governmental actors such as regions and municipalities, private companies and civil institutions, international organizations and cross-border movements. This significantly expands the range of potential stakeholders interested in the development of cooperation, creating a critical mass for subsequent breakthroughs.

Skeptics would argue that this approach has already been tried in the relations between Russia and the West, but failed to prevent the current crisis and therefore should be rejected as inefficient. I would make a counterargument: the current crisis would be much deeper and more difficult to manage if the two sides did not have a thick network of social, humanitarian, cultural, educational and other contacts. Despite an ongoing and intense information war, the West still remains a point of orientation to millions and millions of Russians. It is true that Russians have not become completely immune to anti-Western propaganda, but the depth and the sustainability of anti-Western moods in the Russian society can be questioned.

Whereas the Cold War model proceeds from the premise that the parties are prepared for major deals such as the 1975 Helsinki Accords, and is mainly based on a top-down approach, the regimes model works in situations of strategic uncertainty, in the absence of major deals, and is mostly based on a bottom-up approach. Shoots of cooperation sprout up wherever there are even the most minuscule cracks in the asphalt of confrontation.

The question is whether such different models of Russia's relations with the West can possibly be combined within a single hybrid format. That this is possible in principle follows from the peculiarities of contemporary social organization in Russia and the West, which differs radically from how things were organized in the middle of the 20th century. Thanks to the high level of social, professional and cultural fragmentation in contemporary societies, the existence of multiple group and individual identities, and the extremely intricate mechanisms of interaction within vertical, horizontal, formal, informal, basic and situational ties, both models will have their target audiences, proponents, operators and ideologists in Russia and the West.

It is easy to predict that the logic of confrontation will inevitably restrict and distort the logic of cooperation. One way or another, the two mutually complementary models affect each other, because they simply cannot be isolated. However, the art of foreign policy presupposes, among other things, the ability to play chess on several boards simultaneously, or to be more precise, to play chess, poker and even the exotic Asian game Go at the same time, not just the traditional Russian game of *gorodki*. The most important thing is to delimit the spheres of application of the two models and gradually shift the balance between them from the former to the latter.

Looking Beyond the Horizon

Any significant changes in the current pattern of relations between Russia and the West is likely to be a slow, gradual and long process. At this stage, there are not many compelling reasons for the Kremlin to reconsider its fundamental approaches to the West. On the one hand, the current status quo is perceived as not perfect, but generally acceptable. Potential risks associated with maintaining the status quo are regarded as relatively low compared to risks that might emerge from attempts at changing the status quo. The margin of safety of both the Russian political system and its economy is still quite significant. On the other hand, the trend towards a new consolidation of the West is still very fragile and arguably reversible. There are many political, social and economic problems, to which neither the United States, not the European Union, have found credible solutions.

The status quo-focused foreign policy does not exclude trial balloons, tactical adjustments, incremental concessions, and situational collaboration. All these are important in 2018 and in years to come. However, a more fundamental change in Russian foreign policy is not likely to come as a cumulative effect of incremental adjustments or situational collaboration. Neither will it result from a revelation of a Russian leader, no matter who this leader is likely to be a few years from now. At the end of the day, Russia's foreign policy priorities will be defined by the economic and social development trajectory upon which the nation will embark once it has depleted the potential of the current development model.

Russia can definitely survive without the West generally, and without Europe in particular. It might even prosper without the West if global prices on oil and other commodities go up again and a new golden rain waters the national economy. It does not matter much to whom you sell your commodities—clients in the West or clients in the East, developed or developing nations, mature democracies or authoritarian regimes. With Russia's rent-seeking economy in place, the West is not likely to reemerge as an indispensable partner for Moscow. Moreover, Russia can even stick to a neo-isolationist foreign policy, consistently trying to protect its citizens from the dangers and challenges of the globalizing world.

This foreign policy option will be even more probable if the overall international system evolves in the direction of more nationalism, protectionism, rigid balance of powers, continuous decay of international institutions and international law. If the name of game is survival rather than development, if the top national priority everywhere is security rather than development, then incentives to change anything will remain low.

However, let us suppose that the name of the game is not to maintain the rent-seeking economic model, but to pursue a strategy of encouraging deep structural economic reforms, promoting innovation and entrepreneurship, and unleashing the creative potential of the Russian people. Let us suppose that the modern liberal world order successfully overcomes the ongoing crisis and the international system move away from hard to soft power, from unilateralism to multilateralism, from closeness to openness. In this case connecting to the West, borrowing best Western practices, learning from Western mistakes is going to be a critical precondition for any successful Russian modernization. This has always been the case, ever since Italian architects supervised the erection of the red brick Kremlin walls in Moscow back in 1485.

Given all the uncertainties of future developments in Russia and in the West, it might make sense to define three time horizons for this very complex and uneasy relationship. Each of these has its own logic, priorities, goals, opportunities, and limitations. The first is about de-escalation, which involves a stable cease-fire in Donbass, moderation of inflammatory rhetoric on both sides, a truce in the information war, and resumption of political and military contacts and various levels. The second is about stabilization, including a more general political settlement in Ukraine along the lines of the Minsk Agreements, gradual removal of sanctions and countersanctions, a set of confidence-building measures in Europe, promotion of cooperation in areas of mutual concern (e.g. soft security), unilateral limitations on military deployments, and strengthening European regimes in humanitarian fields. Moving on to the third, long-term horizon, we should review and revise the idea of a Greater Europe that was unsuccessfully tried after the end of the Cold War; our second attempt should be based on lessons learned from the failure of the first attempt.

Chapter 2
Fuzzy Alliances, Flexible Relations

Fyodor Lukyanov

Relations between Russia and the West have reached their lowest point since the Cold War. Unfortunately we cannot be sure that they won't deteriorate even further. It is time to start to mend ties, but the only consensus view shared by both sides is that business as usual is not an option. The relationship cannot be restored; it should be rebuilt. To do this, we first need to reassess the entire international atmosphere, what happened to the relationship, and how it can be transformed based on new realities.

End of an Era

The year 2016 marked the end of a 70-year period in international relations that consisted of two phases: the Cold War from the 1940s to the 1980s, and the transition time after the disintegration of the Soviet Union. The Cold War was characterized by unprecedentedly strong strategic stability, based on a military-political balance between the superpowers. The end of confrontation was accompanied by an unusual urge to spread to the whole world the ideas and values of one group of countries, as if they were universal. Whatever we choose to call the period we may now be entering, it is more likely that we will witness the reappearance of more classical patterns of international relations: an increased role of states; a renaissance of national-interest-based approaches; and interstate competition.

The past quarter of a century was not a time of building a new world order, it was an attempt to adapt existing institutions that had survived ideological confrontation (mainly those that catered to the needs of the Western world) to a completely different international context. These attempts failed.

President Donald Trump, who won the November 2016 election in sensational fashion, is a vivid personification of the end of the previous era. In fact, the United States has never had such a leader before. Regardless of what he may achieve as president and how long he may stay in office,

American—and therefore global—policy will no longer be the same. Trump is a symptom that the previous political and economic model of international development has been exhausted.

For twenty-five years after the end of the Cold War and the dissolution of the Soviet Union, Russia strived to restore (or in some instances even take revenge) its statehood, economy, political system, and international positions. With some simplification, one can say that throughout that period Russian society and the state developed in the wake of what happened in 1991 and the 1990s (and the preceding triggering events). This period combined both historically inevitable and transitory but unnecessary episodes, forced and imagined actions, heroic efforts, and fatal miscalculations. In any event, that era came to an end in Russia, mainly because it came to an end globally.

During this period, not only Russia, but also the West, and consequently world affairs in general, existed in a post-Cold War mode. Russia felt defeated and wanted to make up for its losses. The West was engulfed by euphoria and self-admiration. Between 2008 and 2016 (from the world financial crisis to Brexit and Trump's election), Western delight gradually gave way to anxiety. Eventually, it became clear that things had not gone the way they were intended to go at the end of the last century, and that many, if not all, efforts would have to be started over again, taking into account a new and different situation.

For all the risks and costs generated by the confrontation between the two systems and their mutual reliance on nuclear deterrence, the Cold War kept the world in measurably sustainable order. The superpowers competed constantly with each other in all spheres, but they were well aware (especially after the Cuban missile crisis of 1962) of the red line that could not be overstepped.

A dramatic change in rhetoric after the Cold War ended was essentially followed by an attempt to preserve the existing model of global control. However, it was no longer based on two counterbalancing superpowers, but rather on one hyperpower aspiring to act as a global regulator, due to its enormous superiority in all components of power. In other words, the Cold War and the policies that followed were imbued with the conviction that global processes could be controlled.

The third common feature of that time, which is truly crucial for Russia, was the existence of the West as a single political conception, essentially an institution. The West as an idea appeared much earlier, of course, but until the middle of the 20th century it was a space where great powers were locked in a fierce rivalry with each other. Beginning in the 1940s, the notion of the West became synonymous with Atlanticism. Walter Lippmann, the author of the term "Atlantic community," wrote that America's intervention in two world wars had been necessitated by the need to defend "the enlightened Western civilization," which he insisted included Germany (against which the two wars were fought) but excluded Russia (America's ally in both wars). Lippmann wrote about the need to defend "the security of the Atlantic highway."[1] So the system of coordinates in classical geopolitics (the Eurasian heartland as opposed to oceanic areas) acquired ideological substance.

The results of World War II, primarily the emergence of the Soviet Union as a superpower, for the first time consolidated the West as an ideological, political, military, and economic community. Not only did this community remain after the end of the Cold War, but it became the institutional core of the world system.

While the Soviet Union had clearly positioned itself as a system-wide opponent of the West, Russia faced a double dilemma. One dilemma was between accepting and rejecting Western ideology and values (this issue has been present in Russian discourse for at least 200 years); the other was between agreeing and disagreeing to participate in Western-controlled political institutions, an option never considered before. In other words, Russia had no choice but to determine its position with regard to the West for both purely internal reasons (Europe, as an embodiment of the West at large, has always played a crucial role as a reference point in Russian domestic debate on who we are) and structural ones. The mixing of these two dimensions, hitherto separate, further aggravated painful relations in the 1990s and beyond.

The model of a monocentric world (structured around the United States and its allies), which seemed natural and inevitable a quarter of a century earlier, began to crack in the first several years of the new 21st century. It was seriously shaken by the 2008–2009 global financial crisis, which began not in peripheral states (as was the case during the "Asian" wave in the late 1990s) but in the core—the United States and then the European Union. The mechanism of recovery through nationalization of losses, that is, through rescuing private banks at taxpayers' expense, which

---

[1] Walter Lippmann, "The Atlantic and America: The Why and When of Intervention," *Life*, April 7, 1941.

was adopted at the end of the 2000s, challenged the moral validity of the entire economic model and incited protest against financial and economic globalization.

The world order born out of ideological confrontation in the second half of the 20th century entered the final stage of its crisis in 2014. The European Union and NATO moved to bring Ukraine into their institutional framework and refused to discuss their intentions with Russia. Moscow responded very strongly and became firmly convinced that the West's "geopolitical greed" could only be curbed with "an iron fist," as Sergei Karaganov put it.[2]

Through its decision on Crimea and its support for anti-Kyiv forces in Donbas, Moscow did not just draw a red line, which it is prepared to defend with all available means, including military ones; it also stated its refusal to obey rules created when it was weak and could not fight for acceptable bargains. From Moscow's point of view, the order established after 1991 was not a natural continuation of the agreements that secured peace and stability in Europe during the last years of the Cold War. So Russia did not view the realities that emerged after the breakup of the Soviet Union as immutable, nor did it consider its actions with regard to neighboring countries (created after the concerted decisions of the 1970s and 1980s) a violation of the earlier accords. In other words, Russia never fully agreed with the new world order, which the West took for granted, even though it put up with it as a given until the middle of the 2000s.

Russia's military intervention in Syria in the fall of 2015 reaffirmed its refusal to accept unwritten rules. Moscow started a military operation beyond the sphere of its immediate interests, which until then had been the exclusive prerogative of the United States.

Russia's strong resistance to further expansion of the EU/NATO-centric project into the territory of the former Soviet Union became a catalyst and largely a symbol for crucial changes in global affairs. It really did, because the West continued to believe that the expansion of its model and institutions was historically irreversible and hence undisputable. But the decay of the world system was not caused only by the position of Russia,

---

[2] Sergei Karaganov wrote in December 2008 in *Rossiiskaya Gazeta*, "After Tbilisi's provocation [five-day Russian-Georgian war – Ed.] there prevailed a view, dangerous in politics, that the only argument the West could understand was 'an iron fist'." See "Россия улыбается и показывает кулаки," *Российской газета*, December 24, 2008, https://rg.ru/gazeta/rg/2008/12/24.html.

which failed to fit into the proposed framework, but also by profound problems at the very core of the world order after the Cold War, i.e., European and Euro-Atlantic institutions.

In 2014 NATO officially regained its unity and revived its Cold War goal of containing Moscow—the reason it was created in the 20th century. But the alliance has no answers to the most acute security challenges, such as the spread of conflicts in key regions of the world (Middle East, East and Southeast Asia) or the worldwide rise of Islamic terrorism. The latter is not only an external threat; for most Western countries it is increasingly an internal threat. In addition, Turkey, a key member of NATO, with its second largest army, pursues a policy that is frequently out of sync with that of its allies in Europe and America.

Recipes being proposed to contain Moscow make the remilitarization of politics and even conflict in Europe more probable, even while Cold War mechanisms to manage confrontation and minimize risks are gone. Efforts to recreate them have been slow so far. The West believes that a new dialogue on confidence-building measures would legitimize Russia as an equal military-political partner, which is completely at odds with its philosophy during the 1990s and 2000s.

The Changing Nature of Alliances

Global politics in general has become less and less orderly. After the Cold War, the West made an attempt to Westernize global governance and to expand the competence of organizations that had previously covered only Western countries (WTO, Bretton Woods structures, and at some point NATO) to the rest of the world. But the task appeared to be too multifaceted to solve. Now we see the emergence of other institutions, more formal or less formal, representing the non-Western part of the world: the BRICS, the Asian Infrastructure Investment Bank, the Regional Comprehensive Economic Partnership (initiated by ASEAN and endorsed by China), the Shanghai Cooperation Organization, and others. None has yet to prove its worth, as not all of them have so far tapped their full potential. But their appearance mirrors the general trend: the global economic space is fragmenting, and the idea of universalism (based on Western principles), which prevailed after the West's victory in the confrontation with the Soviet Union, is losing relevance.

The nature of alliances is changing as well. In a famous phrase, Lord Palmerston described the phenomenon as follows: "We have no eternal allies, and we have no perpetual enemies. Our interests are eternal and perpetual." This approach was echoed 150 years later by U.S. Secretary of Defense Donald Rumsfeld in his own famous phrase: "the mission defines the coalition."[3] And then by Donald Trump, who called NATO "obsolete."[4]

At first glance, the very existence of the North Atlantic Alliance proves this approach wrong. But NATO, which was created under completely different circumstances, remains the only and unique bloc based on rigid commitments and shared values and ideology. New blocs of this kind are nowhere to be seen, and are hardly possible. Even within NATO itself, differences in opinions, assessments and priorities are more noticeable than ever before. They can be seen among European allies, but especially between Europe and Turkey.

Other strategically significant relations, including those involving the United States, tend to be more flexible, and this is quite obvious in Asia. Although many of the countries of the Asia-Pacific rim are concerned about China's rise, and would like to receive more security guarantees from the United States, they are not so eager to become fully engaged in the new system Washington is creating to contain Beijing.

Another graphic example is offered by Japan and South Korea, which have close military-political ties with the United States (ever closer due to sharpening problems with North Korea), yet still manage to distance themselves from Washington's anti-Russian policy, and actually to strengthen relations with Russia. Despite Washington's pressure, Seoul did not impose sanctions against Russia after it had reincorporated Crimea, and Tokyo de facto withdrew from the sanctions after a meeting between Prime Minister Shinzo Abe and President Vladimir Putin in the spring of 2016.

Our current environment, which is extremely unpredictable and changing rather chaotically, pushes states to use different methods to protect their interests, yet at the same time pulls them to avoid long-term alliances that could limit their freedom of maneuver. For example, China strongly

---

[3] http://www.washingtonpost.com/wp-srv/nation/specials/attacked/transcripts/rumsfeld_text101801.html.
[4] https://www.reuters.com/article/us-usa-trump-nato-obsolete/trump-says-nato-is-obsolete-but-still-very-important-to-me-idUSKBN14Z0YO.

rejects Western models of rigid alliances with formal commitments, because Beijing believes that failure to fulfill such commitments would lead to moral demise and loss of face, devaluing the status of the leader in the East even more than in the West.

New strategic relations, such as those Russia and China are trying to build, do not presuppose strict hierarchy or full political and security coordination. They are based on mutual complementarity, non-participation in third-party coalitions against partners, and mutual political and economic support if one of the partners comes under external pressure. It would be legitimate to assume, however, that both Moscow and Beijing consider such support obligatory, since each understands that if it were to allow the other partner to be attacked, it could also become a target. The two countries are apparently building unwritten but vital mutual guarantees that may be called strategic as they concern their long-term positioning vis-à-vis each other. Neither Russia nor China wants to forge a binding alliance that would require them to show full solidarity on all issues or accept any risks one of them may create. In other words, Beijing will not back Moscow over Crimea and will keep neutrality, and Russia will not endorse Beijing's claims in the South China Sea, but neither will it offer support to its opponents. However, it becomes increasingly clear that China will lend its shoulder if sanctions push Russia to the verge of collapse, and Russia will not allow direct military blackmail against China if relations in the Pacific sharply deteriorate for some reason.

For China, this type of relationship begins to be much more important now, because even though the country is moving to a more central position in world affairs, it clearly is failing to convince its neighbors of its good intentions. Russian-Chinese ties have never been based on the same values. Their strategic interests do not coincide, although they also do not sharply contradict each other either. Yet each understands that cooperation is simply far more useful than rivalry.

Another example of this paradoxical new type of relationship is that between Russia and Turkey. Their rapprochement, following a severe and very dangerous crisis in 2015, when Turkish forces shot down a Russian military plane, came about after both sides realized how much harm they could do to each other—not only in terms of classical military threats, but their mutual ability to destabilize each other internally. This pragmatic reconciliation led to significant advances in Syria, even though there are no serious reasons to believe that either side trusts the other.

The West Vis-à-Vis Russia: Different Models

Russia's relationship with the West, however complicated it may be, has been a centerpiece of Russian foreign policy since the creation of the Russian Federation in 1991. As mentioned before, Russia faced a politically consolidated West at the peak of its influence.

For decades, the United States has loomed large in European-Russian relations. Washington has been the omnipresent third party in dealings between Russia and Europe, serving both as a guarantor of European security and a stakeholder in the transatlantic system. But now that is open to question.

Growing uncertainty surrounding the future of the transatlantic alliance presents new challenges for bilateral and multilateral relations between Russia, the EU, and the United States. On issues such as sanctions, NATO and EU expansion, the unified transatlantic front of the past has begun to show cracks. Yet Europe, which finds itself stuck between an increasingly activist Russia and the United States, is ill-prepared to conduct a policy of "strategic autonomy" (French term) that some are calling for.

Over the past thirty years, the Western political order has gone through several iterations. The Western Europe of the Cold War, part of a divided European continent, embraced its transatlantic identity by having a shared adversary in Moscow. Then, in the post-Soviet period, the strong political and economic body represented by the European Union presumed less patronage from Washington and a subordinate role for Moscow.

In 1997, Russia and the Euro-Atlantic community established a framework for relations through a series of agreements on defense and cooperation. Thus was born a new model of relations between Russia and the West, one of whose core tenets was Moscow's acknowledgement of Brussels as the center of the new Europe; Russia would become an affiliate of the new NATO/EU-centric Europe, while retaining certain privileges relative to its neighbors.

Yet this system did not, in fact, grant Russia special privileges in treating neighboring countries, nor could it do so, due to the whole philosophy of European integration, which was based on the notion of gradual eastward expansion of a single EU regulatory framework through full (for some) or associate membership—neither of which Russia was offered nor sought.

In the early 2000s, while many of its neighbors sought EU and NATO membership or association, Russia struggled to find its place in such a community, while feeling less and less that it belonged to it. By 2007, the notion of a European Russia had receded, as Moscow rejected westward integration.

More recently, since the beginning of the 2010s, we have seen a Europe in crisis—from the euro calamity, to the war in Ukraine, to the migrant crisis. Consumed with domestic problems, the EU has been too busy putting out fires within and along its borders to seriously invest in widening its European sphere. Europe is, for the first time, contracting rather than expanding, both literally with Brexit and conceptually with its dwindling appetite for enlargement.

After the election of Donald Trump, Europe is also much further from the United States. The statements made by German Chancellor Angela Merkel following the G-7 summit in May 2017: "the times in which we could rely fully on others, they are somewhat over" and "we Europeans truly have to take our fate into our own hands,"[5] were unprecedented, particularly coming from a deeply Atlanticist leader. While this is not yet a firm intention, it is telling nonetheless.

How did Russia fit into the new Europe? While NATO and the EU took great pains to distinguish between the military and political characteristics of each organization, Moscow's perception of them as a unified, creeping threat along its borders never quite faded. In both the 2008 Russo-Georgian War and the 2014 Ukraine conflict, a catalyst for conflict was the question of Euro-Atlantic expansion—in the former, Georgia's NATO aspirations, and in the latter, Ukraine's hopes for EU accession. The Ukrainian revolution and Russia's subsequent takeover of Crimea upended a framework of relations between Russia and the West that had already grown quite fragile by 2014.

Conflict between Russia and the West is hardly new. But the shaky state of transatlantic unity is new. One of the determining factors in the future of relations between Russia and the EU will be the resilience of the transatlantic alliance, and the foreign policy course charted by the United States.

---

[5] Jon Henley, "Angela Merkel: EU cannot completely rely on US and Britain any more," *The Guardian*, May 28, 2017.

One can say with certainty what Russia should not expect. It should not expect an anti-American Europe that will break with Washington in favor of warmer relations with Moscow. Europe would only attempt a new alliance with Russia in close cooperation with the United States. The EU perceives Russia as a threat and—either consciously or subconsciously—as the "other." Russia would also be remiss to expect the model for which it has lobbied since the Gorbachev era: a Europe that approaches Russia as a co-founder of a new order rather than a subordinate. This model is seen from Brussels as little more than an attempt to establish a new sphere of influence in Eastern Europe.

However, it will become increasingly difficult for the EU and the United States to maintain the same kind of unified front against Russia that has held since 2014, especially when it comes to sanctions. Europeans have begun to see the United States as using political pressure to gain economic advantages, i.e., non-market influence over competitors. Some of them view the recent package of congressional sanctions as an attempt to redraw the European gas market in favor of commercially weak U.S. liquefied natural gas (LNG).[6] While NATO remains a strong link between Europe and the United States, the dispute over goals and funding will continue to escalate, regardless of who occupies the White House.

Few Europeans seem able to clearly explain what strategic autonomy would look like in practice. Its champions say that it means boosting Europe's military capabilities to respond to crises in its immediate neighborhood. The French Foreign Legion, which operates on France's behalf in Africa, has been cited as an example. Nonetheless, NATO Secretary General Jens Stoltenberg has pointed out rather sharply that NATO is still Europe's indispensable defense provider. Moreover, the crises on Europe's periphery, from Ukraine to Syria to Libya, are not local spats that can be tidily handled by the French Foreign Legion. They are conflicts that have ensnared the largest military powers in the region, including Russia and the United States. The Permanent Strategic Cooperation (PESCO) agreement, signed by 23 EU member states in November 2017, looks like an attempt to repackage existing programs and very modest ambitions, and to sell them as a strategic breakthrough.

---

[6] See the unusually blunt joint statement by the Austrian chancellor and German foreign minister on June 15, 2017: https://www.bundeskanzleramt.gv.at/-/kern-und-gabriel-zu-einseitiger-verscharfung-der-russland-sanktionen-durch-die-usa. The Trump Administration's general energy strategy is summarized here: https://www.cnbc.com/2017/06/28/trump-america-energy-dominant-policy.html.

With the end of the greater Europe project, the three major players find themselves in a strange position. Neither Russia, Europe, nor the United States are able or want to maintain what it once had. However, a new framework for relations has yet to be established, and the attempt to revive the Cold War paradigm has failed.

This uncertain state of affairs will likely endure until each player achieves a measure of domestic stability. This is especially true for the United States, but also for Russia and the EU on the eve of potentially disruptive elections. China, too, remains an ever-present wild card, given its central role in Russia's new Eurasian policy. Moscow's eastward shift and articulation of a Eurasian identity are perhaps the ultimate signs that the Cold War and post-Cold War eras are over.

In the fall of 2013, *The New York Times* asked experts if, in their opinion, NATO had outlived its usefulness. One of them, Andrew Bacevich, a leading expert in military issues, said it was time the United States left the alliance and let Europeans take care of their own security. He stated that NATO had achieved all of the objectives set when it was founded, while the new functions it was trying to master in the 21st century were no more than a smokescreen for the unilateral and quite imperial policy the United States was pursuing around the world, not in Europe.[7]

Literally six months after that discussion, history sort of reversed itself, and the European issue topped NATO's agenda again. Atlanticism seemed to have gone back to its roots. However even if the conceptual framework for the confrontation between Moscow and NATO is restored for a while (with both sides prepared to play this game for various reasons, including domestic ones), Lippmann's "Atlantic highway" per se will no longer be the core of world politics. The era of Atlanticism, which began with World War II, is coming to end not because the contradictions that engendered it have been resolved, but because the multifaceted world has moved on. The longer the opponents in the previous confrontation try to close that chapter as winners, the more they will fall behind what Americans like to call "the right side of history."

What we can expect from relations between Russia and its Western counterparts in Europe and America? Given the obsession with a Russian menace in Europe and especially in the United States, there is no reason

---

[7] Andrew J. Bacevich "Time for the United States to Leave NATO," *The New York Times*, April 23, 2013.

to expect any common project any time soon. The task should be to rebuild basic trust at least to the level of the Cold War, yet this is very difficult due to the nature of current conflict: lack of self-confidence on all sides coupled with the conviction that the counterpart is about to undermine you from within.

Confidence-building measures should not start between states, but from within each state. Heightened levels of mutual mistrust and fear are largely generated by domestic problems and an instinctive wish to find an outside reason for them. A new beginning internationally presumes first and foremost the restoration of trust within societies. It also requires that and sustainable strategies for self-development be implemented that are adapted to the new era, which is a more fragmented and less coherent global system. That means that many former axioms must be reformulated toward more flexible relationships.

Doing our homework at home is now more important than big initiatives abroad, which are unlikely to succeed because of domestic troubles almost everywhere. This does not mean total inaction, which could exacerbate negative dynamics. Minimizing the risks of unintended collisions, whether among militaries (in Syria or places where NATO and Russia operate in immediate proximity, such as the Black or Baltic sea) or in sensitive political and economic areas, should be seen as an ultimate goal.

In part this means restoring such mechanisms of the Cold War as early warning and interaction between militaries to make their activities more transparent to the other side. It should also include new areas, particularly in the cyber sphere, which has become a new and very dangerous space for competition. In the political field, further fragmentation of our common space, by sanctions or other measures, should be avoided.

Chapter 3

Can Ukraine Change Russia?

Vladislav L. Inozemtsev

Since late 2004, when the Orange Revolution unfolded in Kyiv after a rigged presidential election, many free-minded Russians considered Ukraine's embrace of democracy and Western values as a powerful tool to transform Russia itself and to liberate it from the authoritarianism that had become increasingly evident in Russian President Putin's policies. The fight to get rid of Moscow's dictate was widely anticipated as the battle for "their and our freedom"[1] and a Westernized, prosperous, and democratic Ukraine that could be a beacon for a still-imperial Russia.

Quite soon thereafter, however, it appeared that the Ukrainian political class was so busy safeguarding its commercial interests that the pre-2004 elites regained their powers and secured them until the Euromaidan—this time bloody and cruel—overthrew them in early 2014.

A new revolution cost Ukraine more than a hundred dead and was followed by full-scale Russian aggression, resulting in the occupation of both Crimea and the eastern part of Donbass. But it again generated a feeling that Ukraine might turn into a genuine democracy that would fight corruption, investigate the wrongdoings of previous authorities, bring new people to the top, and sooner or later be admitted to the European Union. Kyiv once again became a sign of hope for many in an already authoritarian Russia.

Three years after the Euromaidan, everything looks entirely different. It seems that Ukraine, stripped of some of its territories, plagued by war and internal problems, unwelcome in the European Union, economically poor and disoriented, is now an example of what Russia must by every means avoid, rather than what it should consider as its best option. Therefore, although I have been for years a strong supporter of Ukraine's cause, if asked whether Ukraine can now, or in the future, change Russia for the better, I would respond no, it definitely cannot—for three reasons.

---

[1] See Vladislav Inozemtsev, "For yours and our freedom [A foreword to the interview with Viktor Yushchenko]" in *Svobodnaya Mysl'–XXI*, 2004, № 10, pp. 3–4 [in Russian].

Changes in Ukraine and its Neighborhood

The first reason has to do with the most crucial question of whether Ukraine might actually be able to transform itself into a more modern, prosperous, law-abiding, democratic, and, most crucially, more European country in the sense of belonging formally to EU structures. For this to happen, Ukraine should be integrated rapidly into the Atlantic community in both economic and political terms, and it should start to change its political system and its methods of governance. Yet none of this is to be seen.

Unfortunately, the Euromaidan and related developments came at a time when the European Union was tired of its new eastern members, obsessed first by the Greek financial meltdown, then by the migration crisis, and finally by the dismal results of the UK referendum. The Europeans had the opportunity to take some very bold decisions vis-à-vis Ukraine, but nothing was actually done. Ukraine offered Europe many unique options that simply were not used.

If the Europeans were bolder, they might consider offering Kyiv EU candidate status immediately, imposing the EU *acquis* and using Ukraine as a major base for relocating their industrial production to the east in a move that could generate additional competitive advantages for Europe. Ukraine is unlikely to become a developed country if it continues to rely on "life support" from international donors. The prospect of EU membership, on the other hand, would be likely to spark a massive inflow of private investment and therefore lower the need for the government-secured loans that Western governments currently need to provide to Kyiv.[2] If admitted to the EU (or even if the EU would drop some restrictions for Ukrainian workers), Ukraine is likely to produce a huge wave of young, competent and Christian migrants seeking to advance their careers in Europe and integrate into European societies, and not because of generous European welfare provisions. They would offer a stark contrast to incoming Muslim migrants, whom the Europeans mistakenly consider to be refugees. Finally, after Brexit, when (or rather if) the UK gets a status similar to that of Norway and Switzerland, who pay the EU for access to its common market, the same relationship could be to be "sold" to Ukraine on the condition that Kyiv pays the EU for access, not vice versa.[3]

---

[2] See Vladislav Inozemtsev, "Ukraine chose Europe. What is to be done next" [in Russian] in: *RBC-Daily*, June 30, 2014, p. 5.
[3] See Vladislav Inozemtsev, "Ukraine's next EU moves," July 19, 2016, http://www.kyivpost.com/

All of these measures are conceivable and could push Ukraine's growth up and secure its European future. Little has been done, with the exception that as of June 11, 2017, the EU agreed that Ukrainian citizens holding biometric passports can travel to the Schengen Zone without a visa for a period of 90 days within any 180-day period for purposes other than working.

Political and military integration has been an even less impressive story. None of the great powers intervened on Ukraine's side to defend its territorial integrity, as had been presupposed by the 1994 Budapest Memorandum. No invitation was issued to Kyiv to join NATO, even though this was the only plausible means to try to stop Russian aggression. Not only did Western powers reject the option of sending troops to Ukraine (even though they have sent troops on other occasions to oppose aggression, for instance in the Persian Gulf in 1990, when they responded to Saddam Hussein's occupation of Kuwait), they also refused to supply the Ukrainian army with modern weapons and munition, thus allowing Russia to keep the current low-intensity conflict in place as a lever to erode Ukraine's will to protect and reform itself. I am convinced that the Kremlin is not prepared to engage into a full-scale conflict with NATO member states, since Putin, while bold, is not prone to suicide. But the West was too cautious in this case, choosing to embark on a pacification strategy resembling the one used in Munich in 1938.

Instead of confronting Putin's Russia, Europe and the United States decided to leave Ukraine face-to-face with Russia, dooming the country to a protracted low-intensity war without any chance of success. This means that Ukraine will not only be deprived of the benefits of EU membership, it will remain the space for Russian-Western confrontation for years. Its government will be preoccupied less with the country's much-needed economic development or administrative reforms and more with the war against its closest and impressively strong neighbor. This simply opens the door to endless corruption and internal quarrels. It not only wastes the resources Ukraine critically needs, it produces more corruption and more nationalism than it can digest. No one should believe that a nation in the middle of a war that threatens its own existence will assign high priority to democratic procedures and the creation of a liberal economy. And there is no sign thus far that the major Western powers are

---

article/opinion/op-ed/vladislav-l-inozemtsev-ukraines-next-eu-moves-418999.html (website retrieved on Sept. 2, 2017).

willing to embrace Ukraine and include it in an effective defense community, which has existed in the Euro-Atlantic area for decades.

Furthermore—and this is the most crucial point—Ukraine does not seem to be willing to change itself from within. The ruling elite has not changed; the "new" people who have emerged on the top came from the same Yushchenko government that proved to be incapable of promoting reforms. Those who enriched themselves under the Yanukovych regime were not prosecuted, their fortunes were not confiscated, and the Ukrainian prosecutor office advanced no claims to stolen assets hidden abroad. The easiest solution would have been to adopt and enforce legislation to reclaim stolen property, and then to hire international private detective firms, which for a fraction of the recovered funds would have initiated a worldwide intelligence operation.[4] Was something like this done? No.

The Ukrainian authorities are still unable to complete the criminal case against those who massacred people in the Euromaidan in February 2014. The economic reforms are progressing very slowly. Instead of becoming the freest economy in Europe (and this actually should be the case, if the country wants to go forward), Ukraine still has one of the highest tax burdens in the world when compared to nations with similar per capita GDP. Mikheil Saakashvili succeeded in turning his Georgia into an orderly and business-friendly country in less than five years; he was unable to do anything of the sort in the Odessa region before he was ousted. The later story of Ukrainian President Poroshenko stripping him of Ukrainian citizenship and the government's efforts to ban him from returning home as he tried to cross the Polish-Ukrainian boarder[5] is emblematic of the Russian-style behavior of the political elites.

Appealing to Western governments to strengthen trade sanctions against Russia, Kyiv proclaimed the occupied Crimea a 'special economic zone' and engaged in profitable trade with the Russians there—until civil activists blocked the border in October 2015, forcing the government to change its smuggler-friendly policies.[6] After initial rumors that a massive team of Western-educated reformers would take over the government,

---

[4] See Alexander Lebedev and Vladislav Inozemtsev, "The West is wrong to write off Ukraine's debts," *The Guardian*, April 14, 2015, p. 19.
[5] See "Saakashvili's breakthrough into Ukraine: the comedy of the century, real-time" [in Russian] at: https://ria.ru/analytics/20170911/1502225720.html (website retrieved on Sept. 12, 2017).
[6] See "The blockade of Crimea: is it working?" [in Russian] at: http://voxukraine.org/2015/11/11/the-blockade-of-crimea-is-it-working/ (website retrieved on Sept. 2, 2017).

those technocrats were deprived of real decision-making authority, and when a decisive moment came, they were thrown out without hesitation. All of these issues came to a head when President Poroshenko appointed a Prime Minister from his home town, thus reviving traditions associated with Kuchma and Yanukovych, and forced the Rada to approve a Prosecutor General without a college degree, contradicting current Ukrainian laws.[7] Poroshenko, who under current law must sell all his assets and hold his money in a special trust fund, is now obsessed with purchasing new television channels and other mass media assets.

Agrarian reform is another example of failure. A moratorium on the free trade of agricultural lands, which has been extended every two years since 2001, was extended once again by the new government in 2016 and might be extended again.[8]

In sum, the current Ukrainian leadership is building a system that is as corrupt as the previous one—but this time it is being built by people who were lifted to the top at a heavy human price, and they have shown that they have no respect for the citizens of their country when it comes to money and wealth. Ukrainian politics corrupts even outstanding reformers; Saakashvili now stands together with Yulia Tymoshenko, who did her best in earlier times to plunder Ukraine with the help of pro-Russian businesspeople.

The record of Ukraine's achievements is short and unimpressive. In 1990, the Ukrainian Soviet Republic's per capita GDP stood at par with that of Poland. By 2015, it was three times smaller.[9] The overall population dropped from 51.9 million in 1991 to 45.0 million people in 2016, including temporarily occupied Crimea. More than 5 million Ukrainians are now living and working outside the country,[10] and most of them do not want

---

[7] See "How Yury Lutsenko became a Prosecutor-General" [in Russian] at: http://novosti-ua.org/news/ 286771-kak_yrij_lutsenko_genprokurorom_stal (website retrieved on Sept. 2, 2017).
[8] See "The authorities decided about the timing of lifting the ban for arable land sale" [in Russian] at: https://ru.tsn.ua/groshi/vlast-opredelilas-so-srokom-otmeny-moratoriya-na-prodazhu-zemli-835903.html (website retrieved on Sept. 12, 2017).
[9] See Jeffrey Sachs. "Poland's return to Europe: lessons for Ukraine, Russia, and the West" at: http://www.huffingtonpost.com/jeffrey-sachs/poland-europe-democracy-anniversary_b_5453823.html (website retrieved on Sept. 4, 2017).
[10] See "At least 5 million Ukrainians have left to live abroad: Ukraine's Foreign Ministry" at: http://112.international/ukraine-top-news/at-least-5-million-ukrainians-left-to-live-abroad-ukraines-foreign-ministry-5834.html (website retrieved on Sept. 4, 2017).

to return to their homeland.¹¹ Industrial production remains 30% below late Soviet levels. After about thirty years, the Antonov company finally succeeded in teaming up with the Chinese to finish and put into commercial use the second iteration of the world's biggest transport aircraft, *Mriya*, which was built in 1988 in just one prototype.¹² But at the same time Rinat Akhmedov, a Ukrainian, appeared to be the wealthiest person in central and eastern Europe, becoming richer than any of the Russian oligarchs in 2008 with an incredible fortune of $31.1 billion.¹³ Public officials are among most corrupted in the world: some estimates put the share of national wealth redistributed through bribes at around 14% of GDP in 2012,¹⁴ or about 60% of state budget revenues. Economic growth actually stalled after 2008, and later reversed—so today the country's GDP is smaller than it was when the Orange Revolution erupted in late 2004. The 2016 inflation rate of 12.4%¹⁵ is relatively low by Ukrainian standards, but it was largely caused by very low personal disposable incomes preventing citizens from expanding their consumption. Sovereign foreign debt climbed to $117 billion¹⁶ and the main lenders are unwilling to reschedule the debt or to provide new loans because the reforms are initiated only under massive pressure from foreign partners. According to IMF, The high risk of sovereign default persists, despite major international efforts.¹⁷

The major problem, however, comes not from the dismal overall economic performance but from the path the nation has trodden recent years. The Ukrainians positioned themselves as the most bold, honest and courageous people in the entire post-Soviet space, doing their best to establish democracy and adopt European values. In this sense they differed enormously from the Russians, who since 1993 have appeared too selfish to revolt against any state authorities. It seems that most Ukrainians deeply

---

[11] The famous letter by a young Ukrainian émigré Iryna Mynich to British Prime Minister Theresa May might be good proof of that. See Tom Bevan, "Ukrainian teenager pens heart-breaking letter to Theresa May in desperate plea to stay in UK," at: http://www.mirror.co.uk/news/uk-news/ukrainian-teenager-pens-heart-breaking-6673823 (website retrieved on Sept. 5, 2017).
[12] See Yanina Sokolovskaya and Natalia Skorlygyna, "Ukraine sells *Mriya* to China" [in Russian] at: http://kommersant.ru/doc/3077551 (website retrieved on September 4, 2017).
[13] See http://files.korrespondent.net/projects/top50/2008 (website retrieved on Sept. 1, 2017).
[14] See Laurence Cockcroft, *Global Corruption. Money, Power, and Ethics in the Modern World* (Philadelphia: University of Pennsylvania Press, 2012), p. 122.
[15] See http://www.index.minfin.com.ua/index/infl/ (website retrieved on September 14, 2017).
[16] See http://ru.tradingeconomics.com/ukraine/external-debt (website retrieved on September 4, 2016).
[17] See "Ukraine approaching a default" [in Russian] at: http://www.gazeta.ru/business/2016/09/03/10174769.shtml (website retrieved on September 6, 2016).

support the European way of life and they might appear very good Europeans. Every time they took to the streets and squares, however, the elite was able to use popular protest to advance its own interests, and one revolution after another resulted in the enriching of one or another faction of the same oligarchy. Few will disagree that, economically, Ukraine has lost at least ten years of its short independent history. This fact is very often used by the Russian political elite to discourage its subjects from any attempts to flirt with both democracy and Europeanness.

So, seen from Russian eyes, Russia's closest neighbor is plagued by all possible misfortunes. It tried to become integrated into the EU and NATO, but nothing actually happened. As a result of democratic revolutions one oligarchic group after another acquired power and looted the country. Real rule of law has never been introduced. Government decisions are made in order to balance the interests of different influential business groups.

Accusations that Ukraine has fallen into the hands of home-grown nationalists and even fascists are simply not true.[18] Nevertheless, Ukraine's history offers the ordinary Russian many examples why she or he would not want Russia to follow the Ukrainian path.

For Ukraine to change—or, better to say, to challenge—Russia, it should become a real part of Europe. Of course, no one anticipates that the country will become as prosperous as Germany any time soon, but it definitely should embrace the rule of law, have a government accountable to the people, demonstrate clear progress integrating into EU structures, and, of course, to demonstrate its capability to rise economically above the late Soviet standards. There are, unfortunately, no signs that the country is moving quickly in this direction.

Ukraine simply still resembles Russia too much—a backward, corrupt, and stagnating country, for it to become any kind of a beacon for Russian society any time soon. Europe could turn Ukraine into an example for Russia, but Ukraine on its own cannot. It may seem disappointing, but a quarter century of post-Soviet transformation should teach the West a simple lesson: those nations that were for so long a part of the Soviet empire can only be reformed once they are included in the West, not before, whether one likes this conclusion or not.

---

[18] See Vladislav Inozemtsev, "Stand up, stand up you giant country: how Russia encountered fascism" [in Russian] in: *RBC-Daily*, June 22, 2015, p. 9.

In Search of a New Kind of Identity

The second set of reasons why Ukraine cannot be a model for Russia is of a somewhat different nature, and deals first of all with the identity issue. Russia was for centuries an empire, even of a very specific kind: the ancient Russian civilization was rooted in Kyivan Rus. The Orthodox faith was adopted there by local pagans in 988. One of the most courageous Russian princes, Danylo of Galicia, who was seeking Western assistance in his fight with the Mongols, converted to the Catholic faith in 1253 and was proclaimed by the Pope as King Daniel, *Rex Ruthenorum*, or *Rex Russiae*.[19] For centuries, the Russian czars were crowned by what was considered to be an ancient Kyiv relic, the Monomach's Cap.[20] Since Kyiv was always considered as a source of Russian statehood and nationhood, the very word Russia replaced the country's earlier name, Muscovy, after the reunification of Muscovy and Ukraine in 1654.

Given this history, the Russian attitude towards Ukraine has been extremely complex: on the one hand, Russians believed themselves to be superior to Ukrainians, since they succeeded in building a vast empire and their neighbors did not. On the other hand, at some subconscious level they understood that Ukraine is a crucial part of the historical Russia without which their nation ceases to exist. In this case, Zbigniew Brzezinski was perfectly right to state that "the loss of Ukraine was geopolitically pivotal, for it drastically limited Russia's geostrategic options."[21] This explains in part the feelings of today's Russians. President Putin is not the only one who believes that Ukraine betrayed Russia by flirting with Europe. The overwhelming majority of the Russian people—even democrats and liberals—shares his views and believes that the occasional rupture between Russia and Ukraine should be overcome by expanding the Russian world and by reestablishing Moscow's predominance over Kyiv.

---

[19] See Serhii Plokhy, *The Gates of Europe: The History of Ukraine* (New York: Basic Books, 2015), p. 55.
[20] According to the official version, traced to the "Story of the Princes of Vladimir (Сказание о Князьях Владимирских)" (1518), the cap was first mentioned as the gift of the Byzantine Emperor Constantine IX to his grandson, Kievan Price Vladimir Monomakh. It was used during all coronations in Moscow until the end of the 17th century. See Boris Uspensky, *The Tzar and the Emperor. Coronations and the Semantics of Monarchical Titles* [in Russian] (Moscow: Languages of the Russian Culture, 2000,) p. 77.
[21] Zbigniew Brzezinski, *The Grand Chessboard. American Primacy and Its Geostrategic Imperatives* (New York: Basic Books, 1997), p. 106.

In this complicated situation, there has been only one possibility for the Ukrainians to claim their own superiority over Russians, and that is to establish a type of promising leadership that Russians may not follow, but could find attractive to team up with. Such a strategy could be based on the premise that Muscovy was actually an offshoot of a unique and united civilization of the Kyivan Rus (as happened many centuries ago), rather than the notion that Ukraine historically is an outskirt of Russia (as actually comes from its very name). In other writings I have described this maneuver in terms of declaring Ukraine the genuine Russia (novo-Rus')—European, Westernized, and democratic—as opposed to the traditionally recognized Russia, obsessed with Eurasianism, imperialistic and autocratic.[22]

Such a strategy could result in two profound consequences. First, if Ukraine positions itself as the core Russia and elaborates a vision of a democratic order for all the heirs of the ancient Rus': Ukrainians, Byelorussians, and Russians, it may become a natural leader for the former Soviet nations; if it declares the Russian language having the same official use as the Ukrainian one, it will emerge as the only one internationalist power in the region deeply obsessed by nationalist ideologies; if it claims that East Slavonic people have been a natural part of the European civilization for many centuries, it may undermine every Russian effort to rejuvenate Eurasianist concepts and to push post-Soviet integration plans eastward. All this will deliver a much more serious blow to Russian imperialism than any victories that might be achieved in Donbass—since for pretending for an empire Russia must prove she is both the historical center and the most dynamic element of all the East Slavonic lands.

Second, Ukraine should be extremely Russians- (maybe not Russia-) friendly for trying to squeeze out from Russia its brightest minds, its most entrepreneurial and adventurous people, and, last but not least, the capital that now flees the country for Europe and offshore jurisdictions. In the years 2009-2015 Russia lost $502.4 billion in private capital. If even one quarter of this amount came to Ukraine it would be more than enough to cover all its external debts. As a former businessman I can witness that many Russian entrepreneurs, who started their activities in the 1990s and now face the aggravating business climate in Russia, might move to Ukraine if they are sure of its European perspective. The mentality of

---

[22] See Vladislav Inozemtsev, "The Island of Novo-Russiya" [in Russian] at: www.snob.ru/selected/entry/105899 (website retrieved on September 4, 2017) and Vladislav Inozemtsev, "L'Ukraine doit guider la Russie vers l'Europe," *Le Monde*, March 23, 2016, p. 23.

Russian and Ukrainian business people is very similar, and such an inflow of independent and self-made Russians would by no means disrupt Ukraine's drift towards Europe or damage the country's economic performance. I would not address these issues if I were not sure of the attitudes of many Russian entrepreneurs—the main problem here comes from Ukrainian side, which too often confuses Russian capital with Kremlin-backed monopolies and, in many cases, fears the competition that in fact is the only plausible means to rejuvenate the ailing economy of Ukraine.

To summarize, I would say that the worst strategy to change someone would be to declare oneself her or his enemy and then try to prove your own superiority. But what we see now suggests Ukraine has already embarked on this desperate path: it wants to change Russia in many aspects, while declaring itself Russia's most radical adversary.

Back in 2003, Ukrainian President Leonid Kuchma published a book entitled *Ukraine is not Russia* (Украина—не Россия)"[23] (the volume was released in Russian by a Moscow publishing house and translated into Ukrainian one year later). In this book Kuchma summarized all the most popular theses about the differences in the two nations' history and worldviews, laying down substantial arguments about why Ukraine can build its future only on the basis of its own clear identity (at that time, alas, it wasn't said this should be an anti-Russian one).

Later, Ukrainian scholars and social activists developed a line of argument that Ukraine had been colonized and suppressed by Russia, and that its liberation in 1991 (which actually came about as a result of the collapse of the centralized power) and its subsequent independence were the results of an anti-colonial struggle.[24] But how can one describe Kyiv as a colony of Moscow if it was not Kyiv that was founded by Muscovites, but Moscow that was founded by a son of Vladimir Monomakh, the Great Prince of Kyiv?

After the revolts of 2004 and 2014 the Ukrainian leaders argued consistently that Ukraine was not only not-Russian, but actually an anti-Russian power—and, moreover, a nation that would defend democratic European states against Russian totalitarianism. President Petro Poroshenko put it extremely clearly, saying: "Today there are we, the Ukrainians, who secure

---

[23] See Leonid Kuchma, *Ukraina—ne Rossiya* [in Russian] (Moscow: Vremya Publishers, 2003).
[24] See, e.g. Ilya Gerasimov, "Ukraine: The First Postcolonial Revolution," *Aspen Review Central Europe*, No 3, 2015, pp. 46–53.

Europe from barbarism, tyranny, terrorism, aggression, and militarism that hung over all our continent. We, Ukrainians, are today at the forefront of the protection of European civilization."²⁵

With all due respect to brave Ukrainian servicewomen and servicemen, I would argue that it was not their valor but the Western powers' diplomatic positions that stopped the Russian forces in eastern Ukraine from pushing further. Even today, it is still the West that effectively defends Ukraine from ongoing Russian aggression, and not so much Ukraine that protects the West from it.

I can easily understand how crucial the establishment of a new national identity may be for a young nation—especially for one that was really stripped off all its national patterns. I would not advise the Ukrainian politicians to change their attitudes, since I realize that only on the basis of national pride and identity can a new and successful nation be built. But I would say that since Ukraine cannot rid itself of its eastern neighbor, Kyiv should try not to oppose Moscow, but rather position itself not the strongest sibling but as an older, more clever and experienced brother who wants not to distance itself from Russia but rather to show it a better path forward to a decent European future that both parts of the formerly one Slavonic civilization desire. The language of hatred should be left to Mr. Putin; Ukrainian leaders should address more intensively the better features of both nations' common character than their readiness to fight each other.

Many decent citizens in Russia, who wish to embrace European values and would like to democratize their country, will think twice about this perspective if their leaders would affirm to them that democratization is inspired by a Russia-hating Ukraine. I fear that what actually Ukraine is now doing for Russia looks like defamation of European principles and values in the eyes of the majority of the Russian people. It is teaching them that they should not follow suit and take to the streets to seek a better future. Unskilled reforms of the 1990s really paupered millions of Russians. They led to a strong rejection of democracy and liberal economic practices by the Russian population. This must be kept in mind, otherwise Ukraine's

---

²⁵ Petro Poroshenko, "Ukraine emerges confidently as a new, promising European country"/An address on Europe Day May 21, 2016 [translated from Russian] at: www.president.gov.ua/ru/news/ukrayina-vpevneno-postaye-v-obrazi-novitnoyi-perspektivnoyi-37147 (website retrieved on Sept. 7, 2017).

"Europeanness" may well turn the great part of the Russians further away from Europe than bring them closer to it.

Ukraine's ability to change Russia depends primarily on two factors. The first is Ukraine's chance to join the European Union and to become a truly European nation, the first among all those who belong to historical Russia. Since even today the majority of Russians pay great respect to Europe, recognizing Russia as a European nation, Ukraine's successful accession to the EU could be of great importance for the Russian public opinion. I believe this is so because neither economic successes, nor the establishment of a democratic and law-abiding society, will turn Ukraine into a beacon for the Russians. The biggest need for a Russian is the need for recognition, and if Ukraine is formally recognized by the Europeans as a part of their community, this fact might be taken into account in Russia, but nothing else.

The second factor is, as I earlier said, the feeling of unity between Ukraine and Russia, and the sense of a shared history, a unique fate, and a common future. Only if Ukraine turns into a state and society that proclaims itself as not only a part, but rather a source, of the Russian civilization, the one that is currently better than Russia itself, could it change Russian society and challenge Russian politics.

One may look at the Baltic countries to understand what I mean: these nations are wealthier than Russia, they succeeded in constructing an effective contemporary state, they have joined the European Union, and they even succeeded in keeping their Russian population from leaving the supposedly hostile nations—but nevertheless they have never been counted as a possible ideal by the Russians living in Russia. To change Russia, Ukraine should be both European and Russians-friendly, which, from my point of view, is next to impossible.

Overcoming Old Prejudices

It is hard to know whether even successful Ukrainian pro-European reforms, however unlikely, will push Russia towards democracy and modernization. In recent years Russian propaganda appeared extremely anti-European, and if in the 2000s it was NATO, and in a few instances the EU, that was criticized and bashed, today Russia tries to reject and damn contemporary European civilization in general. Moscow actively dislikes the spirit of internationalism, the revisionist approach to sovereignty, the excessive attention to human rights, the decadent flirt with sexual minorities, and other contemporary European attributes. Russian ideologues are trying to depict Europe as a source of all the possible vices that might affect Russia, and so turn it away from its unique predestination. Under this perspective, a truly European Ukraine is seen as even more hostile, alienated, and dangerous than the Ukraine of today.

Russia possesses a very strange sense of success. Andrei Kokoshin, a former deputy Minister of Defense and long-time Duma member, argues that a successful country should enjoy unlimited sovereignty, real sovereignty, as he puts it. He and most of Russia's political elite contend that even Germany and Japan aren't really sovereign nations these days, since they have foreign military bases on their territories and are involved in strong military alliances with stronger states.[26] The very idea of being part of a group or an alliance in which another state is stronger than you strikes a Russian as dangerous. In this context, one should pay attention to Russian President Vladimir Putin's extremely equivocal statement made at a Security Council meeting in 2014: "Russia, is fortunately not a member of any alliance. This is also a guarantee of our sovereignty [since] any nation that is part of an alliance gives up part of its sovereignty."[27] If one takes into account that Russia is a signatory of the Shanghai Cooperation Organization, the Collective Security Treaty Organization, the Eurasian Union and other groupings, it appears necessary to consider what Russia's obligations to international treaties really mean. But my point is that today Russia has a very special sense of partnership: it excludes even a possibility to be a partner to anybody stronger than it. This is likely to ruin its relationship with China in the not-too-distant future.

It may not be true that Russia today is not a part of any alliance. But what is definitely correct is that for centuries Russia has had no wish to partner with stronger powers. The only time it happened was in cases of extreme emergency, such as during the Napoleonic wars or during World War II. For most of the country's history, Russia's rulers have faced a basic question: Who is with us, who is against us? Whenever Russia appeared as an alliance-builder, it was the alliance's major power (as can be traced from the Holy Alliance years to those of the Warsaw Pact).

---

[26] See: Andrei Kokoshin, *Real Sovereignty in the Contemporary World-Political System*, 3rd edition [in Russian] (Moscow: Evropa Publishing House, 2006, pp. 63–65).

[27] Vladimir Putin, "Remarks at the Security Council meeting, Moscow, July 22, 2014" at: http://en. kremlin.ru/events/president/news/46305 (website retrieved on Sept. 7, 2017).

For most of Ukraine's history, in contrast, it was a weaker nation that was forced to answer a different question; With whom do we partner? Ukrainian statesmen had to choose which side to take, and of course historically the principal question whether the nation should take Russia's side, or stay with Europe (Grand Duchy of Lithuania, Poland, Germany, the EU, etc.). Therefore, the main question for the Euromaidan was simple, and the people were ready to make their choice.

Russia, however, presents a different case and is confronted by different choices. Even if Ukraine succeeds in Europe, it will be extremely hard for Russia to follow suit. For a Ukrainian, to choose democracy and the European future is to choose revival of her or his state and to save it from reintegration into the Russian Empire. For a Russian to do the same means sacrificing her or his state and abandoning its imperial history and global ambitions. Because of this, Russia will not follow Ukraine in its drift towards Europe, and might become even more conservative and aggressive if Kyiv succeeds on its reformist path.

Conclusion

I cannot imagine how Ukraine may change Russia in coming years. I would agree that the struggle of Ukrainian citizens may challenge and change the lives of many Russians, since they realize the role their own country plays in the ongoing conflict, and because they will make their own individual pro-European choices (look at how rapidly emigration from Russia has grown in recent years). But I cannot agree that many Russians will profit from what is now going on in Ukraine (one may cite dozens of cases where bright and ambitious Russians went to Kyiv, after both the 2004 and 2014 events, and actually achieved nothing)[28] or that Russia might be galvanized by Ukrainian events to the extent that it will abandon its authoritarian legacy or follow Kyiv's road to Europe.

The window of opportunity for Ukraine to transform Russia actually existed only in the mid-2000s, when some political freedom still existed in Russia, when Russia was much friendlier towards Europe, when neo-authoritarian trends in Russia were much weaker; and when the European path was considered to be the right way for Russia, even by many inside

---

[iv] Recent examples include Alexander Stchetinin's work and death, Maria Gaydar's troubles with Odessa's political elite, or former Russian State Duma deputy Denis Voronenkov's ill-fated exile.

the political elite. Vladimir Putin himself said in his Bundestag address that "as for European integration, we not just support these processes, but we are looking to them with hope" since "Stalinist totalitarian ideology could no longer oppose the ideas of freedom and democracy as the spirit of these ideas was taking hold of the overwhelming majority of Russian citizens."[29] The Orange Revolution opened many more opportunities for changing Russia than the Euromaidan did. Times have changed. Ukrainian and Western politicians should abandon the hope that Ukraine's transformation may become someone else's in coming decades.

The transformation of Ukraine into a prosperous and democratic European nation is now at stake. Its success is itself an incredible opportunity, challenge, and priority. What the West should do today is to win the battle for Ukraine, not for Russia.

In coming decades, Russia's story will evolve in its own sovereign way: the country's fate will depend largely on domestic political developments. Today, Russian politics is dominated not so much by its President, Vladimir Putin, as by a long history of antidemocratic and quasi-despotic rule, which was slightly shaken, but not reversed, in the 1980s and 1990s.[30] Since the West appears to have no interest in provoking a sustained transformation in the country (in the 1990s it considered Russia as a normal country, just as Weimar Germany was counted as normal in the 1920s), it will take years, if not decades, for the Russians to experience a new economic meltdown comparable with that of the late 1980s, to realize that all of their geopolitical adventures have failed, and to then rise up and demand a radical change of the existing system.

This will be a tough task. If the Kremlin learned any lessons from Ukrainian history, they are the need to stay firm against the crowd, and to defend your authority through all available means. That means that the prospects for change in Russia, three years after the Euromaidan, look much bleaker than at the time of the 2004 Orange Revolution.

---

[29] Putin, Vladimir. "Speech in the Bundestag of the Federal Republic of Germany, Berlin, September 25, 2001" at: http://en.kremlin.ru/events/president/transcripts/21340 (website retrieved on Sept. 7, 2017).

[30] For greater detail, see: Inozemtsev, Vladislav. "Vernarrt in die Vergangenheit: Die Wurzeln des Putinismus reichen bis in die neunziger Jahre zurück" in: *Internationale Politik*, 2017, № 1 (Januar-Februar), SS. 74–83.

Chapter 4

Eastern Europe's Challenge to Russian-Western Relations

Lyubov Shishelina

Twenty-five years after the crash of the Soviet Union and its geopolitical derivatives COMECON and the Warsaw Pact, which in turn led to the end of the bipolar world order, the globe has experienced a number of local conflicts of varying scale, and we now face a dangerous point of confrontation. Global institutions formed for a different era seem less relevant to this new age. The international order appears unable to cope with unprecedented turbulence in relationships between countries and regions. Political life in both new and old countries is marked by unprecedented instability. The forces of disintegration and destruction unleashed at the end of the 1980s challenge sovereignties and state authority. The rearrangement of territories and peoples that once comprised the space of the former Soviet bloc remains in flux and has not been acknowledged nor accepted by all.

This chaos can be stopped only by means of a new "post-bipolar rethinking," or a reasonable consensus among the relevant parties. Unfortunately, this seems increasingly difficult due to the unwillingness of the main opponents—the United States and Russia—to reach a political compromise Meanwhile, geographic and political gray zones are growing.

What must be done to stop further deterioration of the situation? First, the East–West dialogue must be reset. Second, effective mechanisms must be developed for joint settlement in "gray zones," especially some kind of a common neighborhood policy for eastern Europe. Third, economic and social stability remains important in states—such as Russia—capable of influencing the situation in such gray zones.

All three elements are related; if one is not addressed, efforts in the other areas are likely to be in vain. Moreover, all of the gray zones encompass the space around Russia, thus endangering its own economic and political stability. It is enough to look at the geographical map to understand Russia's engagement and to understand that, on the one hand, Russia could not afford the luxury of inaction—especially if we take into consideration that transfrontier regions everywhere are comprised of Russian-speakers, like in Crimea and Donbass, who often have Russian passports or, like in the Baltic states, non-citizen passports. On the other hand, Russia's own domestic situation is an important determinant of the means it has chosen to address the dangers of instability surrounding it.

Of the three points mentioned above, the situation in Russia itself is of crucial importance. No pressure from the outside world can damage Russia's domestic situation as much as a failure of vision and lack of political will for change inside the country.

Over the 25 years since the collapse of the USSR, no real breakthrough efforts at economic or political stabilization were undertaken, except that by the Yevgeny Primakov government after the default at the end of the 1990s. But that was only a brief effort, and was helped by very favorable oil prices.

Here is the paradox of the situation: if Russia did not react to violations of the rights of the Russian population in the near abroad, its policy would be doomed to condemnation domestically as well as among its compatriots abroad. If Russia does react—like it did after the 2014 winter and spring imprisonment of Russian activists in Ukraine—it is condemned at the international arena. From this point of view the situation looks irreparable.

The Central European Experience: Can it be Useful?

There is much in common between the processes that took place in central and in eastern Europe and those that took place in Russia. All underwent deep economic, social, and political transformations. But the processes in eastern Europe and Russia were more complicated, because in addition to these radical changes they had to establish their new statehoods within the borders acquired within practically one month by "joint efforts" of presidents Gorbachev and Yeltsin. Here arises the difference in central/east European relations with Moscow, and accordingly, in Moscow's relations with them. Thus, although from the beginning they could be considered elements of one process—the collapse of the socialist system—very soon the paths of central and eastern Europeans separated. The decision of the central Europeans from the mentioned point of view had been clear: to adopt the standards of Western integration. Eastern

Europeans, on the other hand, continued for a quarter of a century to try to balance deeper ties with the West with efforts to remain with Russia.

For more than 20 years it has been clear to any professional analyst studying relations between Russia and central Europe that an unstable and disoriented Ukraine poses the major challenge to any effort to develop new forms of cooperation among Russia, its neighbors and the West.[1] Ukraine's chronic instability, aggravated by differences between two parts of the country that have been unable to reach consensus on major issues of statehood, has been a major challenge for East and West alike, and each side has sought to steer the country towards its own camp in a post-bipolar contest for influence.

The situation in central Europe, in contrast, had been stabilized beginning in the mid-1990s, due largely to the decision of those countries to join the European Union and NATO. Reform plans and road maps worked out by common regional and EU expert groups were critical to ensuring a relatively stable, comparatively quick, and ultimately successful transition of these countries toward the European mainstream.

Russia at that time was immersed in its own political and economic reforms, which—let us not forget—were being carried out by the Yegor Gaidar government in close consultation with U.S and other Western experts. They had no intention of including Russia in any integration community, nor did they have a vision for the future of the Russian Federation. Decommunization, deconstruction and massive privatization of state property were urgent orders of the day.

Given Russia's preoccupation with its own internal economic and political restructuring, central Europe ceased to be a major subject of concern. Moreover, following the dissolution of COMECON, Russia agreed to erase the significant debts accumulated by other COMECON countries vis-a-vis the Soviet Union as part of the bloc's various trade arrangements. Moscow had little interest, therefore, in stagnant economies, each facing its own economic challenges, and chose to look to more promising opportunities offered by new open markets emerging from the end of the Cold War.

In short, Russia's relations with central European states, having lost their political and economic glue, began to loosen and drift apart. Russia

---

[1] Концепция внешней политики Российской Федерации. 28 июня 2000 г., http://www.ng.ru/world/2000-07-11/1_concept.html (5.02.2017).

watched its former allies reorient themselves to the West, but given relatively good relations with the West at the time of Boris Yeltsin, and flush with its own sense of opportunity following the collapse of the Soviet Union, Moscow did not undertake any practical steps to block the pro-Western course of the central European states. The high water mark of this approach could be seen in Russia's foreign policy concept from the year 2000, in which only 3.5 lines were devoted to relations with central European countries—less than the space allocated to Russia's relations with African countries.[2]

Russia took a distinctly different approach, however, to countries of the former Soviet Union. Relations with countries of Commonwealth of Independent States remained a priority for all Russian governments during this period.

At the time, Western powers were keen not to irritate Russia. On the eve of accepting these countries into the European Union, several rounds of tripartite talks were held between the newcomer countries, the EU and Russia. They were elaborated in the documents signed by the Russian Federation and the European Communities and the Council of the European Union.[3] As the documents show, the new acceding states adopted the major principles of relations between Moscow and Brussels as consolidated by them in 1994 and 1997.

It is important to mention that, by that moment, the Kremlin's relations with the West—especially Italy and Germany—had become much better than with the parting former allied socialist countries. The formulations of the documents signed in 2004 demonstrate understanding by Brussels about major Russian concerns at least as regards its trade and economic relations with the former COMECON countries:

> EU also confirms that compensatory tariff adjustments accorded in the context of EU enlargement through modifications of the EU tariff schedule will be applied on an MFN basis to the advantage of Russian exporters.[4]

---

[2] Концепция внешней политики Российской Федерации. 28 июня 2000 г. URL: http://www.ng.ru/world/2000-07-11/1_concept.html (5.02.2017)

[3] Protocol to the Partnership and Cooperation Agreement 2004, https://russiaeu.ru/userfiles/file/protocol_to_the_pca_2004_english.pdf; Joint Statement on EU enlargement and Russia-EU relations 2004, https://russiaeu.ru/userfiles/file/joint_statement_on_eu_enlargement_and_russia_eu_relations_2004_english.pdf

[4] Joint Statement, Ibid.

Or the following:

> Agreement has been reached to adapt the EU-Russia agreement on trade in certain steel products *to reflect traditional Russian exports to the acceding countries*.[5] The purpose of the transitional special measures will be to prevent a sudden sharp negative impact on traditional trade flows.[6]

Even the details of transit to the Kaliningrad region of persons and goods had been addressed in the document to give Russia confidence that it faced no dangerous threats to its future economic well-being and security. The protocol, signed on the eve of the European Union's Eastern enlargement, contained very optimistic lines concerning the future of the European continent:

> The EU and Russia reaffirm their commitment to ensure that EU enlargement will bring the EU and Russia closer together in a Europe without dividing lines, inter alia by creating a common space of freedom, security and justice.[7]

This belief grounded in the mutual work of Russian and EU experts on the document *Road Map on the Common Economic Space*,[8] signed on May 10, 2005 in Moscow.

Thus, to a large extent both the NATO and EU membership of central European countries was achieved via consensus between East and West. The manner in which the issues were addressed generated a positive influence on the overall development of relations between central European countries and Russia.

The tenor of the times was illustrated by remarks by Deputy Foreign Minister Alexander Avdyeev at a 2001 conference at the Russian Academy of Sciences on "Russia and Central Europe in the New Geopolitical Realities."[9] Avdyeev touted the revival of Russia's relations with the countries

---

[5] Author's emphasis.
[6] Joint Statement, op. cit.
[7] Joint Statement, op. cit.
[8] Road Map on the Common Economic Space. Approved on May 10, 2005, https://russiaeu.ru/userfiles/file/road_map_on_the_common_economic_space_2005_english.pdf.
[9] Россия и Центральная Европа в новых геополитических реальностях. Сборник выступлений участников III международной научной конференции «Россия и Центральная Европа в но-

of central and eastern Europe[10] and heralded new possibilities, particularly in economic relations, stating that "We are ready to follow this path in relations with eastern European countries as far as our partners themselves would be ready for this." This formula, which was used by Russian officials at different levels, later on gave new impetus to a period of unprecedented growth in economic ties between Russia and central Europe.

These developments tracked with an overall positive turn in Russia–EU relations, including initiation at the 2003 St. Petersburg summit of the so-called "Four Spaces" of cooperation: 1) a common economic space; 2) a common space of stability, security and justice; 3) a common space of international security; 4) a common space for scientific research and education including cooperation in the cultural sphere. At the 2005 Moscow summit road maps for implementing the four projects were adopted. Within this frame there was ample room for central European countries to find their role and place. Good results were registered on all sides until 2006, when Poland blocked the signing of a new EU-Russia agreement and then introduced the Eastern Partnership program.

Was it good or bad that the West was so actively engaged in the shaping of a new central Europe? One can find both positives and negatives. Among the positives was the fact that as soon as Western capitals offered these countries a clear perspective of joining European and Euro-Atlantic structures, they set forth clear conditions to make such integration possible, and helped the countries resolve a number of difficult territorial and other disputes.[11] Western leaders were forthright that joining European structures could only be possible when these countries met EU criteria in spheres ranging from the economy to justice and politics, and they offered road maps towards gradual achievement of these goals. Joining the West gave central European countries a feeling a partnership and security at a time of wars and conflict in neighboring regions, such as the former Yugoslavia, Transnistria and Chechnya. It also helped central Europeans to shape their own positive regional integration, as evidenced by the Visegrad group.

вых геополитических реальностях»/ под. ред. Л.Н.Шишелиной. М.: ИМЭПИ РАН, 2002, стр.18-19.

[10] From 1990 until the mid-2000s the term "Central and Eastern Europe" was used in Russia for the countries of current central Europe, although sometimes the term Eastern Europe was used.

[11] Nationalistic slogans had been among the drivers of crushing the socialist system in this part of Europe.

On the other hand, all of these initiatives were realized at a cost: some national interests were surrendered as traditional domestic industries were challenged, former eastern markets were lost, and central Europeans found themselves confronted with such modern European problems as loss of jobs, migration of the most capable work force, and heightened social inequality. They felt compelled to participate in military actions far beyond their own territories and distant from Europe. Today they find themselves bound by such European rules as the need to accept quotas on migrants.

On balance, however, the clear majority of central Europeans prefer being members of the EU than being left outside it. Of course the absence of an alternative economic-social model of integration is an important factor, given that the previous model ceased to exist in the late 1980s and that the questions of membership in new Eurasian structures has never been on the agenda for these countries. Since the dissolution of the two market integrations in Europe towards the end of the 1980s, there has been to no alternative to EU integration. The projects of CIS and EAES, as well as all intermediate uniting plans, which over the past 25 years have been pushed by Moscow, Minsk, and Astana, never became functional. For central European countries there was only one path—that of integration into successfully functioning Western integration communities.

Perhaps the most effective Russian proposal for trans-European integration was made by Pjotr Savicky, a Russian geopolitician of the 20th century and one of the founders of the Russian school of Continental geopolitics. Savicky advocated for a transcontinental integration plan that would connect its two fragments: integration of countries around Berlin and integration of countries around Moscow.[12] Who knows how the history of the world might have changed if not for one crucial point: the lack of an effective and stable Moscow-oriented integration.

Currently we see how the countries of the region, especially the Visegrad four, are changing their initial perceptions of Western integration. As the outer border of the European Union, they have currently turned into a first line of defense against waves of humanity clamoring to enter Europe, many of whom are suffering refugees, but who also include terrorists and criminals of all shades. Hungary and Poland had to withstand serious and persistent attacks from Brussels on their efforts to make independent political and economic decisions. The migration crisis may mark the beginning

---

[12] Пётр Савицкий. Очерки международных отношений // Пётр Савицкий. Континент Евразия. М., Аграф, 1997. Стр.396.

of a new dynamic within the EU, in which the Brussels bureaucracy and older EU member states will need to listen to the concerns and experience of new member states in central Europe and, at least from time to time, to accept their view of a given situation. These countries today border highly turbulent regions. They cannot afford to wait until Brussels hears them. They must act, otherwise it could be too late for them.

In sum, one important historical lesson is that central European states have tended to seek integration within a community wider than their own national borders, yet have found it difficult to live with outside strictures, whether those are from the East or the West. So learning to live with this region is a great art in itself.

The Challenges of the Eastern Partnership Program

The situation in Ukraine, Moldova, and Belarus has become greatly concerning for Europe, and particularly for the countries of the Visegrad group. These three countries are not only the Visegrad group's direct neighbors, they are—with the exception of Belarus—unstable and divided countries and at the same time neighbors of Russia, sharing a Russian population, tied deeply to the Russian market and economy, using Russian as a major language and, in the case of Belarus, sharing a common Western border and defense potential as well as a quite nominal "Union" state of Russia and Belarus.[13]

During the last 25 years the former Soviet republics countries faced great challenges from both the West and the East. On one hand, they had to adapt to new geopolitical and geoeconomic realities. On the other hand, they had to preserve old economic ties and markets as the only real source of revenue and economic vitality. When the Soviet economy collapsed, modernization took place to their west, while their markets, cultural, and ethnic ties remained firmly centered in the east. Countries such as Moldova and Ukraine, which historically had been part of Western neighboring countries, made cautious forays towards the West. Belarus and Azerbaijan, on the other hand, sought tactical balances that have proved to be rather profitable.

The Eastern neighborhood policy—establishing relations between the enlarged European Union with its new eastern neighbors, had turned into

---

[13] See documents of the Union state: http://eng.soyuz.by/.

a serious call for the European Union in 2000–2001, after the decision on enlargement had been adopted at the Nice summit. It first materialized in 2003 in the form of the EU's Eastern neighborhood policy, and then in 2009 as the Eastern Partnership program.

Neither of these programs, and especially the Eastern partnership policy, generated positive relations with Russia. We can even confirm that the launch of the Eastern neighborhood program correlated with a general worsening of EU relations with Russia. Was it a strange coincidence? Or was it the start to establishing an eastern border of the European Union?

The new EU member states overloaded the EU with issues related to Russia that they insisted must be settled, but which they could not solve bilaterally.[14] In 2006 Poland vetoed a new agreement between Russia and the European Union. According to some Russian experts on EU relations, this move—although initially treated as a mere technical obstacle[15] to developing dialogue—"not only became a serious problem for Russia–EU relations, but also a symptom of a progressive disease affecting the EU's political mechanism."[16] The disease was caused by the EU's eastern enlargement, which had rendered the European Union too diverse and meant that achieving agreement was more difficult. After 2004, some of the former USSR republics (Georgia, Moldova, Lithuania) felt it appropriate to share their personal hostility towards the USSR with the "European family," thus obliging it "to defend" the republics against Russia.[17]

After Poland's claims had been settled, Lithuania was next, vetoing the new EU–Russia agreement anew on account of "post-Soviet" claims against Moscow. As a result the EU had to delay the agreement until the time would be right. Unfortunately the time is still not right. In 2009 the EU took definite steps to freeze relations with Russia because of Russian involvement in the military conflict on the border of North and South Ossetia (Georgia).

---

[14] For more, see Lyubov Shishelina, "Russia's View of Relations with European Union and the Visegrad Group," *International Issues & Slovak Foreign Policy Affairs*, Vol. XXIV, No 1-2/2015, pp.66-83.

[15] Russia had refused to import Polish chicken on sanitation grounds.

[16] D. Danilov, "Rossija—ES: osobennosti politicheskogo dialoga," [Russia–EU: features of political dialogue], in O. U. Potjemkina, ed., *Evropejskij sojuz v XXI veke: vremja ispytanij* [*European Union in the twentieth century: testing times*], Moscow: Vec mir, 2012, p. 538.

[17] Ibid.

By the end of the first decade of the new century, the Eastern Partnership had become more important to the EU.[18] The Russian Ministry of Foreign Affairs declared the Eastern Partnership to be an unfriendly gesture, contradicting the spirit of good relations between the EU and Russia, and forcing former Soviet republics to choose between two different types of integration. In the spring of 2010, Russian Foreign Minister Sergey Lavrov declared that the Eastern Partnership could damage relations between Russia and Partnership countries, especially the integration structures formed within the CIS: "Moscow sees the Eastern Partnership as an attempt to weaken Russian influence in the post-Soviet space and offer former Soviet republics a different development model."[19]

Lavrov's concerns were in response to various EU statements suggesting such a trade-off. As early as 2003 the European Parliament's Committee on Foreign Affairs, Human Rights, Common Security and Defence Policy noted in a report that "the projected establishment of a Common Economic Space together with Russia, Belarus, and Kazakhstan could hamper further cooperation between Ukraine and the EU."[20] Thus, even before the European Neighbourhood Policy was shaped, Ukraine was deliberately forced to choose between Brussels and Moscow, although the economic welfare of millions of its citizens still depended on interaction with Russia. The report went on to state that:

> Ukraine by virtue of its size, geographical location, deep historical, cultural, economic, and other links to Central and Western Europe, as well as to Russia and its potential to become an even more valuable partner of the EU in essential areas, must be given a particularly important role in the context of the EU's Wider Europe-Neighbourhood policy.[21]

---

[18] Nonetheless, this was a very positive period in economic relations between Russia and the European Union. The second half of the 2000s might be considered a time of extensive alternative gas and oil pipeline construction directing attention away from important political issues.

[19] *RIA Novosti materials*, May 13, 2010. http://www.rian.ru, accessed July 29, 2015.

[20] Report on "Wider Europe—Neighbourhood: A New Framework for Relations with our Eastern and Southern Neighbours". COM (2003) 104 -2003/2018(INI). Committee on Foreign Affairs, Human Rights, Common Security and Defence Policy // European Parliament 1999–2004 Session document. Final A5-0378/2003. November 5, 2003, p. 10.

[21] Ibid.

The European Union therefore "supports Ukraine's desire for EU integration." It is notable that Ukraine's link with Europe (including Western Europe) is placed above its links with Russia.

On the eve of the 2013 Vilnius summit, EU–Russia relations were quite positive in the economic sphere, but less so politically.[22] One assumption about Russian integration policy, or rather the lack of visible results in this direction, might be that Russia itself was delaying closer integration with Asian countries and still saw better prospects in resuming its European dialogue. However, some analysts state that Russia had set its main hopes on the possibility of engaging in two integration processes in the post-Soviet region—the EU and the Eurasian Economic Union, and constructing a free trade zone at the point where they intersected.

From this point of view, the worsening relations between Russia and the EU on the eve of the November 2013 summit and the fact that the Association Agreement with Ukraine was not signed in Vilnius, could have been viewed as a no-joy result of cooperation, but was in fact concurrence of Russia and EU on post-soviet space. This might be called "a zero sum game": Russia was defending its "sphere of privileged interests," and the European Union "its circle of friends." As Russian expert Olga Potjemkina puts it, "The latter sounds more elegant, but both are one and the same.[23]

This lack of political culture at the current stage of dialogue between Brussels and Moscow, intolerance, and a lack of responsibility for the fate of the region and continent as a whole were fully manifest on the eve of the Vilnius summit and during preparations for the Association Agreement with Ukraine. It would not be an exaggeration to state that one of the main triggers of the Ukrainian political crisis was the EU's Eastern Partnership Policy. The European Union did not invite Russia to discuss the prospect of joining the economic talks, while Russia was ready to extend EU–Russian plans to create four common areas linking Ukraine, Moldova, Belarus, Georgia, Armenia and Azerbaijan. The EU had provided these new countries with restructuring plans that would widen the gap between them and Russia. Thus, these countries, geographically located between

---

[22] By then Russia had become the EU's third trade partner after the United States and China. In 2012-2013 Russia's trade output with the European Union reached 49.7 percent. O. Potjemkina, "Rossija i Evropejskij sojuz: k edinomu prostranstvu ot Atlantiki do Tihogo okeana," [Russia and the European Union: a common space from the Atlantic to the Pacific Ocean] Русский вопрос [Russian Issues], No. 3, 2013. http://www.russkiivopros.com/index.php?pag=one&id=530&kat=6&csl=63, accessed July 29, 2015.

[23] Ibid.

Russia and the EU, had been transformed from potential areas of cooperation into areas of confrontation and instability.

The response, from Russia's perspective, was Russian reintegration of Crimea—a final signal to the West following the collapse of the agreement achieved in Kyiv through Russian mediation on February 21, 2014. To understand and evaluate the one-sided concessions Russia has made since 1991 it is worth looking at the map of Europe and counting the areas of former Russian influence given up within a quarter of a century in a spirit of good will.

There remains the question whether the European expert community, driven by the euphoria of a quarter of a century of Russian concessions, failed to understand that there was a limit or breaking point to Russia's patience, or was deliberately seeking to draw Russia into confrontation. Perhaps the answer is that those in the West responsible for the strategy (as also happens sometimes in Russia) did not follow the signals coming from serious regional analysts about the importance of Ukraine for Russia.[24] Hungarian diplomat Janos Terenyi, for example, from the very start of the program had been aware that the Eastern Partnership policy puts the European Union into a serious conflict with Russia.[25]

I shall not quote here figures underscoring the economic and humanitarian interdependence of the former USSR republics before the Vilnius summit of the Eastern Partnership, which in fact became a watershed between the "world of yesterday" and "the world today." But they would support the point that Russia had good reason to be anxious about, and ultimately resist, a westward reorientation of Ukraine, Moldova, and Belarus. Currently the number of registered migrants from the former Republics constitutes about 4 million people, and unofficially more than 10 million. Moldovans, Ukrainians, and Armenians occupy the first lines among job seekers arriving to Russia from abroad. They also post the largest sums of remittances to their countries from Russia.[26]

---

[24] For example, Juraj Marusiak, "Russia and the Visegrad Group—More Than a Foreign Policy Issue," *International Issues & Slovak Foreign Policy Affairs*, Vol. XXIV, No 1-2/2015, pp. 28-46.

[25] Keleti Partnerség: terjeszkedés Oroszország felé. *KITEKINTŐ*, 20.05.2009. URL: http://kitekinto.hu/karpat-medence/2009/05/20/szines_tarsasag_kopogtat_az_eu_kapujan/#.UofHeQJdVtU (in Hungarian).

[26] А.Кошкина, А.Баринов «Россия—не место для труда и Отдыха»/ Профиль № 41 (974), 2016. С.33.

What to Do?

We are currently at a threshold: either to continue the current confrontation or to stop and try to find a way out. If we chose the latter, then let us try to reevaluate, from the distance of 25 years, what happened and why it happened the way it did. Thus, the starting point for a reevaluation should be the end of the 1980s and the beginning of the 1990s.

The destruction and chaos wrought by the cacophony of realignments and reforms that characterized that period led the countries of central Europe to address many issues that had been left unresolved over decades and to find a path towards the European mainstream. The same forces of disorder and confusion in eastern Europe, on the other hand, empowered populist extremists and entrenched vested interests who blocked reforms and reconciliation, leading to the turbulence and armed conflicts that grip this region today.

It is clear that such conflicts must be addressed, foremost those in Ukraine and Moldova—but who should do it? Should we stand aside and let these countries settle these disputes by their own means? They have been trying to do this for 25 years. Should the international community intervene? Should neighboring countries—the V4—engage once again, being already once the initiators of the Eastern Partnership policy? Or should we work out a special network for assistance in dampening down these conflicts?

From a geopolitical point of view, the major conflict is being developed in the geopolitical continental sphere between Russia and central Europe. So they should work out their vision of the probable solution. But this is in the narrow context. Besides, we should consider that the countries of central Europe in their foreign policies are restricted by subordination within the EU. In a wider context, both in Ukraine and Moldova we have characteristic features of a bigger-scale confrontation that could be defined as the clash of two systems of values, two geopolitical trends. So, the solution at the regional level might not be enough and need the inclusion of the European Union—which is lately more associated with Germany, especially after Brexit—and the United States, if after the current presidential elections its policy will follow the Euro-Atlantic trends.

If the European policy of the new U.S. administration remains unclear, some initial steps, such as talks between the newly elected US president Trump with the presidents of Russia and Ukraine, have left Moscow and

Kyiv with some hope. Now that the Minsk process has entered the phase of a frozen conflict and cannot prove its effectiveness, perhaps some new positive signals could come from across the Atlantic?

Russia, representing the bordering country, the center of the Eurasian space, and a world power, thus is a part of all three proposed configurations of talks. Beginning with the lower—regional—level, a kind of scheme for settling the conflict became apparent during the Kremlin's talks with Moldova's newly elected president Dodon. He proposed to settle the Transnistria problem through the unification of Moldova, rather than via a federal solution that would grant special status to Tiraspol. This vision of a settlement corresponds with current Russian propositions and possibilities. The challenge, however, remains the intensive inner conflict between the pro-Russian presidential line in Moldova and the European inclinations of the cabinet of ministers. This deep political conflict does not add confidence to the determination of Transnistria to start realization of this plan of settlement immediately.

As to foreign policy trends in the European Union and Russia, the EU has stepped back a bit from the most far-reaching aspects of the Eastern Partnership, even though it began 2017 by granting visa-free regime to Georgia and in June 2017 granted visa-free travel to Ukraine. Russia, on the contrary, has continued to underscore the priority of moving ahead with initiatives to advance all levels of integration in the post-Soviet space.

For the moment, Russian ministries have not presented any constructive plans to realize such initiatives. Yet just as Brussels was keen on mediating with Russia during the accession of the central European countries to the EU in the early 2000s, Russia and the EU might also seek to find overlap in their partnership policies with regard to Belarus, Moldova, Ukraine, and the Caucasus. Such efforts could offer a serious chance both for reconciliation and for modernization of these gray zones and really pave the way towards an "integration of integrations." This has already been proposed under the program of the so-called "Four Common Spaces" between the European Union and Russia, until the one-sided policies of the Eastern Neighborhood and Eastern Partnership pushed broader EU-Russia considerations aside.

If the European Union and Russia could find their way back to constructive dialogue about common spaces, the conflicts in gray zones will eliminate themselves. The interest of each of these countries in joining such a broader effort would become an additional incentive for each of them to stabilize the political situation in their country and to consider constructive administrative reforms that might include also federalization.

In short, the task for Russia and the United States is to revive and reset the dialogue, and the task for Russia and the European Union is to return to the idea of Four Common Spaces. The task for Russia and other neighboring countries (V4 among them) is to start the Common Neighborhood dialogue. And the task for Russia itself is to work out and to start deep and overwhelming economic reform for the benefit of the nation.

Chapter 5

Russia and the West: Energy Warfare

Mikhail Krutikhin

The nature and shape of the Russian oil and gas industry is not just Moscow's concern. The ups and downs of Russia's energy production and exports are factors that affect the global political environment. The influx of revenues from hydrocarbon sales determines the way the Kremlin behaves in the world arena, and the notorious unpredictability of the Russian political leadership becomes even more pronounced when oil prices show an appetite for instability.

Russia is a major energy supplier. In 2015 it accounted for 11.6% of global oil production and 17.8% of global natural gas production. Its natural gas export sales equaled 19.1% of the world's total. Russia remains the world's largest supplier of piped gas (covering about 30% of the EU's total demand), even though it plays a much smaller role in global LNG trade.

It would be wrong to assume that Russia and foreign consumers of its oil and gas are equally dependent on each other. While stable revenues from energy exports are an important to domestic socioeconomic stability and even survival of the incumbent regime, international consumers' dependence on Russian supply is shrinking. Recipients of Russian oil can relatively easily switch to other sources, and the EU, the principal market for Russian natural gas, is slowly adopting very practical measures to enhance its energy security by encouraging energy saving, energy efficiency, the use of alternative types of energy, diversifying suppliers, building interconnectors, and raising the proportion of LNG in its gas imports.[1]

Russia's financial health depends much more on exports of raw materials (predominantly represented by oil and gas) than is officially recognized. In June 2016, Prime Minister Dmitry Medvedev said that the share of oil and gas revenues in the federal budget had fallen to 34%, from 45% in

---

[1] In the last quarter of 2014 and the first quarter of 2015, President Putin ordered Gazprom to cut its gas deliveries to Western Europe to a minimum, to prevent "reverse" gas sales to Ukraine, yet gas prices at European trading hubs were unaffected.

the previous year.[2] Pro-government media hastened to declare that the decline was caused by an increasing share of revenues from other sectors of the economy. In fact, both figures are open to doubt.

According to the economy research team at the Carnegie Moscow Center, the Russian federal budget received over 90% of its revenues from the sale of mineral resources in 2014, and the following year 2015 witnessed another decline of other revenues.[3] In Russia, taxes from citizens do not constitute a significant part of federal revenues, and the majority of the population's income (from salaries of government-fed labor force to pension funds) has to be subsidized by revenues that come from exports of mineral resources. These vitally important revenues have been shrinking since the fourth quarter of 2014, when oil prices started plummeting in the wake of the shale revolution in North America.

Foreign factors such as low energy prices and poor prospects for global energy demand are amplified by domestic issues: politicized investment decisions, monopoly practices, inefficient government-run corporations, an investment-discouraging fiscal system, rampant corruption, discrimination of private business and foreign investors, a notoriously unfair judicial system, lack of rule of law, and other issues. Russia's intervention in Georgia, Ukraine, and Syria has led to international self-isolation of the Russian regime and aggravated its economic problems. Western sanctions against Russia have made it hard for petroleum operators to procure long-term funding and gain access to sophisticated technologies as well as credits for investment.

Confronted with challenges that may result in a catastrophe for the national economy, the Russian government has been unable to respond adequately. One of the main reasons is the specific economic system of today's Russia. The system is based on collecting and distributing natural rent, and the deficiencies of such an arrangement are aggravated by a management pattern that can be referred to as "crony capitalism." A few people associated with the president of the country control cash flows from the federal budget to specific businesses, and from these businesses to the budget, and then appropriate part of the flows in the interests of themselves and the whole group. The key questions for the rest of the world, and especially for the developed nations, is how Russia's basic industry may evolve, and how to engage with Russia and its regime.

---

[2] http://www.ntv.ru/novosti/1634737/.
[3] https://www.facebook.com/andrei.movchan/posts/1268406526548888.

Accelerated Depletion

Russia produced 547.5 million metric tons (MMT) of oil and condensate in 2016 (10.965 million barrels per day (MMbpd)), consumed 284.3 MMt domestically, exported 235.8 MMt beyond the former USSR, and sold 18.4 MMt within the Commonwealth of Independent States (in Belarus). Overall production of liquid hydrocarbons was 2.5% larger than in the previous year.[4] The physical volume of oil and condensate exports from Russia increased 7% in 2016, but low prices eroded the value of these sales by 17.7% to $73.676 billion.[5]

The growth of oil production in Russia deserves a closer look. The factors that exert a depressing effect on upstream operators' activities are obvious:

- Low prices of oil, generally expected to continue for at least a few years with an uncertain outlook, prevent companies from investing in new projects that require large capex and a protracted period of negative cash flow.[6]
- Low prices also make it hard for investors to finance development of tight reserves—and about 70% of Russia's remaining oil reserves are officially recognized as "hard to recover."
- Most of the large Russian oil projects that are currently on stream are past peak production and their reserves are facing depletion. New discoveries are minuscule in size. According to the Ministry of Natural Resources, Russia's recoverable oil reserves would be depleted by 2044 at the current rate of production.[7]
- The government definitely wants to tap the oil and gas industry for extra taxes. It has already frozen the promised decrease of the oil export tax after a markup of the mineral extraction tax and intends to undertake other actions for increasing the tax burden on oil and gas producers (there are no other sectors in the national economy

---

[4] https://rg.ru/2017/01/02/dobycha-nefti-v-rossii-za-2016-god-obnovila-rekord.html.
[5] https://rns.online/energy/Dohodi-Rossii-ot-eksporta-nefti-v-2016-godu-sokratilis-na-178—do-737-mlrd-2017-02-08/.
[6] Oslo-based Rystad Energy estimated in June 2016 that the breakeven price of barrel for Russian oil projects that have not yet seen a final investment decision averages $110, although this estimate covers all types of projects, including Arctic offshore and hard-to-recover reserves.
[7] https://rg.ru/2016/03/16/glava-minprirody-rasskazal-kogda-v-rossii-zakonchitsia-neft.html.

that can be used as a source of additional income for the ailing state budget).[8]

The factors that work in the opposite direction and enable the oil and gas companies to remain in business, and even contribute additional volumes of oil to the country's overall output are also evident:

- The majority of Russia's ongoing oil projects have had their capital expenditures reimbursed long ago, and production costs there do not include an investment amortization component. Sunk costs make it commercially viable to continue production.
- Final investment decisions were made for a large number of projects well before oil prices started their downward slide in the last quarter of 2014, and significant funding has been approved. Companies are going ahead with the projects because dropping them at this stage would mean a big loss of cash. Still, they maintain a no-fringes regime at such projects to minimize costs.
- The depreciation of the Russian national currency (from 35 rubles per U.S. dollar in the middle of 2014 to 60 rubles in December 2016) has enabled companies to save on costs of labor, power, domestic materials and equipment, taxes, etc., while earning hard currency for exported gas, crude oil, and refined products. As a result, the breakeven price of Russia's exported crude oil from brownfield projects is tentatively estimated to average in the range of $24 to $27 per barrel of Urals blend, which ensures a comfortable profit against the 2015–2016 average of around $45 per barrel of Brent.[9]
- Fiscal incentives available for specific categories of Russian upstream projects help them remain commercially viable.[10]
- Three grandfathered projects that operate under production-sharing schemes (Sakhalin 1, Sakhalin 2, and Kharyaga) enjoy special tax regimes that enable them to maintain, and even increase, production levels.

---

[8] http://www.vedomosti.ru/business/articles/2016/08/25/654406-minfin-sobrat-neftyanikov.

[9] When Russian government officials quote a figure around $2 per barrel as "production costs" of regular oil and over $20 for tight and offshore oil, they mean only lifting costs (opex). Effective (total) production costs have to include capex, administrative and marketing expenses, transportation costs, taxes, interest on credit, etc.

[10] http://www.ey.com/GL/en/Services/Tax/Global-oil-and-gas-tax-guide---XMLQS?preview&XmlUrl=/ec1mages/taxguides/GOG-2016/GOG-RU.xml.

Driven by those conflicting factors, Russian oil companies are pursuing strategies that lack long-term vision. They keep recording high-volume investment programs (in rubles) but the structure of investments has changed dramatically in comparison with the high-price period prior to 2014. In the low-price environment Russian oil producers prefer to focus on quick gains from marketing whatever cheap oil they still can recover from ongoing (brownfield) projects rather than investing in exploration and development of new (greenfield) projects. An onshore greenfield project may take between seven and fifteen years to reach payback, and the price of oil during that period is a great uncertainty, especially in view of the poor quality (and high recovery cost) of Russia's untapped yet reserves.

Even as companies assure the government that they are not trimming down their investment programs, investments are mostly made not in development but in drilling extra wells at the most productive reservoirs and in enhanced oil recovery (EOR) methods from the reservoirs that are already on-stream. This approach translates into an accelerated depletion of underground reserves. In the Khanty-Mansi Autonomous District of western Siberia, Russia's main oil producing area, production fell from 270.6 MMt in 2009 to 239 MMt in 2016, and is expected to decrease by another 20% by 2030.

According to Fitch, the Russian oil industry is already in the red. The main companies' costs (including the dividend and investments in future production) exceed the size of their cash income. The agency estimates that each barrel of produced crude oil removes an average of about $0.50 from the companies' financial balance.[11]

Paradoxically, the same companies that boast ridiculously small production costs and ability to remain in business in the low-price environment warn the government that oil production in Russia is going to drop sharply without additional tax incentives. When the Ministry of Energy collected oil companies' forecasts of their performance for the next twenty years in 2015 and summed the forecasts up, it discovered that the industry was predicting a decline of national oil production from almost 11 MMbpd to less than 6 MMbpd (297–310 MMt a year) by 2035.[12]

Some of these dire predictions have to be ascribed to the companies' desire to blackmail the government into fiscal benefits for the industry,

---

[11] http://www.finanz.ru/novosti/aktsii/Fitch-rossiyskiy-neftyanoy-sektor-teryaet-po-$0-5-na-kazhdy-barrel-dobychi-1001379462.
[12] Draft General Scheme of Development of RF Oil Industry through 2035.

Figure 1. Russian Oil and Condensate Production Outlook with New Projects, thousand bpd

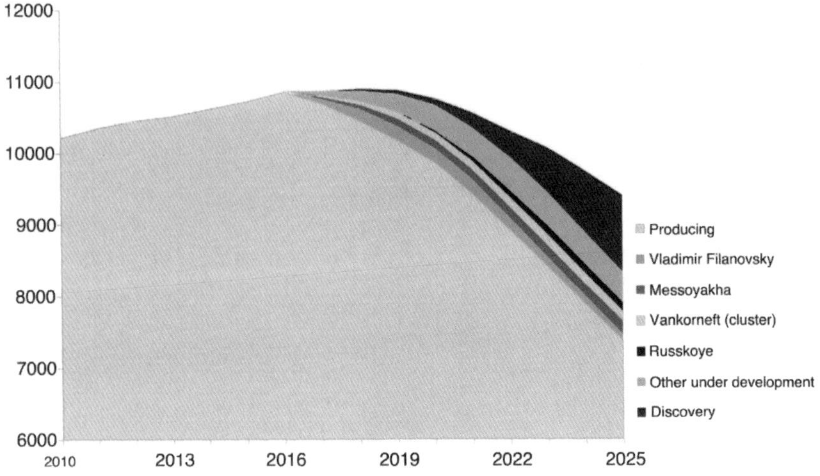

- Producing
- Vladimir Filanovsky
- Messoyakha
- Vankorneft (cluster)
- Russkoye
- Other under development
- Discovery

Source: Rystad Energy UCube (2016).

but the negative tendency cannot be avoided in view of the depletion of brownfields and shortage of newly discovered and developed reserves of cheap oil. The Ministry of Natural Resources and Energy estimates a peak of oil production in Russia to occur around 2020.[13]

Gas Galore

The natural gas sector of the Russian economy is also ailing, but not from lack of commercial production capacity. Gazprom's records for 2014 are a good example. The company's CEO Alexey Miller told President Vladimir Putin[14] that the company could have produced 617 billion cubic meters (bcm) of gas, but had been able to sell only 444 bcm during the year. The sold category included 217.2 bcm to the domestic market, 48.0 bcm to former Soviet republics, and 126.2 bcm to the far abroad, that is, to western Europe and Turkey. Some of the gas volumes Gazprom posts as sales were not physical exports from Russia but gas consignments the

---

[13] https://regnum.ru/news/economy/2173652.html.
[14] https://www.1tv.ru/news/2015/06/15/19333-vladimir_putin_vstretilsya_s_glavoy_gazproma.

Figure 2. Natural Gas Production by Gazprom Group, bcm/year

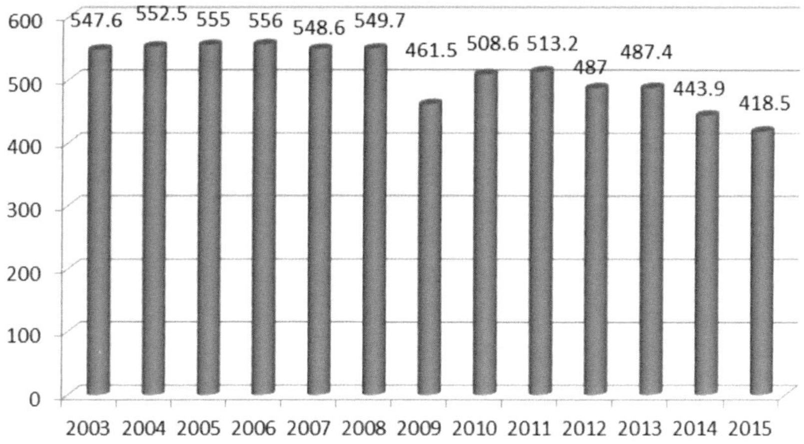

Values by year: 2003: 547.6; 2004: 552.5; 2005: 555; 2006: 556; 2007: 548.6; 2008: 549.7; 2009: 461.5; 2010: 508.6; 2011: 513.2; 2012: 487; 2013: 487.4; 2014: 443.9; 2015: 418.5.

Source: Gazprom

company's overseas trading arms obtained from non-Russian producers and resold (e.g., Gazprom delivers no Russian gas to the UK but reports sales of gas there.)

The overcapacity of gas production by Gazprom exceeds 200 bcm a year, and the Russian gas export monopoly could have easily added another Europe to the list of its customers, but there is no such thing as another Europe close to Russian gas fields and gas pipelines. Natural gas demand in Europe, the principal market of Gazprom, is not growing significantly and the company has had to slow down development of new fields on the Yamal Peninsula, which are expected to replace semi-depleted old ones. The domestic market is suffering from stagnation, and non-Gazprom gas producers snatch whatever opportunity appears to increase their hold on Russian consumers. LNG projects in Russia are somewhat questionable, mainly due to the scarcity of deep-water ice-free ports that are located close to major gas producing areas. Long-distance transportation of natural gas toward such ports is not economical.

Gazprom's attempts to play a role on the global LNG market have been unsuccessful. After some governmental pressure, the Russian monopoly acquired a controlling stake in Sakhalin 2, an international consortium (Shell, Mitsui, and Mitsubishi) that operates an LNG plant exporting about 10 MMt a year, but expansion plans in this business are still little more than declarations. The project of an LNG plant near Vladivostok on the Pacific coast is now forgotten, although Gazprom did make the investment decision on Putin's orders. There is neither adequate gas supply, nor finance, nor proof of commercial feasibility to go ahead with this project.

Russia's only LNG project that is actually going ahead is Yamal LNG, under a consortium of Russia's private company Novatek, France's Total, and two Chinese partners. To make it commercial, the Russian government has granted an exemption from all taxes and provided financing for costly infrastructure for the project. Without this unprecedented assistance, Yamal LNG would have been a commercial disaster.

The underlying reason for the overhyped pivot to China in Gazprom's plans is evidently political rather than commercial. On September 1, 2014 Vladimir Putin said that the Power of Siberia pipeline to China would enable Russia to switch gas flows from the west to the east and backwards depending on the price arbitrage.[15] And Gazprom managers claimed on multiple occasions that the volume of Russian gas exports to Asia would soon exceed that of westbound exports—an utterly unrealistic plan.

The problems with the pivot to China are obvious. To begin with, China does not need all the gas the Russians would like to deliver across the border. Moreover, as a monopoly buyer at the receiving end of the great transportation infrastructure, China will certainly insist on special terms. While Gazprom hoped to collect as much as $350–400 per thousand cubic meters for its gas in China to make the Power Siberia marginally economical, the spot prices in Asia have fallen by the middle of 2016 to about $130 ($4.40 per MMBtu), and the Russian project is now hopelessly infeasible.[16]

Russia's intention to double the capacity of its Nord Stream pipeline in the Baltic Sea is open to doubt as well. Moscow insists that the current transit route across Ukraine is insecure and wants European customers of Gazprom to switch to alternative routes, such as the Nord Stream or the abortive South Stream instead. This is not an economically feasible solution. While Gazprom is currently selling gas in Germany at prices that are on the verge of breakeven figures or below it, the idea of transmitting

---

[15] https://lenta.ru/news/2014/09/01/pipeline/.
[16] http://www.focus.de/finanzen/news/milliardengrab-power-of-siberia-warum-gazproms-giga-gasdeal-mit-china-fuer-putin-in-eine-katastrophe-ausartet_id_4890036.html?drucken=1.

this gas from Germany to Austria and then, via as-yet inexistent pipelines to Italy, Greece and Balkan nations defies commercial logic.

Meeting the Challenges

Two obvious solutions may be suggested for the alarming situation in the oil industry, and both require radical reforms, both structural and fiscal. The current structure of the industry does not encourage small-scale and medium-sized upstream businesses. Large integrated companies enjoy a domineering status even though the quality of remaining oil reserves calls for a larger role of small players: new discoveries are usually smaller than 3 MMt each, and cumbersome giants prefer dealing with large fields. Small enterprises that are prepared to assume financial, geological and other risks and take a stab at a new advanced technology are a rare case in Russia today.

Of course, it is impossible to expect a drastic change in the Russian legislation that makes the state the sole owner of mineral resources and allows developers to use subsoil riches under a license. The North American legal system (when the owner of a few acres of land possesses all the mineral wealth underneath) is unthinkable in Russian traditions, but an extra incentive for small privately-run companies would definitely help a lot.

Unfortunately, privatization in the Russian petroleum industry has been just a slogan for many years. Quite a few private, and commercially efficient, companies (e.g., Yukos, Udmurtneft, Slavneft, Sibneft, Itera, TNK-BP, Bashneft, et al.) have been taken over by either Rosneft or Gazprom, the quasi-governmental giants under politicized management. Government-controlled companies accounted for 61% of revenues in the oil and gas industry in 2014 as compared to 48% in 2005.[17]

Direct foreign investment in exploration and development is restricted by law (e.g., if a company discovers reserves in excess of 70 MMt of oil or 50 bcm of gas, the license may be transferred to a state-controlled company because such discoveries are recognized by law as strategic federal reserves.) Equity participation in offshore oil and gas production is banned. Foreign companies can only be partners in special vehicle companies, the operators of projects without any chances to book some reserves or claim a share of production.

---

[17] http://ac.gov.ru/files/publication/a/8449.pdf.

A tax reform could also benefit the Russian oil industry. The main obstacle to launching new innovative projects is the need to pay taxes on volume of production rather than on profit. For many years the industry has been lobbying for some form of a windfall tax (dubbed a tax on financial result, or a tax on extra profit), but the Ministry of Finance has successfully derailed all attempts at this reform stating that any such changes would leave the state coffers without a large portion of revenues for several years. Debates about a specific form of tax reforms can go on for a very long time, especially because the financial problems of the federal budget make it hard to endure even a short period of missing revenues because of the reform effort. Instead, the government keeps nurturing plans to increase the tax burden on the oil and gas industry.

Challenged by the prospect of seeing natural gas prices remain at a very low level for a long time, and with weakening demand for gas on the global market, the Russian government is behaving unreasonably. It is prepared to spend extravagantly on new export pipelines. Evil tongues allege that the only purpose of these infrastructure megaprojects is to make pipeline contractors richer (often without any tenders). And, since the lucky contractors are personal friends of the Russian president, such as Arkady Rotenberg and Gennady Timchenko, the allegations are not without foundation.

Investments in Russia's oil and gas industry are hardly growing. The Ministry of Energy expected them to increase from 16.7% from 1.2 trillion rubles in 2015 to 1.4 trillion rubles in 2016, but admits that growth could be eroded by new tax markups and inflation.[18] To make it worse, the structure of investments is a cause of worry. Oil operators prefer to intensify recovery at brownfield projects rather than explore new possibilities, and the major gas player, Gazprom, invests mainly in politicized projects of gas transportation infrastructure, which cannot yield any profit for a long time, if any.

Comparative statistical data for the period of January–July in various years demonstrates the gravity of the crisis. In that period of 2012, state revenues from oil exports equaled $105.8 billion but in January–July 2016 they amounted to just $39.4 billion. Revenues from gas exports in the same period plummeted from $37.46 billion in 2014 to $17.05 billion in 2016.

---

[18] http://abnews.ru/2016/03/23/investicii-v-neftegazovuyu-otrasl-rossii-vyrastut-v-2016-godu-na-167-minenergo/.

On Deaf Ears?

The energy sector of the Russian economy is of particular concern not only for the Kremlin but also for the international community. A deterioration of Russia's relations with the rest of the world in the vitally important energy business might lead to dire political consequences. It may make the Russian regime more confrontational and dangerously unpredictable in its self-imposed isolation. It may tempt Moscow to continue ascribing domestic economic problems to allegedly unfriendly activities of the West and to indulge in a new round of hostilities. Given the importance of the oil and gas sector for the Russian economy and the stability of Russia's regime, the international community may choose to influence the policy of Moscow by providing either an impediment for this sector or encouragement of cooperating with it.

Efforts have been made to find a way for improving the environment for cooperation with Russia in the energy industry and other sectors of economy. The Rand Corporation, for instance, has been pursuing this goal since 1997 through its Business Leaders Forum.[19] In 2015–16 Germany's SWP organized a "Saturday Club" of Russian and European corporate and academic experts to prepare a position paper that could be a road map for developing energy cooperation with Russia through specific common projects.[20] The EU–Russia Energy Dialogue is also going on, but its half-frozen activities are limited to contacts on the expert level without involving actual decision makers.[21] These efforts have been fruitless so far.

Russia's domestic community of experts in economics and politics is ignored by the Kremlin. Formerly influential analysts, who could be sure their opinion was heard and appreciated by the political establishment in the past keep complaining: "After Crimea, nobody listens to our recommendations up there." An expert told the author: "People in the presidential administration said we can write and publish whatever we like but the word 'recommendation' is a taboo nowadays."

The current economic crisis in Russia is evidently going to be a slow-evolving affair and can hardly lead to serious social unrest or mutinies in the foreseeable future. The majority of the population is adapting to the

---

[19] http://www.rand.org/international/cre/forum.html.
[20] http://ac.gov.ru/events/09172.html.
[21] http://www.interfax.ru/russia/533356.

crisis by trimming consumption in both quality and quantity. A recent poll demonstrated that 66% of households were looking for an extra job and 87% were already following an economy regime or planned to start such a regime.[22]

It remains to be seen how the West would react to an increasingly belligerent Russia whose behavior is determined by a mafia-like structure of government, ailing and failing economy, and shortage of cash (mainly because of low energy prices but also because of the government's inability to prevent corruption and to efficiently manage economic processes).

What the West Could Do

Essentially, there are three possible ways the West might act vis-à-vis Russia in these circumstances.

1. An appeasement strategy may eliminate some tensions in Russia's relations with other nations and create a better environment for economic cooperation (an improved investment climate, larger trade exchange, cooperation in important issues such as climate control, etc.) As former U.S. National Intelligence Director James Clapper said, commenting on Putin's arrogant attitude:

> I think he has this vision of a great Russia, as a great power. It's extremely important to him that Russia be treated and respected as a global power on a par with the United States. And I think that has a lot to do with impelling his behavior.[23]

In the energy sector, such rapprochement would open tremendous opportunities for international business. Even if the Russian government continues restricting direct involvement of foreign players in large oil and gas production projects, a softer set of sanctions (or elimination of sanctions) would benefit suppliers of advanced technologies and equipment, as well as international creditors. Cooperation with the outside world would help delay the imminent decline of Russia's oil production.

---

[22] http://www.vedomosti.ru/opinion/articles/2016/10/11/661884-tunnel-sveta and http://www.bbc.com/russian/business/2016/03/160304_zubarevich_russian_regions.
[23] http://www.rferl.org/a/potention-us-russia-conflict-seen-clinton-syria-no-fly-zone-plan-trump-clapper-/28075466.html.

The strategy is not flawless. The soft approach will certainly be interpreted by the Kremlin as weakness, and the Russian leaders will feel free to engage in new aggressive actions on the global scene. Moscow has proven many times during the past two or three years that it was not ready to follow a joint course with the United States or with European nations and prefers a confrontational attitude.

As outgoing Defense Secretary Ash Carter said in an interview, Vladimir Putin's efforts to blunt American influence have been increasing and are making it harder to find areas in which Washington and Moscow can work together:

> It seems to be part of his self-conception. And one of the ways he defines the success of his policy is not by results on the ground but the level of the discomfort he can create in the rest of the world and show to his people as the point of his policy.... That's what makes it so difficult to build a bridge.[24]

It would be naïve to assume that the Russian leader

> hopes to scale back tensions with the United States and secure Washington's assent for a new, multipolar world order based on the spheres of influence of the great powers rather than on the liberal norms and institutions that dominated the post-Cold War era.[25]

Efforts of some Russian non-governmental foreign policy organizations, such as the Russian International Affairs Council, to propagate a dialogue with the West for the sake of a multipolar world are either ignored or resented by Kremlin decision makers. A senior official of the Presidential Administration told the author angrily during a rare frank conversation: "They are making more harm than benefits for us. In a nutshell, we want a new Yalta."

Efforts to either contain or accommodate Russia are failing, associate fellow at Chatham House Lilia Shevtsova warns, explaining:

---

[24] http://www.wsj.com/articles/ash-carter-says-putin-is-making-it-harder-for-u-s-to-work-with-russia-1483698600.
[25] https://www.foreignaffairs.com/articles/2017-01-04/rapprochement-russias-terms?cid=soc-fb-rdr.

The new mantra of "transactional relations" (a policy expected to be supported by U.S. president-elect Donald Trump) does not exactly inspire hope, either. Moscow is ready for a new "grand bargain" and has made its demands clear. It wants not only a "New Yalta," but also Western endorsement of Russia's right to interpret global rules as it sees fit and to build an order based on a balance of interests and powers.[26]

To make it even more hopeless, the issues of Crimea, southeastern Ukraine, and Syria make it hard to hope for success of any dialogue or, in a larger sense, détente, for the time being.

2. An opposite approach, a containment and stop-and-punish-the-aggressor strategy, may also work in unpredictable ways. The most effective measures would have to include international sanctions against Putin's close associates and Putin himself (especially targeting their assets abroad); international persecution of Russian officials accused of war crimes; enhancement of the West's relations with the countries in Moscow's sphere of interests; accelerated development of energy sources and methods that could erode Russia's domination on some energy markets; and a propaganda and counter-propaganda campaign.

A new set of sanctions against Russia,[27] including probably a ban on investing more than a few million dollars in Russian oil and gas projects, would undermine the Russian energy industry's ability to maintain the current level of oil production and expand gas exports. An abrupt decline of oil and gas revenues to the federal budget would affect the socioeconomic vitality of the regime and probably lead to social unrest. It is hardly possible to expect a turn toward democratic reforms and liberalization of the economy because of new hardships. The regime will probably resort to new belligerent acts abroad and ascribe the problems to foreign conspiracies. The duration of such attitudes, as well as the survival potential of the Russian regime in these circumstances, are open to speculation.

This confrontational strategy would provide the Russian leadership with new fuel for its domestic propaganda (the nation is surrounded by enemies, let's tighten our belts, eliminate the fifth column, and support the great leader). Moreover, driven into a corner, the Russian regime may

---

[26] https://www.chathamhouse.org/expert/comment/efforts-contain-russia-are-failing.

[27] http://www.cbsnews.com/news/senators-introduce-sweeping-russia-sanctions-in-response-to-hacks/.

become desperate and nasty. In addition, the interests of European business in Russia have to be taken into account—and the Kremlin will do its best to capitalize on European unwillingness to spoil relations with Russia.

3. A wait-and-see strategy aimed at outliving the Russian regime is another option. The international community may opt for monitoring the situation in Russia without much interference and make attempts at minimizing the impact of negative developments. The goal would be to expect the internal processes in Russia to reach a critical phase, which would require a radical change from within in the economic and political management of the country.

Looking for the limelight is evidently the Russian president's major weakness. "Indifference of the world to statements and actions of Putin would be the worst punishment for him," as a prominent political analyst in Moscow says off the record. Combined with a containment strategy, it might be a powerful instrument in dealings with the Kremlin. On the other hand, accommodating Putin's desire for publicity—without actually making serious concessions—may become a lubricant for maintaining some sort of a détente.

The question remains whether a dialogue for the sake of confidence building is still possible in view of Russia's determination to maintain the status of its military involvement in Ukraine, Syria and, probably, in some other regions in the future. Without a real dialogue, the West will have to resort to developing a joint effort to defend its interests against Russia's arrogant and provocative attitude—all the way to a dangerous military buildup. In these circumstances, Russian oil and gas potential will undoubtedly become a political instrument and a weapon in the confrontation. However, the probability that the West would adopt a united position against Russia's aggressiveness and lack of cooperation appears too small. In any case, it will take a lot of work in Washington to spearhead such efforts and to convince other Western partners to go along.

"Iron Fists in Kid Gloves?"

It is hard to develop a rational modus operandi for dealing with a frequently irrational player, but there exists a model that has proven to be effective. When Rex Tillerson, the new U.S. Secretary of State, headed ExxonMobil, the company's strategy and tactics in Russia gained it respect in the Kremlin and a carte blanche for pursuance of its own goals—often regardless of the Russian government's wishes.

On January 11, 2017 Tillerson, speaking at his Senate confirmation hearing as the future secretary of state, described some specifics of Russian leaders' ways of action, saying that they usually have a plan, then make a step and watch for reaction before making another step.[28] The pause between the steps could be a good opportunity for showing firmness or approval by the West.

The behavior of ExxonMobil in Russia from the very beginning has been unlike the conduct of other major oil and gas players. While Royal Dutch Shell and BP have opted for a model based on absolute obedience and loyalty towards the Russian leadership (and suffered quite a few humiliating losses because of this), Tillerson's company rejected such proposals and demands of the Kremlin that contradicted interests of ExxonMobil shareholders. Having established good personal contacts with Vladimir Putin and Rosneft CEO Igor Sechin, Tillerson has never made any real business concessions to the duo that could have harmed his company or his country. This is what they respect and accept in the Kremlin: firmness based on strength plus well-publicized friendly personal relations.

Rex Tillerson is apparently going to follow this model of dealing with the Russian leadership during his tenure at the State Department.[29] It looks like the most appropriate and efficient line of behavior under the circumstances, especially if the new U.S. administration manages to mobilize wide international support of its policy vis-à-vis Moscow.

The factors that determine the attitude of the United States and EU toward the energy industry of Russia differ greatly, and this difference makes it an uphill task to develop a joint policy in this respect. While for the Americans, Russian oil and gas are a big market for equipment, technologies and services (and mainly a nuisance in international politics), the Europeans remain dependent on supply of natural gas from Russia in addition to that. Moreover, being close neighbors of Russia and forced to coexist with Russian agents in the heart of the EU, they have to be very cautious in order to prevent or avoid Moscow's military outbursts.

---

[28] http://www.cbsnews.com/news/rex-tillerson-confirmation-hearing-for-secretary-of-state-live-blog/
[29] https://www.washingtonpost.com/news/josh-rogin/wp/2017/01/04/rex-tillerson-talks-tough-on-russia-in-private-capitol-hill-meetings/?utm_term=.747ed0bbecf9.

Choosing the right strategy in relations with Russia means encountering many ambiguities. A soft approach—a mixture of scenarios 1 and 3 in various proportions—may strengthen Russia's belief that the West is hopelessly weak, and encourage Moscow to get engaged in new expansionist actions. For Russia's energy industry, a softening of sanctions would help delay the imminent downfall of oil production and exports. In the Russian gas sector, hardly anything would change.

If a containment scenario becomes the preferred option for the West, tighter sanctions would undermine the Russian energy industry's potential for generating revenues to the state budget and accelerate a decline of the Russian economy. Under a worst-case scenario, the Russian government will be unable to support economically depressed regions by transferring funds the federal budget gets from oil-and-gas-rich areas, and the integrity of the Russian Federation will be in jeopardy.

The choice of the scenario in the West would depend on opting for one of the principal goals: helping Russia to survive regardless of the ruling regime's qualities or assisting Russia's economy to deteriorate, with dramatic consequences for the country as a whole.

Chapter 6

The Worst Friends: EU-Russian Economic Relations at a Time of Hostility

Andrey Movchan

When we mention Russian–Western economic relations, we implicitly mean Russian—EU cooperation: of overall Russian exports of $333.5 billion in 2015, 57% went to the EU and only 3.2% to North America. The difference is easily explained without relying on traditional rhetoric about historical hostility between Russia and the United States: the two countries are located quite far from each other, making shipments more expensive, and in addition Russia's major way of exporting—through pipes—is impossible as far as the United States or Canada are concerned. The United States and Canada also have much closer and more flexible sources of hydrocarbons, which is Russia's major export item. Russia's trade balance with the United States (about $6 billion in 2015, with imports of about $10 billion and exports of about $4 billion) is less than the difference in calculation of the amount of imports from China to Russia made by Russian and Chinese statistical agencies. Such trade isolation affects financial relations: 75% of loans to Russian banks are extended by European financial institutions; only 15% came from the American banks. Moreover, the United States accounts for only 0.7% of foreign direct investment in Russia.

It would be rather natural to conclude that such mutual economic indifference makes political confrontation easy and harmless. Knowing there is little to lose, politicians from each side of the Pacific use downright political hostility between the United States and Russia as a means for achieving domestic political goals. It is quite hard to expect elites in either country to forgo the clear advantages such confrontation may offer them in favor of pursuing unclear and rather limited opportunities that may arise from potential economic cooperation. Hence, while discussing the potential developments of Russia–West economic relations, it is more logical and meaningful to focus on EU-Russia cooperation.

In this chapter I review the recent history of economic relations between Russia and European Union member states in an attempt to understand the habits and rationale behind the actions and inactions of the parties, and offer a rough forecast of the future of such relations.

EU-Russia Economic Relations: Worst Friends

EU–Russia political relations have had their ups and downs, ranging from hostility to dormancy to renaissance and even active discussion of potential Russian membership in the EU. Behind the curtain of politics, however, economic and in particular trade and financial relations between Europe's two major players have been driven by mutual pragmatism and remained quite stable for decades. Geography as well as complementarity in resources and technologies have over time made the EU and Russia essential trade partners, with the opportunity cost of potential substitution being unaffordable at least in the short run.

Although relations are critical to both parties, Russian international trade is much less diversified and more EU dependent. Russian merchandise trade with the EU has historically constituted over 50% of Russian trade with the entire world, while EU trade with Russia does not exceed 10-12% of its worldwide trade. Russian trade turnover with the other Great Neighbor—China—rarely exceeds 20% of that with the EU, despite China's GDP constituting 60% of that of the EU, China's population exceeding the population of the EU by a factor of 2.5, and Chinese production costs being China is remarkably lower. The strength of Russian-EU economic ties over Russian-Chinese economic relations cannot be explained simply by marginally lower transportation costs and/or better quality of European goods. Other factors are at play.

At First Glance: Hydrocarbons for Machines

At first glance, EU-Russian economic relations are in large part limited to the Russian supply of hydrocarbons (85–90% of EU imports from Russia, 30–35% of total EU imports of fuels and chemicals) and EU supply of machinery and equipment (over 65% of Russian imports from the EU, however only 6-7% of overall EU machinery exports). The figures can lead to the conclusion that while the EU is definitely dependent on Russia in such a sensitive area as energy security, Russia is highly dependent on the EU in a wide range of supplies, and, beyond that, Russia is dependent on its appetite for hydrocarbons, which still account for almost 50% of Russia's total exports. Sales of hydrocarbons still bring Russia over $160 billion a year, accounting for 13% of Russia's GDP, almost 90% of its imports and 10 times its current account balance.

Beyond the obvious monoproduct nature of Russian exports, trade relations between Russia and the EU from the quantitative side look well balanced: Russia's trade-to-GDP ratio with EU members is similar to that of an average EU member state. Russia's GDP in 2014 was roughly 9% of that of the EU28 on the whole, and its trade turnover with the EU was roughly 10% of intra-EU trade turnover. Even Russian neighbors such as Poland, which could have been more active in relations with their eastern partner, show the same proportion: Polish trade with Russia is limited to 9.5–10% of Polish trade with the rest of the EU.

Gas Exports: Stable Volumes, Lower Prices

Oil and gas are the main components of Russian exports to the EU. The demand for natural gas in Europe was rising until 2010, and along with rising demand figures most forecasts were predicting even greater future need for fossil fuels. That was a time of huge infrastructural projects, ranging from new pipelines from Russia to new LNG ports. However, the pressure of high oil prices on economies resulted in the rapid growth of emerging energy-saving technologies and employment of renewable energy sources. As a result, since 2010 gas consumption has declined. In 2014 it fell to 1995 levels, and even marginal growth of about 7% in 2015 due to colder weather did not alter the trend. On the other hand, the decrease in EU gas consumption has been less than the decrease in EU domestic gas production, hence EU28 gas imports of gas are steady if not growing.

Russia supplies 30-40% of EU gas imports. The amount supplied has grown 17% since 2005, despite the decline in EU gas consumption. In fact, Russia is the only importer of gas to the EU with extra capacity: its pipelines to Europe have a total capacity of 309 bcm; total Russian gas exports to the EU do not exceed 160 bcm. Even with the dramatic changes in the political landscape in 2014 and 2015, which resulted in the consecutive alienation of Ukraine and (temporarily) Turkey, the collapse and sudden rebirth of the South Stream project, and the seemingly final decision to eliminate the transit of gas through Ukraine, the capacity of the remaining pipelines (still putting South Stream aside as not reliable) is around 120 bcm. In addition, the famous Nord Stream project (where Russia deliberately pays a high fixed price for gas transportation regardless of physically transported volumes to the consortium where Gazprom Switzerland has a significant share, thus legally transferring much money to Switzerland) offers an additional possible increase in capacity that is both rather easy and obviously beneficial for the Russian side, especially if we consider the large amounts of money cronies of the Russian leadership earn from such construction projects.

Indeed, Europe can physically substitute Russian gas supply with a combination of Algerian and other North African gas (unused capacity 40-45 bcm), an increase in consumption of Norwegian gas (20 bcm more) and by taking a larger share of the LNG received through Regas terminals (a potential increase of up to 128 bcm based on current and soon-to-be-built capacity)—not to mention future potential pipelines from Iran/Turkmenistan and/or the Persian Gulf. However, the prices of liquefied gas are still substantially higher than that of pipeline-transported gas, and Russia with its spare capacity and enormous sunk costs has shown itself to be very flexible in pricing when it comes down to tough negotiations.

It is therefore reasonable to believe that the supply of Russian gas to the EU will be sustained over the long run. The only change we could expect concerns the role of Germany in EU–Russian gas relations. With the rise of the role of Nord Stream, Germany will gradually become not only the largest importer of Russian gas, but also the largest distributor and the key hub for Russian gas to other European countries. It is still unclear how the distribution will be organized, and it definitely will need more investments. Not everyone in Europe is in favor of this, given the persistent idea that the EU should reduce its gas dependency on Russia through greater diversification of suppliers. But because German companies and budgets will benefit from this new situation we can expect that the project will obtain enough support.

Oil Exports: Preparing for Decline

The EU is still the world largest oil consuming region, although demand has dropped 17% since 2005 to below 12.5 mbd (being flat in 2015 for the first time in 10 years). A number of analysts expect demand to continue to slide 0.5% per year over the next five years. However, the EU is still heavily dependent on oil imports—in 2013, 83% of EU consumption was imported.

Russia is the single largest supplier of oil to the EU, with about a 29% share of total EU imports (for comparison, Norway supplies 12.6%, Nigeria 9%, Saudi Arabia 8.9%). Russian dependence on European oil consumption is even higher: the EU share of Russian oil exports is about 75%, with over 70% of it being transported by pipelines (and hence hard to divert to another destination).

Russian oil exporters to the EU are facing a range of challenges, including declining EU demand for imported oil, European programs seeking to boost energy efficiency (including those targeting the shift to hybrid engines from currently mostly diesel ones—75% of oil consumed in Europe is used as a fuel for ground transportation vehicles), active competition from the United States and Middle East countries, the current increase in transportation capacity from the Middle East to Europe through the Suez Canal, and the future potential increase of such capacity due to the construction of trans-Turkey and trans-Syria pipelines. However, the situation is even more complicated: starting in 2018 Russian upstream capacity is about to decrease, and by 2025 could fall as low as 50% of current capacity. In this regard, decreasing sales to Europe could result more from failing supply than shrinking demand.

The EU and Russia should prepare themselves to a gradual loss in turnover. Russians must look for other products they may be able to offer to the EU to substitute for the decreasing amounts of oil in the trade balance. European refineries, in turn, should prepare themselves for a switch to other sorts of oil from the Urals. Unfortunately, since none of these changes will occur in the short run, no one in Russia is dealing with these issues. It is as if the threat of the declining Russian oil production never existed. Although the best probable response would be to try to utilize the Mexican scenario and try to diversify imports from the EU by winning the outsourcing production market for EU companies, Russia's traditional policy of industrial isolation does not suggest that such a way out will be considered any time soon.

Machinery Imports: Vital for Infrastructure

Russian equipment purchases from the EU have long exceeded €50 billion per year, with transport equipment accounting for at least €14–15 billion per year, and two-thirds of that represented by passenger cars and trucks. Imports of elecommunications and data processing equipment from the EU constitute at least €10 billion per year. While a larger share of consumer electronics imports comes from China, Korea and other countries, the EU still supplies most of the industrial telecom and data equipment, and uninterrupted provision of such equipment, as well as spare parts and services, is critical to Russia's infrastructure.

Two other critical areas of import are speed trains and railroads operation equipment and civil aircraft: the EU sells over €4 billion in non-automotive transportation vehicles to Russia each year officially, and this does not include lease arrangements with aircraft and spare parts used for offshore servicing: 93% of passenger turnover in Russia is served by imported aircraft, mainly from Airbus and Boeing.

In addition, the EU supplies over €25 billion worth per year of other machinery (most of which is non-electrical). Although theoretically other types of machinery currently imported from the EU could be more easily substituted by non-EU suppliers, in practice the vast majority of the industrial equipment is being bought for the replacement of particular elements in complex technological chains and requires specific models; spare parts and consumables are also a large part of such supplies.

Investment Balance: Limited but Important

Net investment into Russia from EU countries (due in large part to the use of Dutch, Cypriot and other holding structures by Russian investors) has averaged over 80% of total foreign investment in Russia over the long term. Although this fact does not prove that European investors have a special attitude towards Russian markets, it is a clear sign of the deep structural dependency of Russian financial and investment markets on European infrastructure and legislative systems. Major Russian tycoons keep their assets in European and quasi-European structures—OAO Novolipetsk Steel through Cyprus, Alfa Group through Gybraltar, etc. Beyond that, true European investors have also heavily invested in Russia. German investors only hold stocks for over €25 billion. 611,500 employees (about 1% of the workforce) are employed by EU28-affiliated companies in Russia. European infrastructure has also helped to attract capital to Russia. The amount of external debt outstanding raised by Russian companies through issuance of Eurobonds on the European stock exchanges exceeds $180 billion—over 35% of Russia's total external debt.

The reverse process has also been in place at least since the collapse of the Soviet Union: Russian entrepreneurs (mostly legally) and officials (mostly illegally) have exported at least $1 trillion dollars from the country, and while the major part of the funds are nested in Swiss banks, according to different unofficial sources over $100 billion have been put in German and Austrian banks. Even Cyprus had up to €35 billion from Russian sources at its peak. The number of houses and apartments bought by Russians in Europe is estimated by the Russian press as exceeding 500,000 (most of them in eastern Europe). Although this may be an overestimation, the degree is correct: Russians are important buyers of real estate not only in Bulgaria, but also in London, Berlin and Frankfurt. Russian beneficiary owners own 3% of companies registered in the EU.

The freeze in incoming foreign direct investment hit Russia in 2014; since then the flows have been negligeable. In 2016 and 2017, however, German and Finnish companies started to return to the market, along with other European enterprises, ahead of their peers from other parts of the world (except for a vague transaction with Rosneft shares allegedly made by Glencore and Qatar Fund, which had all the features of a disguise for the theft of the shares by current stakeholders). In private conversations many European companies express their willingness to increase their exposure. On the other hand, the capital flight to Europe from Russia has never stopped.

New Bureaucratic Reality: Tender Pressure

The EU and Russia have long been cooperating along the terms of their 1994 Partnership and Cooperation Agreement. Many discussions have been held about the need to provide a more comprehensive framework, to shift to more substantive and legally binding commitments not only in civil areas such as security, justice or education, but also in economic cooperation, trade and investment. At the 2008 Khanty-Mansiysk summit an attempt was made to move to a new version of the agreement, but the negotiations were never completed. Since 2003 the EU and Russia sought to advance their cooperation within the framework of the so-called "common spaces program." This resulted in many different initiatives, ranging from an unsuccessful attempt to allow visa-free travel to much more successful cooperation in a space work program. In 2010, following the Rostov summit, the Partnership for Modernization program was launched. The program included substantial economic elements as well as joint technical modernization aspects.

In 2014, however, following the annexation of Crimea and destabilization in eastern Ukraine, all programs were suspended and a number of sanctions were imposed: European development banks put all financing projects on hold; several companies and individuals from Russia were banned access to financial markets and financing (a number of European bankers told the author that recently the banks in the EU were unofficially recommended not to place any Russian financial instruments on new issue). Export to Russia of dual-purpose technologies, complex oil extraction technologies and equipment and few other advanced technologies and goods was also prohibited.

Although the contemporary rhetoric is rather hostile, and the sanctions are actively used by the Russian government as an excuse for the current economic downturn, the real effect from sanctions is minimal: the ban on financing coincides with the period when the Russia's balance shrank due to recession and its overall external debt decreased almost 30% even without sanctions. The oil price drop led to a suspension of any development of high-cost oil wells, thus the respective technologies are neither in use or in need. The export of dual-purpose goods has been minimal, and the ban does not have any significant effect on Russia's economic situation.

Russia symmetrically responded to the sanctions by banning imports of a number of agricultural products. The measure, which was officially targeting import substitution, in reality caused temporary deficits, substantial loss of quality of several food products on the Russian market, and significant inflation of prices of core food—with little negative impact on European suppliers.

Food Imports: Much Ado about Nothing

The export of food and agricultural products to Russia (so much in discussion now with regards to sanctions) has never exceeded €10-11 billion per year—a pathetic 3.5% of the turnover between the countries on average and 8% of EU food exports to the world. This figure dropped more than 20% in one year due to the worsening of EU-Russian relations, the subsequent sanctions war and the drop in demand in Russia, and some sources suggested it could cause damage to the economies of the EU countries. WIFO (wifo.ac.at) claims in an article "Disputed trade relations between the EU and Russia" that the current decrease in trade turnover and tourist flows can in the long run cause an increase in overall unemployment of up to 1% of workforce, and up to 0.8% decrease in GDP in the EU.

The reality, however, is that such effects are not likely to materialize even partly. The scale of the problem is too small compared with the adaptive resources of the European economy. On top of that, substitutional effects have already taken place. Despite sanctions and countersanctions, the production of most of the sanctioned products in the EU is increasing because of the overall increase in demand in the world. While Russia is not being able to substitute sanctioned goods with domestic production, it simply buys them from new suppliers (Turkey substituted for Greece, then Chile substituted for Turkey, the Faroe Islands substituted for Norway, Tunisia substituted for France, Belarus for Poland, etc.), causing both the redistribution of flows and black market intermediation by quite a few countries, which are now making a good deal of money by affixing new labels on sanctioned goods and then smuggling them into Russia. To compensate for losses in those smaller product lines where the sanctions were really sensitive for particular businesses, local governments and EU authorities stepped in to provide financial aid and purchase excess production, redirecting it for charity.

In this regard, a Polish story of apples exports is both typical and enlightening. Poland was the biggest supplier of apples, with over 55% per cent of the crop going to Russia. After the Russian sanctions were imposed, many farmers in Poland began to panic, causing applie prices in Europe to drop and the margins of those selling during the season to halve. The rebound, however, was quick: those who stored apples until winter lost little in price and sold almost 100% of the harvest. Serbia and Belarus took an active part: for as little as €500 per truck, the delivery's documentation would be changed. The government stepped in and bought 15% of "should have been sold to Russia" apples. Canada, UAE, Hong Kong and other countries started to buy Polish apples. Eventually, the overall food exports of Poland rose by 4.5% in 2014 and preliminary estimations indicate there was a further increase of 8% in 2015—altogether 3 times the overall food export from Poland to Russia before sanctions.

Russia, in turn, experienced a short-term growth of agricultural production (overall reaching a cumulative growth of about 8% over 3 years), which coincided with antisanctions, a sharp devaluation of the ruble that made domestic production much more competitive, and good harvests in 2015 and 2016. 2015 was also a year of substantial domestic investment in the agricultural infrastructure in Russia, made mostly by the government with funds borrowed from the state agricultural bank at a discounted rate. This growth appears to be unstable, however, and 2017 brought a noticeable decrease in the growth rate as new investments vanished, leaving Russia with an insignificant achievement in the area, not exceeding 0.2% of total GDP.

Global changes in tourist flows seemed to help the European tourist industry regain revenues from lost Russian tourists. The short-term contraction in tourist flows to Europe because of the sharp decrease in households earnings in Russia was followed by the fall of the euro-dollar exchange rate and political and security problems with two major tourist alternatives, Egypt and Turkey. During the 2016 season there was a partial return of pre-crisis numbers of Russian tourists to EU resorts, and in 2017 Russian tourists, attracted by the rebounded ruble, flooded European resorts, especially Cyprus and Greece.

Russian Prospects: Gloomy Perspectives for Change

Since 2000, Russia has experienced two well-known interconnected phenomena: a classical commodities boom and a serious case of Dutch disease, in which over-reliance on energy exports has badly damaged and distorted the economy as a whole.

The rapid rise in oil prices at the start of the century dramatically boosted state revenues and relieved the government of the need to both broaden its tax base and spend more efficiently. In addition, because the state captured the lion's share of oil revenues due to the peculiarities of Russia's taxation regime and distribution of major assets, it was able to consolidate its control over the energy and banking industries and therefore the entire economic and political life of the country. This hampered the development of non-oil-related businesses and made economic and budgetary decision-making much less effective.

By 2008, hydrocarbon export revenues effectively comprised 65–70% of Russia's budget directly or indirectly, according to the calculations made by the Carnegie Moscow Center. There is a 90-95% correlation between the levels of GDP growth, federal budget revenues, and reserves on the one hand and changes in oil prices on the other hand—proof of the extremely tight relationship between hard currency inflows generated by oil exports and the country's overall economic realities. It was no surprise that the massive influx of petrodollars significantly distorted the ruble market exchange rate, which at peak times exceeded the inflation-adjusted rate by more than 35%.

In its effort to control financial flows, the regime deliberately made the investment climate worse by refusing to protect the rights of investors and entrepreneurs. This led to a decline in investment, further distortions in exchange rates, lower entrepreneurial activity, and ever-increasing financial and human capital losses. Capital flight amounted to over $1 trillion during this period, and many of the best business people and professionals left the country.

The copy-paste from the old Chilean copper reserve fund policy by the Russian finance ministry, depositing extra profits into reserves while also borrowing extensively in international markets at a significant spread, together with high risks associated with domestic investing, led to a disproportionate increase in the price of debt capital. That made investments even less attractive and held back the development of capital-intensive and slow-growing sectors of the economy.

The combination of an overvalued ruble and populist government policies (e.g., unjustified wage increases and higher taxes) drastically increased production costs and made domestic production a losing proposition.

In the end, all sectors of the Russian economy suffered. The manufacturing sector never became competitive, despite overall higher revenues fueled by hydrocarbon exports and greater-than-anticipated consumption growth. Hydrocarbon extraction constituted up to 20% of Russia's GDP. In 2014, another 29% came from trade, according to Rosstat. This was a disproportionately high number inflated by the enormous influx of petrodollars, a figure that twice exceeds the average in most developed countries.

Rosstat reprts that the domestic energy market and infrastructure comprise another 15% of Russia's GDP. Public projects make up a further 15%, while the financial sector accounts for almost 10%, which means that about 10% of the country's GDP comes from the independent service sector and non-resource production.

On top of this has come a decidedly unreasonable social policy. Personal incomes have outstripped GDP growth even when the oil factor is taken into account. The public sector employs 30% of the workforce directly and another 8% indirectly, thus shouldering an excessive burden. Half-hearted and indecisive government policies have led to the failure of pension reforms (and Russia had at least 3 of them in the last 20 years). The federal budget was further overloaded by ambitious but inefficient projects and inflated defense and security spending. Finally, massive corruption blew budget spending out of proportion.

As oil prices declined, Russia was stuck with an undiversified, quasi-monopolized economy lacking the resources to stimulate growth. The desolate landscape observed today is the result of a situation that long predates the current stagnation. It reflects years of chronic failure to adapt to changes in the global economy.

Russia's industrial production capacity has a long history of underinvestment. Utilization of production capacity is nearly 85%, even at the currently modest levels of output. But a large part of Russia's production capacity (more than 40%, according to some estimates) is technologically and functionally obsolete. Many Russian-made products cannot compete in the world market, mostly because of the technological gaps and inefficiency of industrial equipment.

One reason for the decline is that the total machinery stock in Russia has shrunk by almost half over the past ten years, a problem that can only partly be explained by old, inefficient machinery being replaced by new high-tech and more productive equipment. A new spurt of economic growth requires accelerated capitalization of production and the creation of new capacity, but this is something that Russia simply cannot afford.

In 2015 the budget deficit exceeded 4% of GDP, and the government then adopted a 3-year budget plan that provided for a GDP deficit of 3% for the next year. State budgets shrank in real terms almost to half of the size of those 5-6 years earlier, and state financing of the economy was planned to shrink 20% more over the ensuing three years. Only recently did the government take into account the rebound of oil prices, which has led it to revise its forecast, suggesting that the budget deficit will decline to 2% of GDP per year in coming years. Indeed, welfare funds helped Russians to survive during 2014–2016 period, and the remaining funds are slated to be used for the financing of the deficit in years to come, together with an increase of internal debt amounts, which are currently quite low. Still, state companies do not have the funds to catch up on investments, and Russian and foreign private players alike are unwilling to invest because of the overall crisis of confidence in Russia.

Russia has fallen far behind its international peers in efficiency. Russia uses four times as much energy per dollar of GDP as Japan and the cost of transporting, storing, and processing goods through customs is very high by world standards. Moreover, Russia's workforce is shrinking by 0.5% per year. It is concentrated in sectors with very low or nonexistent value added, such as the civil service, law enforcement, private security, retail, agriculture and the highly inefficient banking sector. There is a skills shortage, with a disastrous lack of engineers, technicians, and other skilled workers, not to mention competent managers and administrators.

For years, Russia's municipal services have been maintained through the exploitation of the labor of millions of migrants from neighboring states, most of whom are in Russia illegally. Until recently, cash remittances from these workers were the main source of revenue for Kyrgyzstan, the second-largest source for Tajikistan, and a major component of revenue in Uzbekistan, Moldova, Ukraine, and Belarus.

Today, however, the number of labor migrants is dwindling because of the devaluation of the ruble and the decreased purchasing power of the Russian population. As a result, all businesses that rely on unskilled labor—particularly municipal services, but also the retail sector—are short of workers. Overall, shrinking demand has led to closure of a significant number of outlets and termination of quite a few new construction projects, but the corresponding decrease in demand in the workforce really did not compensate for the outflows of foreign low-skilled labor.

Inconsistent and illogical government policies have exacerbated the situation. The absence of a solid legal framework for property rights, the economy, and entrepreneurship means that investors and businessmen both in Russia and abroad harbor nearly unshakeable impressions that the government is unreliable, unable to enforce laws fairly and consistently, hostile toward the business community, corrupt, and likely to prioritize state interests over private ones.

This lack of trust in the government has converted a growing number of Russian businessmen from skeptics to expats. Over the past 16 years, total capital flight has exceeded total revenues from oil and gas sales. The share of private business in GDP (not counting quasi-private companies effectively owned by individuals working for the state) has fallen to 30–35%. Foreign debt has dropped below 50% of GDP due to lack of interest in maintaining business development and the knock-on effects of divestment by Russian players.

The Russian private sector is so undeveloped that it generates less than $3,000 per year per capita in GDP, a figure that puts Russia outside the top 100 countries worldwide in this ranking. According to official statistics, the proportion of small and medium businesses in GDP was close to 20% in 2014 and was close to 18% in 2016, compared to 40–55% in developed countries. In 2016 over 70,000 small and medium-sized enterprises were closed in Russia, according to the national statistics agency Rosstat. Yet Russian citizens and ex-Russians have bank account deposits totaling more than $1 trillion in banks in Switzerland and other European countries, as well as Hong Kong and Singapore.

That brings us to the brain drain. Although official statistics do not distinguish a prominent professor or a talented manager from a seasonal worker or a crook fleeing from justice where emigration is concerned, indirect estimations suggest that every year since the late 1990s on average about 20,000–30,000 professionals and businessmen leave Russia. The flow increased dramatically in 2012-2013 after the election related protests and subsequent repression, and has remained high ever since. Aggression in Ukraine, continuing deterioration of the economy, and violations of human rights are among the major reasons for emigration, along with such pragmatic reasons as lower tax levels in many European countries, lower cost of doing business, less bureaucratic burden and many fewer personal risks.

Meanwhile, hopes that the devaluation of the ruble may improve Russia's long-term productivity are misguided. Devaluation has certainly helped exporters, expanded the budget, and softened the worst of the economic shock. But it is unlikely to boost GDP growth. Potential GDP growth in Russia depends largely on domestic demand, which is measured in rubles and is basically not growing. Eventually, growth in exports requires capital investment and technologies, neither of which is available at the moment. Moreover, in almost every sector of the Russian economy, production depends to some degree (anywhere from 15-80%) on the import of raw materials, parts, or equipment. The devaluation of the ruble is increasing the ruble-denominated prime cost of goods and even services faster than consumer demand is rising.

The investment and business resources Russia needs for diversification of the economy are not there and will not appear unless and until Russia's governance model undergoes radical change. So far there is no sign of any change in attitude towards reforms by the Kremlin. Indeed, the new reform plans are being produced (recently two of them were ordered and presented to the President by two independent groups—Kudrin's and Titov's—representing the mix of left- and right-liberal economists and more or less state-dependent businessmen), however they are not much different from the plans produced years before, and peacefully buried in multiple committees and commissions without any attempt of even partial implementation. The current situation, as seen from the Kremlin towers, is close to stablilization, the long term GDP growth forecast is in a range from zero to 1% per annum, households incomes almost stopped falling, having found support at about 65% of their 2013 levels, and the government is leery of risking stability for an unclear perspective of any reforms. Sources from the goverment confirm that the general understanding is that due to accumulating problems with infrastructure and the financial system, such stability would not last for longer that 8-10 years from now. Then, every one rightfully concludes that it is far beyond the current government horizon and out of focus.

Approaching a Closer Framework with Russia and its Neighborhood

The European Union is purposefully trying to develop deeper and more efficient trade and production cooperation relations with the markets around it, paying more attention to the potential of those markets than to their current size.

Establishment of rather political bodies like the Euro-Mediterranean Association Agreement or the Union for the Mediterranean, or the Eastern Partnership with its eastern neighbors, was followed by the launch of the Deep and Comprehensive Free Trade Area (a weak form of an old European Free Trade Association and integral part of the European Association Agreement)—in essence a set of bilateral agreements with neighboring states covering trade tariffs, custom operating regulations, sanitary and technical standards, transparency and public procurement issues and other aspects of facilitation and unification of trade and production processes, based on EU standards. So far only three countries—Moldova, Georgia and Ukraine—have signed a DCFTA, and it could have looked like a specific attempt to penetrate the former USSR economic space, however current active negotiations about DCFTAs with Tunisia and Morocco prove that the new form of close economic cooperation proposed by the EU is conceived for broader use.

The EU's attempt to push the borders of the free trade and co-production based on EU standards and regulation faces resistance from the other center of economic gravity concerned with its *Lebensraum* in a contemporary format—the Russian Federation. In parallel with EU activities, Russia has developed a so-called ECU—the Eurasian Customs Union—born in 2010 and having Russia, Kazakhstan, Belarus, and (later) Kyrgyzstan and Armenia as participants. Russian authorities put enormous efforts to prevent other former USSR republics and CIS members from associating with the EU in any forms, trying to convince (and even force) them to join the ECU—with success. European Union officials currently consider Russia a threat to their plans and thus are foregoing an opportunity of looking at Russia as yet another potential partner, which, if attracted, may deliver others into the net by virtue of its regional economic dominance. Russia still has a domestic market of over 145 million people, with a Chinese average level of household income and consumption, and (although 1/15th of the EU)—a GDP that is 4 times greater than the combined GDP of all the current DCFTA members and candidate states. The ECU market is too big and too close to be ignored as the EU contemplates wider integration and development.

The differences between the EU and the ECU are not limited to their respective size. While the EU has no dominant economic force (some may argue that Germany pretends to be it, yet its GDP is only 20% of the EU total), Russia represents over 80% of the ECU's GDP and trade. The EU is a well-established political union with fully developed rule-books and procedures. The ECU pretends to be a political union, however there is no clear political body developing its framework and establishing common rules. Unlike the EU, where there is always a queue of candidate countries willing to get associated or/and become a member, the ECU has no volunteers to join, and Russia has to use a combination of seduction and coercion to try to gain new members. The ECU's external focus is on trade diversion, on protection of the inner producers allowing them to avoid competition and ultimately deteriorating value for end customers. The EU's focus is on free trade expansion. Although the ECU is weaker than the DCFTA (it focuses mostly on establishment of a common custom area, principles and tariffs), it makes its members inflexible enough to be unable to participate in any other significant economic blocs or associations.

There is a chance that closer cooperation between the EU and ECU still may be initiated via through the belt of intermediary states. Successful integration of Ukraine, Georgia and Moldova into the DCFTA framework, and even further inclusion of other non-ECU countries such as Azerbaijan or Uzbekistan, will definitely strengthen the position of the EU towards negotiations with the ECU and Russia.

DCFTA membership does not necessarily prevent countries from trading with the ECU. Nothing in a DCFTA prohibits its members from having specific bilateral agreements with other countries and unions, unless they contradict DCFTA itself. Having said that, ECU members can have bilateral free trade and custom agreements with other countries, however a DCFTA is not viewed as a form of bilateral agreement and we should not expect the EU to agree to treat it as an FTA under any circumstances.

One of big issues standing in the way of the development of EU/DCFTA—ECU cooperation are the technical standards changes imposed by DCFTA. Most newcomers have outdated GOSTs [state standards] as a legacy of the Soviet Union. Russia is also changing its standards base, and as of today almost half of the most-used technical standards in Russia are already compatible with those of the EU. (And in the Ukrainian case, ironically, a big part of trade with Russia is still in military equipment, which is not covered by DCFTA). Eventually, DCFTA does not prohibit imports of goods not matching EU standards, and certainly does not limit members' ability to produce and export non-matching goods to non-EU countries. In that regard, the signing of a DCFTA in and of itself cannot significantly influence the ability to trade; however, the unification of standards that can facilitate the entry of new members' products into the EU market will significantly change trade patterns, and not necessarily in favor of external trade.

A DCFTA is broader than a trade agreement. It requires its members to change a number of fundamental laws, liberalize major service sectors, adopt EU intellectual property rights, thus rendering DCFTA members incompatible and unacceptable for any form of association with the ECU in its current form. Deeper cooperation between the ECU and EU/DCFTA members is hardly possible unless either of them implements serious changes in policy. Recalling the relative weights of the economies of the EU/DAFTA and the ECU, the dependency of the ECU on the European market and the current negative trends in ECU member economies, we may assume that the ECU is the one that will face the need to change if it wants to have closer economic ties with the EU. This is difficult, and raises the fear—expressed by Russia many times—that cheap European goods will flood the ECU market should countries with specific trade agreements with Russia also become members of a DCFTA. This fear is grounded: the accession of Kirgystan, having a specific duty free trade arrangement with China for private traders, immediately led to a massive flow of Chinese goods through this country into Russia.

In light of the situation, EU members, supported by the new associated partners who are seriously interested in retaining economic ties with Russia, should develop and maintain a pragmatic strategy of very slow convergence (not to frighten off the beast)—a sort of the new, more realistic, yet less broad and more gradual Common Economic Space Program (instead of the one put on hold a few years ago). There is also a good chance that the political position of Russia will evolve and become less isolationist as mineral resources play a lesser role in Russian trade and the Russian economy. Unfortunately, the current hostility means that such changes are less likely in the short run.

Future Scenario: Little Change After All?

According to the EU Trade and Investment Strategy approved by the EU Council on November 27, 2015, "The EU's strategic interest remains to achieve closer economic ties with Russia. The prospects for this will, however, be determined primarily by the course of Russia's domestic and foreign policy, which so far gives no signs of necessary changes."

One should doubt the ability of the two partners to seriously improve their cooperation should Russia undergo a magic change and start behaving differently, however, given the failure of all previous attempts to generate substantial improvements during two decades in which a relatively good political atmosphere prevailed. The fact that recent Russian actions in and around Ukraine and massive ideological anti-European pressure on Russian society did not cause serious damage to commercial relations with Europe proves the real unwillingness of the EU to connect commercial issues with political manoeuvres. European countries had all the tools they needed to force Russia to retreat: a ban on supplying of new aircraft, railroad, telecom equipment and spare parts and services; a suspension of operation of banking accounts and legal entities opened by Russian commercial and state bodies; and a declaration of intent to gradually decrease the consumption of Russian gas and oil until all hydrocarbon imports from Russia are halted within five years—these are just three of a handful of measures at the EU's disposal, each of which could make Russia stop.

Taking the above into consideration, we can conclude that commercial relations between the EU and Russia will most likely remain stable for many years, but that their scale will diminish. We can expect a gradual decrease of Russian oil exports and most probably gas exports to the EU; Russian imports from the EU will also fall, simply because economic recession and shrinking exports will limit Russia's ability to buy abroad. Russia is likely to remain unable to diversify and enhance its economy. As currency inflows dry up, Russia will seek to diversify suppliers of essential equipment, and over time will succeed in substituting European higher quality and more expensive machinery and systems for more affordable and often lower quality equipment, whether from China or other countries. Over time, Russia will return, at least partially, to the production of necessary machinery as it did during Soviet times. While today the share of foreign passenger cars sold in Russia exceeds 80% of the total market, and 71% of cars, officially produced in Russia, are in reality foreign cars, assembled on Russian industrial facilities, 25 years ago AvtoVAZ, together with a few other automotive plants, were the only sources of the cars for the internal market.

We may expect that in 10–15 years the EU will become much less dependent on Russia in the field of energy security, and Russia will gain independence from Europe both in financial, industrial and infrastructural spheres, due to a range of circumstances, including growing cooperation between Europe and developing countries from the Middle East, North Africa and the Asia-Pacific region, the development of alternative energy sources and transmission channels, and the steady relative decline of the Russian economy. These processes will take place irrespective of political developments, regardless of whether for example Ukraine will join the EU in any capacity, or, after an unsuccessful attempt to develop a western democracy will rush back to the Russian embrace. Russia will however remain a European neighbor, a large resource-rich country with a poor but relatively wide market of over 140 million people, and a territory, strategically positioned between the EU and the Asia-Pacific region, that makes Russia the permanent reserve transportation channel between the East and the West. Given all of these considerations, trade relations between the EU and Russia, including the extensive trade of services, will remain in place—as will political tensions and bureaucratic declarations about the need to improve cooperation and achieve closer economic ties.

Chapter 7

Russian Foreign Policy in the Middle East: New Challenge for Western Interests?

Nikolay Kozhanov

The current Russian presence in the Middle East is unprecedented for the region since the fall of the Soviet Union. Records of diplomatic and political contacts show increased exchanges of multilevel delegations between Russia and the main regional countries. Since 2012, Moscow has attempted to cultivate deeper involvement in regional issues and to establish contacts with forces in the Middle East, which it considers as legitimate. Moreover, on September 30, 2015, Russia launched air strikes against Syrian groupings fighting against the regime of Bashar al-Assad. Before that time, Russia had tried to avoid any fully-fledged involvement in the military conflicts in the region. It was also the first time when it adopted an American military strategy by emphasizing the use of air power instead of ground forces.

Under these circumstances, the turmoil in the Middle East, which poses a political and security challenge to the EU and United States, makes it crucial to know whether Russia could be a reliable partner in helping the West to stabilize the region or whether, on the contrary, Moscow will play the role of a troublemaker. In this context, this paper addresses the following questions:

- How did the changes in Russian–Western relations affect the evolution of the Kremlin's Middle Eastern strategy?
- What influence did Russian domestic political dynamics have on Russian foreign policy in the Middle East?
- What are Russia's main interests in the Middle East?

The answers to these questions will help to understand whether regional dialogue between Moscow and the West is, at least theoretically, possible.

The Soviet Heritage and Russia's Approaches to the Middle East 1991–2011

By the fall of the USSR in 1991, Soviet authorities had created a solid foundation for the development of fruitful cooperation with the Arab world and Iran. The Soviet Union had relatively good relations with Algeria, Egypt, Syria, Iraq, Libya, the People's Democratic Republic of Yemen, and the Palestinian Authority. Moscow's dialogue with Iran and Kuwait had substantial and positive potential. From the political point of view, the USSR was quite appealing for Middle Eastern countries as a certain ideological alternative to the capitalist West and as a counterbalance to the American presence.

From the economic point of view, the Soviet presence in the region was also visible. Since the 1950s, Moscow had been involved in the construction of huge and ambitious industrial projects such as the Aswan High Dam and the metallurgy complex in Isfahan. During the 1950s–1980s, the USSR constructed about 20 hydro and thermal power plants in the region. By 1991, the track record of Soviet accomplishments in the region included 350 industrial projects. All in all, the Arab states received about 20% of the technical assistance allocated by Moscow to countries of the developing world. In addition to this, by the fall of the USSR, the annual volume of Soviet trade with the Arab countries reached $7–12 billion. This figure comprised about 30% of USSR trade with developing countries and made economic relations with the Middle East an important source of income for the Soviets. The military cooperation between the USSR and the Arab countries was also impressive. The largest part of this sum was related to the Soviet–Iraqi ($24 billion) and Soviet–Syrian ($11 billion) deals. However, Egypt, Yemen, Algeria and Libya could also be named among the clients of the military-industrial complex of the USSR.[1]

Apart from that, Moscow was an important creditor of the Arab regimes. The real volume of the debts of Middle Eastern countries to the Soviet government is still unknown. According to the most moderate estimates, by 1991 the USSR had $35 billion of unreturned credits out of which the large part belonged to Iraq, Syria, Algeria, and Egypt.[2]

---

[1] Mediastl, *Ekonomicheskiye Otnosheniya mezhdu Rossiey i Arabskimi Stranami v Proshlom, Nastoyashchem i Budushchem*, www.mediastl.ru/upload/docs/5_analytic_reference doc, accessed on October 4, 2013; Vladimir Isaev and Aleksandr Filonnik, "Rossiya—Arabskiye Strany: Politicheskiye Imperativy i Ekonomicheskoye Sotrudnichestvo," *Novoye Vostochnoye Obozreniye*. October 9, 2012. http://journal-neo-ru.livejournal.com/47496.html, accessed October 4, 2013.

[2] Ibid.

Yet, after 1991, Moscow largely neglected the potential for development of its ties with the region that had been created during Soviet times. In other words, from the fall of the Soviet Union until our current decade, Russian cooperation with Middle Eastern countries has had a relatively low profile. This can be explained by domestic political and economic turmoil in Russia during the 1990s and by the Western orientation of Russian diplomacy under President Boris Yeltsin (1991–1999).

Both political and economic contacts were mostly curtailed, if not cut. This situation was determined by a mixture of objective and ideological reasons. On one hand, the economic crises which periodically hit Russia during the first decade of its existence, political turmoil, the short-sighted privatization policy of the Yeltsin government, and the grip of criminal groups over the country's economy seriously limited the export capacities of Moscow and diverted the attention of the Russian authorities from foreign to domestic policy issues. The ports of Odessa and Ilyichevsk on the Black Sea, which were the main trade gates of the USSR to the Mediterranean, became part of independent Ukraine, which also negatively influenced Russian business contacts with the Middle East. According to various estimates, by the mid-1990s, the share of Arab countries in Russia's volume of trade was less than 1 percent.[3] On the other hand, political and economic cooperation with the Middle East contradicted the new ideology of the post-Soviet elite of the Russian Federation, who saw their country as part of the Western world and refused to develop those vectors of diplomacy that they viewed as non-Western. As a result, the Middle East was considered a region of secondary importance for the new Russia. The only exception was Israel, whose relations with Moscow improved considerably during the 1990s (mainly due to the strengthening of the political and business positions of the Jewish community in Russia and the fact that this country was considered a Western splinter in the Middle East).

During the 1990s and 2000s, the development of constructive dialogue with Washington was still unofficially considered a top priority of Russian diplomacy. This intention was supported by the gradual strengthening of semi-official and unofficial ties with the West by the Russian economic, political, and cultural elite. Such an approach, in turn, determined Moscow's perception of the Middle East as a leverage and trade item in Russian relations with the United States and Europe. In fact, Russian authorities have played this card during periods of both U.S.–Russian rap-

---

[3] Ibid.

prochement and severe tensions between the two countries, by either freezing their cooperation with the opponents of America in the Middle East or boosting it, respectively.

Russian–Iranian relations serve as the most notable example of this approach. Thus, in 1995, Russia and the United States signed the so-called Gore-Chernomyrdin agreement. According to this confidential document signed in the wake of reconciliation between Moscow and Washington, the Russian government agreed to stop the implementation of existing military-supply contracts with Iran by 1999 and not to conclude new deals with Tehran in this field. U.S. authorities, in turn, were expected to develop cooperation with Russia's military-industrial complex while halting unauthorized provision of American military equipment to both the Middle East and the countries bordering Russia. In addition to this treaty, Moscow decided in 1998 not to implement its contract for the supply of a research reactor to Tehran. The reason for this decision was the same as in the 1995 agreement: the need to bridge relations with Washington. The subsequent tensions between Washington and Moscow during the first years of the new millennium were accompanied by the improvement of Russo–Iranian dialogue. In 2000, Putin and the then-president of Iran, Mohammad Khatami, met in New York, which led to the Iranian president making an official visit to Moscow in March 2001.

In 2001, both Khatami and Putin positioned their negotiations as the beginning of a new chapter in Russian–Iranian relations. It is necessary to admit that the rapprochement between the two countries was determined not only by their difficult relations with Washington. The substantial role in bridging relations between the two countries was played by Khatami's firm intention to implement his doctrine of "the dialogue of civilizations," Khatami's cultural and diplomatic strategy that implied the development of contacts between Shia Iran and other countries of different religion and traditions. On the Russian side, Putin's plan to develop Russian ties with non-Western countries as a part of his doctrine of the multi-polar world also pushed the two countries towards each other. In the early 2000s, the Russian president for the first time formulated his idea that Moscow should not be solely focused on its dialogue with the United States and Europe but try to have equally intense relations with the countries of the Middle East, Asia and South America. And Iran was one of those non-Western countries that seemed to be appealing for Russia as a potential partner within the framework of the multi-polar world doctrine.

Yet, the tense relations with the United States still remained the main factor determining the dynamics of the Russian–Iranian rapprochement of the early-2000s. Thus, the terrorist attacks of 9/11 and subsequent improvement of both U.S.–Russian and U.S.–Iranian relations slowed down the tempo of the interaction between Moscow and Tehran. It again intensified after the American invasion of Iraq in 2003, when both Russia and Iran were dissatisfied with the U.S. decision to occupy this country. Nevertheless, the U.S.–Russian reset of 2009 once again offset the Russian–Iranian dialogue, compelling Moscow to adopt a harsher stance on Tehran and its nuclear program. The Russian vision of the Middle East as the region of the secondary importance has changed after 2012.

Putin's Third Presidential Term and Russian Foreign Policy in the Middle East

After 2012, Russia has substantially increased its presence in the region of the Middle East. Its foreign policy also became more consistent. Moscow not only improved its relations with traditional Soviet/Russian partners in the region (such as Iran and Syria), but also reestablished ties with those countries where its leading positions were believed to be lost for good (Egypt, Libya, Iraq). The Russian authorities made several attempts to increase their presence in those sub-regions that were believed to be the zone of exclusively Western (primarily U.S.) influence (for instance, the GCC countries). Moscow also intensified its interaction with regional organizations, paying special attention to the development of ties with the Middle Eastern members of the OPEC (an organization from which Russia deliberately distanced itself prior to 2012). Finally, for the first time since the fall of the USSR, Moscow deployed its military forces in the Middle East when it started a military operation in Syria in 2015.

It is possible to say that, after 2012, the Russian leadership adopted a more strategic approach to the Middle East by seeing it as a region of growing importance for achieving Russian political, economic, and security goals. This period of Russian diplomacy in the Middle East could be titled as the period of Moscow's return, main goal of which was to re-establish Russia as an important player in the region—a status that was lost by Moscow after the fall of the USSR. Yet, the main difference between current times and Soviet times was that now the Kremlin was more pragmatic, less ideology-driven, but also less economically capable than the Soviet Union. The intensification of Russian foreign policy in the Middle East was determined by a number of factors. The key role in shaping Moscow's approaches was played by the growing confrontation with the West outside of the Middle East that naturally reoriented Moscow's diplomacy towards the non-Western countries. Yet, it was also the domestic situation in Russia and regional events that determined Moscow's new stance on the region. First of all, 2012 was the year of Putin's return to the presidency. The Putin of 2012 was different from the Putin of 2000 and 2004; more authoritarian, more decisive, more anti-Western, and extremely disappointed by the failure of the reset in Russia–U.S. relations. This could not but affect Russia's stance on the Middle East. At least initially, the support provided to the Assad regime was, in fact, revenge for what Russia saw as political and economic losses from the fall of dictatorial, but pro-Russian regimes in Libya and Iraq after the Western military intervention.

Public discontent with Medvedev's government and the controversy over Putin's re-election in 2012 compelled the leadership to shore up its support. From 2012, official propaganda started to appeal to the nationalistic sentiments of the population. These appeals received a positive response. A large portion of the Russian population wished to see Medvedev's successor more actively protect their perceived national interests and cement relations with non-Western powers. Under these circumstances, Russian support for Damascus, closer relations with Tehran, and rapprochement with Egypt were supposed to symbolize a return to the old traditions of the Soviet Empire for those missing the superpower glory of the USSR. Prior to its fall in 1991, the USSR had good political and economic relations with these countries. The image of the Soviet Union as an active player in the Middle East contrasted vividly with the behavior of post-Soviet Russia that did not see the development of its strong presence in the region as a top priority. Prior to 2012, a serious attempt to return to the Middle East was undertaken by the Kremlin just once. This sluggish effort took place in 2003–2008, when Putin decided to test the ground for the development of future relations with the Middle East and made a number of visits to the regional capitals. Yet, relatively modest gains of his trips stalled during Medvedev's presidency (2008–2012); like Boris Yeltsin in the 1990s, Putin's successor was not interested in building ties with the region.

Under these circumstances, the image of Russia in the Middle East itself was changing. While still considered as a political alternative to the West Moscow was seen as a weak and not always reliable player. Its inability to prevent the United States from invading Iraq in 2003 vividly demonstrated the limits of Russian capabilities; that year Middle Eastern newspapers were often repeating the claim that under the USSR the military occupation of Iraq would have been impossible.[4] This image of a weak but still internationally active country stuck to Russia until 2012. Putin also wanted to change this narrative.

Putin's return to power coincided with the end of the Arab Spring of 2011–2012. Moscow explained the social uprisings within its traditional narrative of accusing the West of attempting to destabilize the international system with color revolutions and to impose its improper democratic values on other nations. Considering the Arab Spring as, at least partially, a U.S. and EU plot, the Russian government felt it had no choice but to become more deeply involved in the situation on the ground in order to balance the destabilization of the political situation in the Middle East by Western powers and to prevent repercussions in Eurasia. The experience of Iraq and Libya, where the fall of the dictatorial regimes of Saddam Hussein and Muammar Qaddafi launched the chain of bloody events that completely destabilized these countries and turned them into sources of regional instability only fortified Russian concerns (especially when some Libyan anti-regime fighters suddenly moved to Syria—a fact that was seen in the Kremlin as a proof the conflict is overspilling country's borders).

By intensifying its current activities in the region, the Kremlin is pursuing the following three groups of goals:

- Economic: compensating for the negative effects of sanctions on the Russian economy; securing existing sources of income; protecting the interests of Russian energy companies and their share in the international oil and gas market.
- Political: avoiding complete international isolation; creating leverage which can be used to affect U.S. and EU behavior outside of the region; propagandizing Moscow's conception of the "right world order"; shaping Russian popular opinion.
- Security: reducing potential security threats for Russia and the post-Soviet space posed by the situation in the Middle East.

Russian strategy in the Middle East comprises several elements. First, Moscow is persistent in defending what it sees as its red lines in the region. It does not welcome forced regime change if it leads to the destruction of

---

[4] Irina Mokhova, "Obraz Rossii v Arabskom Mire: Ot Sovetsko-Arabskoy Druzhby do Problemy Poiska Novogo Obraza," http://www.iimes.ru/?p=16683, accessed October 4, 2013.

existing state mechanisms. The Kremlin is also concerned about any change of borders in the Middle East. Moscow's flexibility has enabled it to talk to different forces in the region and, if necessary, play the mediator's role.

Second, Russia seems to be trying to reclaim its Cold War role as a counterbalance to the United States in the region. The Kremlin does not directly oppose Washington, but rather exploits the region's pre-existing disappointment with the United States through practical moves, which contrast with Western behavior. Thus, Moscow's stubbornness in protecting the Assad regime, and its readiness to help the police and authoritarian governments of the Middle Eastern countries with weapons supplies, allowed Russia to garner additional respect and popularity among the local elites when compared to Obama's attempts to promote democracy in the region and his intention to disengage from regional affairs. In 2013, the White House's failure to play an active role in overthrowing Bashar al Assad only strengthened the perception among U.S. allies in the GCC that American leaders wanted their country to leave the region and abandon its old partners. Meanwhile, the old perception of Russia as a weak and incapable country was replaced with the understanding that Moscow had become a force to reckon with.

Third, Moscow avoids using ideological rhetoric in its official dialogue with the countries of the region. It remains extremely pragmatic. Russia does not raise the question of political freedom in Iran, and tries not to be vocally critical of Israel's policies in Palestine and Gaza, in spite of its support for a two-state solution. Finally, in its economic efforts, the Kremlin focuses on those areas where it has market advantages: nuclear energy, oil and gas, petro-chemicals, space, weapons, and grain. Although the Middle Eastern share of overall Russian trade and investment remains small, the region still holds great interest and, in some cases, even key importance for selected Russian industries, including the agricultural and military-industrial complexes, and the petrochemical, space, and oil and gas industries. Israel and the UAE buy up to 16% of the precious stones and metals exported by Russia. The Middle East is the main destination for exports of Russian grain; by 2016, the largest buyers of Russian wheat, rye, and barley were Egypt, Israel, and Saudi Arabia, respectively.[5] The Middle East is also an important market for some small and medium enterprises. For them, trade with the region often represents the main (and, in some

---

[5] See http://stat.customs.ru/, accessed July 13, 2015.

cases, only) export market for their products.[6] At the same time, Russian business in the Middle East builds its market strategy in the Middle East on the principle of a "Chinese price for European quality" by offering its products and services at a lower price than its Western rivals.

Nevertheless, Moscow is not omnipotent. Its success is more often than not determined by the policy mistakes made by the EU and United States. This suggests that corrections in Western approaches to regional issues would limit Russia's capacity to maneuver. The Kremlin's financial and economic capabilities will never match those of the West, so Russia has a market advantage in only a few areas—and these are gradually decreasing with the failure of economic diversification and the growing technological gap with the West. Moscow's strategy of balancing between different powers in the region in order to maintain good relations with them all is also fragile and can be upset in the future by the necessity to take sides. Thus, the intensification of dialogue with Tehran raises Iranian expectations of closer cooperation. Yet, the formation of any alliance with Tehran could harm Russian dialogue with other states, including Israel and the GCC countries. Russia's partners in the region are not reliable. Egypt, Turkey, and Israel are using Russian interest in closer contact as leverage to shape their own relations with the West; they intensify dialogue with Russia in order to make Washington more flexible on sensitive bilateral issues, but this instrumentalization does not make for good relations.

Vectors of Russian Diplomacy in the Middle East

Currently, there are several key vectors of the Russian diplomacy in the Middle East.

Iran

Moscow is extremely interested in keeping Iran in its sphere of its influence. First, Iran's geostrategic position allows it to influence the situation in the Caspian Sea region, the Caucasus, Central Asia, and the Middle East. This, in turn, compels Moscow to discuss a wide range of foreign policy issues with Tehran. Given the shared visions on how to handle most of these problems, Iran's support is believed to be important to the success of Moscow's activities to restore and strengthen Russia's regional position

---

[6] Igor Naumov, "Rossiyskiye Ubytki ot Arabskoy Vesny," *Nezavisimaya Gazeta*, February 29, 2012 http://www.ng.ru/economics/2012-02-29/1_arab_vesna.html, accessed October 4, 2013.

after the fall of the Soviet Union. Second, Moscow perceives Tehran as one of its last reliable partners in the Middle East, and tries to secure Russian positions in Iran. Finally, Russia and Iran are deeply involved in Syria, where they are trying to save the remnants of the Assad regime.

In 2013–2015, the Russian authorities also intensified their efforts to settle the Iranian nuclear issue. Moscow helped to facilitate Iran's negotiations with the international group of negotiators, whereas Lavrov's 2012 proposals on the settlement of the nuclear issue laid the necessary groundwork for the resumption of talks. In this case, Russian motives were determined by a number of factors. First of all, Iran armed with a nuclear bomb was not desirable for Moscow, as this would change the balance of power in the region and encourage other, even less stable, Middle Eastern regimes to join the nuclear club. Secondly, Russia believed that an unsettled nuclear issue could hypothetically lead to the destabilization of Iran as it created pretexts for potential military conflict between Washington and Tehran. Under these circumstances the Kremlin did not want Iran to become another failed state near the border of the post-Soviet space in addition to Syria, Iraq, and Afghanistan. Third, Russia's role in the multilateral negotiations on the Iranian nuclear issue helped to promote Moscow's importance as a constructive international player. The latter was also important given the negative reaction on the international community to the annexation of Crimea and Russian support to the separatist forces in eastern Ukraine. Thus, Moscow's involvement in the negotiation process on Iran was considered by some U.S. analysts as one of the main factors that guaranteed the success of the negotiation process.[7] In July 2015, U.S. President Barack Obama even telephoned Putin to thank him for Russia's role in reaching the P5+1 agreement with Iran.[8] Finally, by helping Tehran to settle the nuclear issue and lift international sanctions, Moscow was creating the positive image of Russia as a reliable partner. The latter brought obvious results by helping to revitalize Russian–Iranian relations.

Both Moscow and Tehran are interested in saving the remaining government institutions in Syria. This common goal favors Russian–Iranian

---

[7] Suzanne Maloney, "Three Reasons Why Russia Won't Wreck the Iran Nuclear Negotiations," March 25, 2014, http://www.brookings.edu/blogs/markaz/posts/2014/03/22-russia-us-tension-sabotage-iran-nuclear-deal, accessed June 18, 2016; Multiple interviews with U.S. and UK diplomats and experts on Iran. London, June–August 2015; Washington DC, January 2016.

[8] "Obama Thanks Putin for Russia's Role in Iran Nuclear Deal," *NBCNews*, July 16, 2015, http://www.nbcnews.com/storyline/iran-nuclear-talks/obama-thanks-putin-russias-role-iran-nuclear-deal-n392976, accessed June 18, 2016.

cooperation, although each country certainly has its own reasons for saving the remnants of the regime. Russia is largely driven by its security concerns and strong beliefs that the building of a new post-conflict Syria is possible only through the evolution of the old regime, not through its destruction. By supporting the Assad government in Syria, Iran fights for its place in the system of the regional affairs. Under these circumstances, Moscow and Tehran formed a marriage of convenience where each partner tries to reach its own goals through joining efforts. Such an approach implies that the partners not only coordinate their activities, but also try to avoid unnecessary confrontation over issues of secondary importance.

Another reason for the intensification of Russian–Iranian cooperation is the economy. Since the late 1990s, Iranian authorities have been promising to help European countries decrease their dependence on gas supplies from Russia. In most cases, the statements by Iranian officials on Tehran's intentions to enter the European gas market still remain the part of the political game played by the Islamic republic's authorities to make the West more inclined to lift sanctions and restore its economic ties with Iran. Yet, Russian authorities do not consider the challenge of Iran's natural gas to their interests in the European market as negligible. Indeed, within the next decade Tehran will hardly be able to represent a threat to the Russian presence there. However, Moscow tries to see the situation in a long-term perspective. Under these circumstances, the Kremlin does not exclude the long-term scenario that Tehran will finally implement its promises to reach the European market.

Nevertheless, even seeing Iran as a potential rival in this field, Russia still prefers cooperation to confrontation. Moscow follows the principle of judo, which implies staying in full contact with your opponent and keeping him close. Consequently, wherever possible, Moscow tries to ensure the flow of hydrocarbons in the direction necessary for itself, or at least to make sure that it has a stake in the energy projects of Iran. As a result, Gazprom and other Russian energy corporations demonstrate open interest in the development of Iran's gas production and gas infrastructure. This strategy of involvement in Iran's gas sector is supported and promoted at the top level of the Russian political elite. However, by March 2017, Moscow did not progress beyond the mere discussion of potential investments projects in the gas sphere with Tehran.[9]

---

[9] https://www.gazeta.ru/business/2017/03/13/10574165.shtml.

During the Baku summit of the Azerbaijani, Russian, and Iranian presidents in August 2016, Putin called for the necessity of closer cooperation and coordination in the oil and gas sphere, particularly over the shared use of existing pipeline infrastructure and joint development of Caspian hydrocarbon resources.[10] He formulated a plan to supply the northern provinces of Iran with natural gas via Azerbaijan in exchange for Iranian liquefied natural gas that Russian companies will receive in the Persian Gulf. The implementation of this project would allow Iran to decrease its dependency on Turkmenistan as its sole supplier of natural gas to the northern districts, while the Russian authorities would be able to ensure that at least some Iranian gas will not reach Europe but, instead, it will be channeled by Russian companies to other regions.

Syria

Russian involvement in the Syrian civil war was determined by a number of factors. At the initial stage, growing confrontation with the West and Putin's plans to reestablish Russia as an influential world power were the key factors determining Moscow's decision to support the Assad regime in its struggle. Moscow wanted to demonstrate to the United States that it could stir up trouble if its opinion were not taken into account. Thus, in early 2013, Russian Foreign Minister Lavrov stated that in Syria the Russian government was eager to make the Americans "learn the lesson" that they should deal with Moscow only "on the basis of equality, balance of interests, and mutual respect." In order to protect its interests, Russia used its veto several times (on October 4, 2011, February 4, 2012, July 19, 2012, May 22, 2014) to prevent the adoption of UN Security Council resolutions that, in Moscow's view, could have led to a further aggravation of the situation in and around Syria. Finally, in 2013 the Russians managed to do what was previously believed to be impossible: they stopped what had appeared to be an inevitable military operation by the West against the Syrian regime. On August 21, 2013, international media sources reported the usage of a chemical weapon in one of Damascus's neighborhoods. Neither side in the conflict took responsibility for it. The Western powers and their Middle Eastern partners accused the Assad regime of this. Subsequently, they tried to use their suspicions as a pretext for military intervention in the conflict. However, the reluctance of the Obama administration and the failure of the

---

[10] https://www.pravda.ru/economics/materials/gas/09-08-2016/1309352-iran-0/.

British government to get the approval of the UK Parliament gave Moscow the necessary time to offer its own solution.

This was the first time during the Syrian conflict when Russia demonstrated that it had a number of opportunities for leverage at its disposal to shape the development of the situation in the way that would most benefit the Kremlin. Moscow's tough stance on Syria also had a positive influence on Russian relations in the Middle Eastern region. Thus, in the eyes of those regional states with a positive or neutral attitude to Moscow, the Russian authorities managed to rehabilitate themselves from their failure to protect the Qaddafi regime. Moscow proved that it was capable of protecting its partners and, thus, made the Arab countries once again interested in Russia as a political counterbalance to the United States. Regional rivals of Russia such as Qatar and Saudi Arabia were, in turn, compelled to recognize the Kremlin as an important player in the Middle East whose opinion needed to be taken into account. Thus, such influential newspapers as *Al-Sharq Al-Awsat* and *al-Hayat* considered the failure of Obama to persuade Putin to change the Russian stance on Syria as a pure victory for Russia whereas the U.S. administration was accused of "opportunism and weakness."[11]

At the same time, Syria as a country paid a high price for Moscow's ambitions. Russian stubbornness in protecting the Assad regime for the sake of the Kremlin's success in its confrontation with the West gave Damascus much-needed protection and made it more confident in its actions against the opposition. As a result, during the first year of the conflict, when most existing problems had the chance to be settled through negotiation and reforms, the Syrian regime responded to the peaceful appeals of its opponents with brute force. By doing this, it hardened and brutalized further confrontation. It is true that Moscow made some reluctant attempts to persuade Assad to make concessions to the opposition. Thus, on February 7, 2012, Lavrov and the director of the Russian Intelligence Service (SVR), Mikhail Fradkov, visited Damascus to discuss the situation in the country with the regime. Yet, while seeing its confrontation with the West as the top priority Moscow did not demonstrate sufficient persistence in persuading Assad. However, with the further development of the conflict the Kremlin started to reassess its priorities. Consequently, in 2015, Russia's decision to send troops to Syria was determined not only by Moscow's

---

[11] Grigoriy Kosach, "Pozitcsiya Rossii po Siriiskomu Krizisu v Arabskoy Presse posle Vstrechi G8," http://www.iimes.ru/?p=17779, accessed October 5, 2013.

intentions to confront Western intentions to displace Assad but by a reason not related to the Russian–U.S. standoff.

Multiple interviews with Russian officials and decision-makers showed that, by 2015, one of Russia's main concerns was that the fall of Assad's regime could lead to the spread of instability and radical Islamism to the post-Soviet space. By September 2015, Moscow's assessment was that the military, technological, and financial assistance by Russia to the Syrian regime would extend its existence but not save it. Intervention was the result of a choice between a bad and a very bad scenario; between a costly military operation to support Assad or doing nothing as his power—and Russian influence—crumbled. The Russian leadership was motivated by its perception of what had happened in Libya and Iraq, where—in its view—nothing good came of the complete destruction of the old regimes. In this case, the dynamics of Russia's relations with the West was of secondary importance in the decision-making process.

The idea that saving the regime from complete collapse was the only way to prevent Syria from going the way of Libya and Iraq determined Russia's military tactics. Its air force never took IS as the major target. Instead, it concentrated its firepower against the opposition groups that represented the greatest threat for the Assad regime. Russia's military intervention was largely about keeping the regime in power.[12] Nor is Moscow concerned about the collateral damage of its bombings. Reports of civilian casualties clearly demonstrate that little has changed in Russian tactics since the second Chechen war of 1999–2000.[13]

Nevertheless, Russia does desire to bring an end to the Syrian war. Moscow understands that it simply does not have enough economic and military resources to bring Syria back under Assad control by force. For Moscow, a settlement is only viable through a national dialogue between the regime and opposition. However, Russia would like to launch this reconciliation process under its own conditions. These include the preservation of the territorial integrity of Syria, the immediate formation of a united anti-IS coalition, saving the remaining state structures and the

---

[12] Interviews with Russian military experts. San-Francisco, Moscow, St.Petersburg, January – February 2016; Krishnadev Calamur, "A Strengthened Assad's Welcome at the Kremlin," *The Atlantic*, October 21, 2015, http://www.theatlantic.com/international/archive/2015/10/syria-russia-assad-putin/411658/, accessed March 27, 2016.

[13] Natalie Nougayrede, "We Are Watching the Destruction of Aleppo," *The Guardian*, October 8, 2016, https://www.theguardian.com/commentisfree/2016/oct/08/destruction-aleppo-russia-massacre-civilians-grozny, accessed March 16, 2017.

transformation of the regime only within the framework of the existing government mechanisms. This is why Russia gives so much attention to the Astana negotiation process: it creates a necessary basis for launching the sluggish political process while allowing Moscow to keep the initiative of shaping the format of the Syrian reconciliation in its hands. It was not a coincidence that the beginning of Astana consultations coincided with the presentation of the Russian draft of the future Syrian constitution.

On the one hand, Moscow is relatively comfortable with the possibility of political reforms in Syria and the perspectives of a post-Assad situation, as this is inevitable to achieve national reconciliation in the country. Russia does not exclude the possibility that Assad could be replaced, but this will not happen before there is confidence that the new leaders are able to control the situation in Syria and guarantee Russia's interests. On the other hand, Russia's vision of the future of Syria is unstable. Moscow's views on the depth of Syrian regime transformation depend on the dynamics of the dialogue between Moscow and the international community and developments on the battleground in Syria. The more Assad is successful in gaining territories back, the less Moscow is inclined to support changes beyond the facelifting of the regime. From this point of view, the regime's victory in Aleppo played a dual role. On one hand, it made the Kremlin excessively self-confident in its capacities to influence the situation in Syria. On the other hand, the stubborn resistance of the anti-Assad forces also showed Moscow that it needs to communicate with a wider range of forces fighting against Damascus than just a systemic/official opposition. As a result, Moscow stopped labeling all fighting opposition forces as terrorists and recognized at least some as legitimate players.

By March 2017, Moscow felt quite comfortable in Syria. The Russian authorities managed to achieve their first goal—to save Assad regime and ensure its success in retaking certain parts of the Syrian territory. Yet, the end of the game was still far away for Russia. Moscow would like to put an end to the civil war in Syria, or at least ensure the sustainable ceasefire on a large part of the country's territory in order to be able to facilitate partial Russian military withdrawal (Moscow intends to keep its presence in the Tartus naval base and Khmeimim airbase after the end of the war in Syria). However, this is only possible through the revitalization of the political process, and that is where Moscow did not achieve much success. Negotiations in Astana that started in early 2017 and were initially welcomed by the international community as an attempt to launch a full-fledged peaceful settlement have come to a deadlock.

Another challenge that Russia will face in Syria soon is the issue of ISIS. As it was mentioned, so far Moscow has not been enthusiastic about fighting the Islamic State and saw the saving of the Assad regime as its top priority. According to the Kremlin's vision, it was not the radicals themselves but the fall of the old political regimes that led to the destabilization of the region. As a result, the Russian authorities preferred to address the source of the problem (regimes' volatility) and only then deal with the outcomes of the system crisis (the rise of jihadists). Yet, after the regime success in Aleppo and gradual defeat of the opposition forces, Russia will inevitably have to intensify its struggle against the radical Islamists. However, Moscow does not want to fight against ISIS on its own. Yet, forming any effective coalition with other international forces is hardly possible due to mutual mistrust existing between Russia and the U.S.-led coalition as well as due to differences existing between them in the vision of the Assad regime's future.

Libya

In 2017 Russian involvement in the Libyan civil war has grown substantially. Along with active political consultations with General Khalifa Haftar, a commander of one of main military groupings in the Libyan civil war, Russia is believed to be supplying him with weapons with the logistic help of Egypt (it is believed that Cairo persuaded Russia to support Haftar and Moscow agreed to do this to flatter its partner)[14] and financial support of the United Arab Emirates (UAE). By doing so, Moscow obviously pursues a number of goals. First, by providing active political and material support to General Haftar in Libya, Russia also demonstrates its readiness to affect the domestic political dynamics in Middle Eastern countries beyond Syria and in those areas of the Middle East that are located close to the post-Soviet space. Moscow's recent involvement in the Libyan civil war could be considered as the final stage of the evolution of Russian foreign policy in the region that started in 2012. Russia tried to approach to the region from largely neutral positions avoiding direct involvement in the Middle Eastern affairs. Its active support for the Assad regime after 2012 demonstrated the Kremlin's readiness to respond more decisively to those regional events that are believed to threaten Russian interests. Meanwhile, Moscow's involvement in Libya showed Russian intentions not only to give a response to the emerging challenges, but to take pre-emptive

---

[14] Interview with Russian experts on the Middle East. Berlin, February 2017, Rome, March 2017.

steps to determine the development of the situation on the ground. Second, the instability in the region caused by the Arab Spring has been a serious blow to Russia's economy. Moscow lost up to $20 billion in planned investments in military infrastructure, road construction, energy, and other areas following the fall of the Qaddafi government. By supporting General Haftar, Moscow has sought to create an influential pro-Russian group in the future Libyan government that Russia might use to compensate for some of its loses.

Finally, by increasing its involvement in Libya, Moscow continues to leverage the West. It tries to make sure that Russia's active role in Libyan affairs will make the United States and the EU less determined to put pressure on Russia in other areas in order to prevent the Kremlin from becoming a serious troublemaker in the Middle East.

Israel and Palestine

In 2017 the Kremlin managed to deepen its dialogue with Tel Aviv to a previously unseen level, although Russia retains its close contacts with the Palestinian administration. The Russian and Israeli authorities have finally come to the understanding that there will always be certain restraints on the development of bilateral ties, and have focused on the exploitation of opportunities rather than discussing fundamental problems. Consequently, in 2015 Israel secured Moscow's guarantee that the issue of the Iranian nuclear program would be settled in such a way as to eliminate any security threats to Israel. In return, the Israelis took a neutral position in the Russian–Ukrainian confrontation, abstaining from the UN General Assembly vote on Resolution 68/262 against the Russian annexation of Crimea, and silently supported Russian military involvement in Syria. The Israeli authorities also refused to support the main sanctions imposed by the United States and the EU on Russia, although some restrictions on cooperation with Russia in the military and banking spheres were still supported.

The Russian–Israeli rapprochement creates certain concerns that Russia is not always interested in the implementation of the two-state solution if it goes against Israeli interests. For Moscow it is more important to create a buzz around its diplomacy in the case of Palestine and Gaza than to actually settle the issue. Russian influence and resources are insufficient to bring the sides to agreement, but the Kremlin sees itself as profiting simply from participation, which demonstrates its importance to the Arab world and West as part of the negotiation process. A solution would mean that Russia is no longer needed.

In 2017, Russian-Israeli relations were on the rise. Moscow and Tel Aviv actively cooperated both economically and politically. Israel was the first to establish effective de-confliction mechanisms with Russian air forces in Syria. In exchange Russia *de facto* opened Syrian skies for Tel Aviv by closing its eyes to occasional airstrikes conducted by Israeli air forces to prevent the transfer of Iranian and Syrian arms to Hezbollah.[15]

Yet, Moscow and Tel Aviv prefer not to draw much attention to their cooperation, as this may harm Russian relations with some other Muslim countries of the region. Nevertheless, Russian relations with Israel may still become a restraining factor for the further developing of Russian–Iranian relations. By allying with Tehran, Moscow would most likely harm relations with its silent partner in the Middle East—Israel. In December 2015–January 2016, statements by Israeli officials demonstrated concerns about growing Russian_Iranian cooperation in Syria and beyond. Previously, Israel tolerated the rapprochement between Moscow and Tehran as long as it was not considered a threat to national security. Yet, by 2016, Israeli officials had started to openly worry that the Russian government was beginning to close its eyes to anti-Israeli moves by Tehran.[16] Although these speculations seem to have little basis, active Russian support of Tehran in Syria would almost certainly be considered in Israel as further proof of the growing Russian–Iranian alliance.

Egypt

Russian military involvement in Syria produced a harsh anti-Russia backlash throughout the Middle East. This compelled Moscow to intensify its attempts to bring some of the Arab countries onto the Russian side, as a means of diluting anti-Russian sentiment in the region. Subsequently, the Kremlin tried to find support in Egypt. Russia's efforts brought the expected effect: Cairo supported Moscow's actions in Syria and facilitated Moscow's arms supplies to Libya by providing necessary logistic support. Egypt also became actively involved in the revitalization of the diplomatic

---

[15] "Syria Predupredila Izrayel," *Interfax*, January 13, 2017, http://www.interfax.ru/world/545163, accessed March 16, 2017.

[16] "Rossiya i Izrail Dogovorilis o Konsultatciyakh Zamnachalnikov Shtabov po Sirii," *Vzglyad*, 4 October 2015, http://www.vz.ru/news/2015/10/4/770399.html, accessed on October 29, 2015.

track of the Syrian crisis settlement by arranging dialogue between the different groupings of the Syrian opposition.

The substantial improvement in relations between the two countries within the last four years should not be considered as exceptional, unexpected, or based solely on their common interest in fighting against Islamic radicals. The intensification of the Russian–Egyptian dialogue was a result of a gradual strengthening of the bilateral ties during the last two decades. It is notable that Egypt's interest in establishing closer relations with Moscow was demonstrated by Egyptian authorities both under Hosni Mubarak and Mohamed Morsi.[17] It was they (not Abdel Fattah al-Sisi) who essentially prepared the groundwork for what some Russian and Egyptian experts consider "Russia's return" to Egypt. Therefore the choice of Moscow as one of Cairo's potential partners was determined not only by the current developments in the Middle East, but also by deep and strategic calculations of the Egyptian elite that tried to improve its relations with Moscow even when Russia was not that much interested in this during the first two decades after the fall of the Soviet Union. Egyptian memories of Soviet assistance provided to Cairo under Gamal abdel Nasser also played some role, as did the gradual understanding that it was too risky for the Egyptian elite solely rely on the United States as a key international partner. Obama administration attempts to put pressure on al-Sisi, limits on arms supplies to his country, and criticism of the Egyptian government for human rights and democracy issues only convinced Cairo that Egypt should diversify its foreign policy and find new allies.

The personality of Vladimir Putin has also played an important role in the spirit of Russian–Egyptian cooperation. Putin's political agenda aimed at the creation of a multi-polar world and Russia's increased interaction with non-Western players inevitably pulls Egypt (as one of the key players in the Middle East) into the zone of Moscow's interests. However, Russian analysts and diplomats are also arguing about Putin's personal positive attitude towards al-Sisi. Some members of Putin's administration have even discussed that a certain chemistry exists between the two presidents, which helps them to find a common understanding.[18]

---

[17] Evgeny Bezushenko, "K Vizitu Prezidenta Rossii V.V.Putina v Yegipet," February 13, 2015, http://www.iimes.ru/?p=23524, accessed on March 16, 2017; Pervin Mamed-zadeh, "Rossiya-Yegipet: Dvizheniye v Storonu Sotrudnichestva," January 14, 2005, http://www.iimes.ru/?p=3428, accessed March 16, 2017.

[18] "Peregovory Vyzvanniye Simpatiyey," *TASS*, February 9, 2015, http://tass.ru/politika/1753188, accessed March 16, 2017.

Russia also seems to be trying to reclaim the Soviet Union's role as a U.S. alternative in Egypt. From this perspective, the memory of a Soviet presence in the region serves as an additional benefit to the Russian government. However, Moscow plays this card very carefully. As opposed to the Soviet Union, modern Russia clearly understands that it cannot compete with the United States in the scale of possible economic and political influence. The Kremlin does not oppose Washington directly, but exploits existing Egyptian disappointment with the United States through practical moves that contrast with American and European behavior. Thus, the reluctance of Washington to protect Mubarak when compared to Russian support provided to Assad makes Cairo think about Moscow as a more reliable partner. The decision of the United States and the EU to limit weapons exports to Egypt in 2013 was one of the reasons for the intensification of the Russian–Egyptian discourse on military cooperation.

Gulf Cooperation Council (GCC)

In 2011–2012, the growing confrontation between Moscow and the Gulf monarchies caused by the Russian position on Syria tangibly limited Russian options for strengthening cooperation with the GCC. For instance, during 2010–2011, Russia offered to involve Qatar in a number of investment projects worth $10–12 billion in different fields of the Russian economy (especially in the oil and gas, construction, and gold mining sectors).[19] However, all these proposals were ignored by Doha. Political factors (such as Russian–Qatari differences over approaches to the Arab Spring and the Syrian conflict) were, according to some analysts, critical in determining the lack of a response.[20] Moscow's contacts with the other GCC countries also became problematic. Even the UAE, where the Russian presence was probably the strongest in the GCC, was considered as an unreliable partner from the beginning of the Arab Spring.

All in all, the events of the Arab Spring and their aftermath formed a serious stress test for Russian foreign policy towards the GCC. The initial results of this test, however, suggest that Russia has managed to transcend it. During 2013–2016, the growing energy independence of the United States, Washington's intention to bridge relations with Tehran, and the U.S. failure to use force against Bashar al-Assad created grounds for Wash-

---

[19] Eldar Kasaev, "Rossiya i Katar: Prichiny Ekonomicheskoy Stagnatcii," http://www.iimes.ru/?p=17847, accessed October 4, 2013.
[20] Ibid.

ington to split with its traditional allies—the Arab monarchies of the Gulf. The potential division between the United States and the GCC created new opportunities for Russia, which had been trying unsuccessfully to increase its presence in the Arab part of the Gulf since 2003. The rumors about U.S. withdrawal from the region compelled Saudi Arabia and its Gulf partners to look for other non-regional countries capable of compensating for a future decrease in the U.S. presence. As a result, some attention was now paid to Moscow, and, in spite of all existing contradictions, the members of the GCC were compelled to continue the dialogue with Russia. By the beginning of 2017, it became obvious that in spite of existing contradictions over a variety of political issues, neither Moscow nor the GCC intend to cross the red lines that would deprive them of the option of rapprochement. The events of the Arab spring clearly demonstrated to Moscow that it should recognize Saudi Arabia and Qatar as regional leaders. At the same time, Moscow's determination in defending its interests in Syria, while at the same time being ready to continue the dialogue with the GCC, proved that Russia was an important player in the region that should not be either neglected or underestimated.

Although the economic relations between the countries of the Gulf and Russia remain underdeveloped, they have certain potential. Moscow is unable to challenge the West's economic presence in the region, nor the growing influence of China (and other Asian countries). Yet, Russia is probably capable of finding its own niche in the Gulf system of economic relations. In its economic efforts, the Kremlin currently focuses on those areas where it has market advantages: nuclear energy, oil and gas, petrochemcals, space, weapons, and grain. Price and reliability are among the main reasons for Middle Eastern countries to become interested in Russian technologies. The Russian government also needs to demonstrate considerable patience, vigilance, and courtesy in developing its relations with the Gulf. The established ties with GCC members are still young and fragile, and they are exposed to the negative influence of external factors such as the unstable situation in the Middle East.

Balancing on the Verge

The overview of the main directions of the Russian diplomacy in the Middle East allows making the following conclusion: Moscow's success in reclaiming its long lost role as an important player in the Middle East was largely determined by its pragmatism and intention to talk to every force in the region it sees as legitimate. Given the complexity of Middle Eastern realities, this strategy of balancing between all major players was not supposed to work. And yet, it does.

First, Moscow managed to persuade its political interlocutors that it will be much more useful to concentrate on discussion of those areas where Russia and Middle Eastern countries can cooperate rather than spend all their time on trying to persuade Moscow to abandon some partners for the sake of strengthening cooperation with the others.

Second, the overall regional disappointment in the United States and the West compels Middle Eastern countries to accept Russia, due to their perceived need to diversify their foreign policy.

Third, Moscow's capacity to deal with all the major players is appealing in a certain way. Russia is among only a few countries that sustain positive relations with Tehran, Ankara, Damascus, Riyadh, Cairo, and Tel Aviv. This makes Moscow a perfect candidate for the role of a mediator.

Nonetheless, Moscow's strategy of balancing between different powers in the region in order to maintain good relations with them all is ultimately risky. The region still wants Moscow to take its side. Thus, the intensification of dialogue with Tehran raises Iranian expectations of closer cooperation. Yet the formation of any alliance with Tehran would harm Russian dialogue with other states, including Israel and the GCC countries. Under these circumstances, the decision by Moscow not to veto UN Resolution N2216 on Yemen, adopted in April 2015, was a stress test for Russian–Iranian relations; the document imposed a ban on the export of weapons to Yemen's Iranian-backed Houthi rebels.[21] Russia managed to avoid an overtly negative Iranian reaction in this instance, but it will not be able to pull off this trick every time.[22]

Is Russia a Threat to Western Interests in the Middle East?

There is no one answer to this question. The active Russian presence in the Middle East should not automatically be considered a serious threat to U.S. and EU interests. To begin with, Russia's capacities in the region

---

[21] "MID: SB OON Otvetstvenen za Mir v Yemene Posle Prinyatiya Rezolutcii," *TVC*, 16 April 2015, http://www.tvc.ru/news/show/id/66195, accessed July 13, 2015.

[22] "Moscow Backs Iran's Yemen Proposal," *Mehr News Agency*, April 19, 2015, http://en.mehrnews.com/news/106722/Moscow-backs-Iran-s-Yemen-proposal, accessed July 13, 2015.

are limited. This limits its ability to engage in direct confrontation with the West there. In most cases, Russia tries to safeguard its existing political and economic interests. Even in Syria, its goals are not completely contrary to Western interests: it accepts the idea of a post-Assad Syria but wants to guarantee Russian presence there.

Moreover, there are several issues where Russian interests fully converge with those of the West. These include protection of the non-proliferation regime in the Middle East, the stabilization of Iraq and Yemen, and counteracting the spread of jihadism. Success on these issues would create further grounds for cooperation. Thus, Russia has been working hard to secure an effective dialogue between Iran and the West on the settlement of the Iranian nuclear issue. The main reason for this is that Russia appeared to be actually interested in the outcome of its efforts and not only in what it could gain during the process. An Iran armed with a nuclear bomb is not desirable for Russia, as this would change the balance of power in the region and encourage other, even less stable, Middle Eastern regimes to join the nuclear club. This, in turn, would pose a genuine threat for Russian security. Under these circumstances, it would be logical for the West to choose issues for cooperation with Russia carefully, where the latter is genuinely interested in an actual solution. Such grounds for interaction can likely be found in issues related to IS, Iraq, Afghanistan, and even Syria and Libya.

Nevertheless, Russia also believes in the success of its current Middle Eastern strategy based on the principle of balancing among different regional players. Success in Syria, rapprochement with Iran, the strengthening of ties with Egypt, and the development of dialogue with Israel and the GCC add to the Kremlin's confidence. As a result, Moscow demonstrates its readiness to defend its interests in the region with the use of not only diplomacy but by military force, if necessary. Consequently, any attempts to change Russia's approaches towards the Middle East will be challenged. While it will remain interested in dialogue with international players on key Middle Eastern issues, Russia will try to impose its own vision of the region's future with little inclination to make concessions.

Under these circumstances, dealing with Russia in the Middle East will be challenging but not impossible. Moscow is extremely suspicious about the West and believes that it has good reasons to blame the United States and EU for its previous misfortunes. The unprecedented (since, at least, the end of the Cold War) scale of the current tensions between Russia and the United States and the EU makes Moscow see its diplomacy in the

Middle East as another avenue that could be used in the confrontation with the West. Thus, the Russian authorities believe that they can exercise additional pressure on the United States and the EU via its contacts with the regional pariah states. Under these circumstances, Russian ties with Assad have special importance for the Kremlin. Even before the Ukrainian crisis of 2014, the issue of Russian–U.S. relations was one of the factors determining Moscow's stance toward the situation in Syria. Russia was certainly taking what it saw as revenge on the United States for its previous losses in the region. Given the outcomes in Iraq and Libya, Russia learned that the fall of longtime partners inevitably leads to the loss of economic and political influence in those countries. Whether Russia stays out of the conflict (as in Iraq) or unobtrusively helps the West to overthrow its old allies (as in Libya, where Moscow was the first government to stop exports of military equipment to Qaddafi), the result is the same: Russia is compelled to leave countries liberated from dictators (after the fall of Saddam Hussein in 2003, Russian companies lost their stakes in the Iraqi energy sector, and it took more than six years for them to begin their sluggish return). Therefore, without solid guarantees regarding the security of its interests, Russia has been fighting hard for Syria, increasing its involvement in Libya and strengthening ties with Iran and Israel.

It is still unclear, however, how substantial Russia's declared turn to non-Western countries really is. There is a suspicion in the region that Moscow may once again change its policy towards the Middle East as soon as its conflict with the West is over. Although challenges to Russian security that come directly from the region have also become some of the main drivers of Russian policy in the Middle East, so far Moscow's activities there are still largely determined by factors not directly related to the Middle East—namely, relations with the West. A substantial change in Russian–American relations will inevitably affect Russia's stance on Middle Eastern issues, although a complete revision of Russian approaches is unlikely. Even during the current fallout with the United States and the EU, Moscow is cautious about direct confrontation with the West over the Middle East unless it is determined to be in the interest of Russian security (as it happened in Syria). In April 2015, Putin decided to lift the ban on the export of S-300 missile complexes to Iran. However, even the sale of the S-300s should be considered as part of Russia's message to the West rather than a real attempt to change it, given that the number of S-300s delivered to Iran is not enough to change the military balance.

Consequently, it is important to talk to Russia even if the outcome of this talk is not always substantial or immediate. The trust-building process will require time. Moscow also wants to be heard. It also has ambitions to secure the role of an international player whose opinion on key issues matters. As a result, asking Russia for assistance could have an unexpectedly positive role in allaying existing tensions between Moscow and the West. Otherwise, any attempts to isolate Russia can turn it in the serious and not always predictable troublemaker. Yet, while being ready to talk to Russia the West should also be prepared to defend its red lines in the Middle East. Putin and his team respect strong counterparts and neglect weak ones. Being unpunished for crossing red lines convinces the Kremlin of Western weakness and tempts it to be more brutal and decisive.

The set of topics that could be discussed with Moscow is limited, but still there are quite a number of issues to talk about. First, Russia is interested in preventing the spread of nuclear weapons in the Middle East. From this point of view, Moscow could be an effective partner in ensuring Iran's adherence to the nuclear agreement reached in 2015. Moscow also understands that the settlement of the Syrian crisis is impossible without launching an international discussion on the future of the post-conflict Syria. In general Russia would like to minimize the number of sources of instability existing in the region. As a result, Moscow's involvement in the discussion of the futures of Libya, Iraq, Yemen, and Afghanistan can be desirable. Finally, there are some opportunities for economic cooperation. For instance, Russian companies appear interested in forming joint energy consortia with foreign companies to develop Middle Eastern hydrocarbon resources. In 2016, one of the Russia's energy behemoths, Gazpromneft, acknowledged its experience of working in a consortium on the development of the Badra oilfield in Iraq as successful. This in turn creates opportunities for cooperation between Russian firms and those Western and local companies that eye Iran as a potential market. Russian energy companies have interests in other places. In fact, Moscow sees Egypt, Libya, Israel, the GCC countries, and even post-war Syria as potential markets.

Chapter 8

Russian and Western Engagement in the Broader Middle East

Mark N. Katz

There are many problems in the greater Middle East that would be in the common interest of the United States, its EU/NATO partners, and Russia to work on together in order to resolve, or at least contain. These problems, many of which are overlapping, include: the challenge of Islamic State (IS), al-Qaeda, and other jihadist groups; the war in Syria; the multifaceted problems posed by Turkey and by Iran; the conflicts in Yemen, Libya, Iraq, and Afghanistan; and, of course, the Israeli-Palestinian conflict.

Whether America, Europe, and Russia can work together on these issues, however, is not at all clear given not just the quantity and severity of the problems facing the greater Middle East, but also the difficult state of Russian-Western relations, rising populism within the West, and the election of Donald Trump—a president whose foreign policy priorities appeared at first to be very different from those of previous U.S. presidents. On the other hand, the stated willingness of Trump and Putin to improve U.S.-Russian relations and work together on common problems raised the possibility that the Middle East is a realm where they could cooperate. Trump, as well as Putin, called for Moscow and Washington to work together against IS in Syria in particular. Further, if such Russian-American cooperation came about, it is difficult to imagine that America's EU/NATO partners would not support it. However, the hopes for improved Russian-American relations present at the beginning of the Trump administration seem to have already met the same negative fate as similar hopes at the beginning of the Clinton, Bush, and Obama administrations.

Yet even if Russian-Western relations remain poor and their interests largely diverge, there may be some instances in which they converge—including in the Middle East. In looking at Russian-Western engagement in the broader Middle East, then, both optimistic and pessimistic scenarios regarding how the United States, EU/NATO, and Russia might or might not cooperate on the many conflicts and problems of the region must be looked at since both are plausible. Something must first be said, though, about what the spectrum of possibilities from optimistic to pessimistic might be.

The most optimistic scenario is one in which all three sides of the triangle—the United States, the EU/NATO partners, and Russia—work together towards common goals. There are also several combinations of two out of these three working together: America and its EU/NATO partners but not Russia; America and Russia but not the EU/NATO partners; and the EU/NATO partners and Russia but not America. The first of these three would probably be an adversarial scenario (West vs. Russia), whereas the other two might occur if either America or the EU/NATO partners chose not to be actively involved in dealing with one or more of the greater Middle East's problems, and let the other take the lead in working with Russia. There is also the possibility of little or no coordination among the U.S., EU/NATO partners, and Russia in the Middle East, thus maximizing the prospects that they would work at cross-purposes. The most pessimistic scenario, from a Western perspective, is one in which the U.S. and EU/NATO both prove unwilling or unable to be actively involved in much of the Middle East, and so leave Russia as the most assertive great power in the region. With this in mind, an assessment will now be made of the prospects for Western and Russian engagement on various issues affecting the greater Middle East.

Islamic State (IS), Al-Qaeda, and Other Jihadist Groups

Since Sunni jihadists are a common threat to America, Europe, and Russia (as well as all the states of the region); joint cooperation against them is clearly a common interest. Putin has called for working with "Western partners" (among others) against this common threat in Syria in particular. Trump has called for working with Russia in Syria against IS as well. Indeed, considering that Sunni jihadists are such a common threat, it might not seem that the United States, EU/NATO partners, and Russia would actually need to cooperate on too much else in order to see the value in working together on this issue.

Yet even if, under the best of circumstances, all three recognized the benefit of working together against IS and al-Qaeda, this will be difficult. For if and when IS and al-Qaeda could be eliminated or seriously weakened in various places, the West and Russia (as well as their various Middle Eastern partners) will worry about who this will benefit. In Syria, for example, the West will not be happy if the elimination of IS and al-Qaeda merely serves to strengthen the Assad regime. Reports abound that while Moscow calls for joint action against IS, it is mainly targeting other opposition groups opposed to Assad. This suggests that Russia views the latter as more threatening. Moscow may also want to eliminate Assad's non-IS opposition in order to force the West to choose between Assad and IS in anticipation that it would prefer the former. Similar concerns will arise elsewhere: if IS is defeated in Iraq, will this mainly benefit Iran through strengthening its Arab Shi'a allies in Baghdad, or will it enable Baghdad to be less dependent on Tehran? Or will the main beneficiary be Iraqi Kurds, who (if they are regarded as America's allies) will be seen by others as benefiting the United States?

Thus, even if the desire for joint cooperation between the West and Russia against IS (as well as al-Qaeda and other Sunni jihadist threats) is great, it may not be able to advance very far unless they can also agree on a common approach to the greater Middle East as a whole. For if they cannot do so, and especially if their actions against IS and similar groups are not coordinated, then each will fear that the other's actions against the jihadists are designed to harm its and its allies interests.

Syria

Since the outbreak of the Arab Spring rebellion in Syria in 2011, Russia and the West have differed sharply on Syria. Moscow (along with Tehran) has firmly backed the Assad regime, while America and certain European states have called for Assad to step down. The Obama Administration provided some (largely ineffective) support to the "moderate" Syrian opposition, but some of its allies—Turkey, Saudi Arabia, and Qatar—have provided a much greater degree of support to various Syrian rebel groups. As a result of the war in Syria, refugees have fled in massive numbers not just to neighboring states, but also to Europe where there has been an anti-immigrant political backlash against them.

The Obama Administration argument was that Assad should step down because his brutal rule contributed to the rise of jihadist opposition against it. Moscow's argument, by contrast, has been that while Assad may be bad, his most likely replacement, the jihadists, would be worse, and so the West should join Russia in supporting Assad. The Trump Administration seemed to be persuaded by this logic (and European governments do not now seem to oppose it even if they do not fully embrace it), but the U.S. military strike on a Syrian air base in response to Assad's use of chemical weapons against his opponents and civilians in April 2017 showed that there are limits to how much Trump accepts Putin's logic about Assad.

Yet if all Trump's one bombing raid on Syria does is pressure Russia into halting Assad's use of chemical but not conventional weapons, and if the U.S. along with the EU/NATO partners effectively acquiesce to the Russian viewpoint that Assad is the least worst viable option in Syria, then the prospects for Russian-Western cooperation on Syria may still remain despite the rise in Russian-American tension as a result of this incident. The trouble, though, is that while Russia and Iran may have succeeded in preventing Assad from being overthrown and even clawing back important territory that he had lost, they do not seem capable of ending internal resistance—which may well continue to receive external support from some governments in the region. Even Moscow recognizes that the Assad regime needs to accommodate at least some part of the opposition, and so is sponsoring peace talks between the regime and some rebel groups in Astana. However, it is not clear whether Iran will go along with this process or whether it will help the Assad regime resist any Russian pressure to make concessions it does not want to make. In other words, even if they act in concert, Russia and the West may be unable to persuade or cajole either the internal parties to the Syrian conflict or their regional supporters to agree to a settlement. The lack of Russian-Western cooperation would only exacerbate this problem.

Turkey

Turkey's relations with America began to deteriorate at the time of the U.S.-led intervention in Iraq in 2003. One of Ankara's concerns was that American actions enabling the Kurds of northern Iraq to govern themselves would fan Kurdish secessionism inside Turkey as well. While Ankara now has reasonably good working relations with the Kurdish Regional Government in northern Iraq, the Turkish government has become angry with the United States over several issues, including American support for the anti-IS Syrian Kurdish forces (which Ankara views as linked to Kurdish separatists inside Turkey), Obama Administration criticism of Erdogan's increasingly authoritarian policies, and Obama's refusal to extradite Fethullah Gulen, the Turkish oppositionist residing in the United States whom Erdogan blames for the July 2016 coup attempt against him (It is not yet clear if Trump will reverse this policy). European relations with Turkey have also turned sour over the lack of progress in negotiations on Turkey's accession to the EU, European criticism of Turkey's human rights record, and acrimony over the Syrian refugee issue. Even Turkey's continued willingness to remain part of the NATO alliance is uncertain.

Putin courted Erdogan for years, but this did not prevent their relations turning sour when Turkish forces shot down a Russian military aircraft in the vicinity of the Turkish-Syrian border. Since mid-2016, though, Russian-Turkish relations revived after Erdogan apologized for the incident and Putin was much quicker than Western leaders to express support for Erdogan at the time of the July 2016 coup attempt. Instead of being at loggerheads, Turkey and Russia are now coordinating some of their actions in Syria. But the potential for Turkish-Russian discord remains, especially since Moscow has also been supportive of Syria's Kurdish opposition (though it has downplayed this since the Moscow-Ankara rapprochement in mid-2016) and because they take different sides in the dispute between Armenia and Azerbaijan, which could well revive.

Russian-Western cooperation would reduce the opportunity for Turkey to play the two sides against each other, while the lack of such cooperation gives Ankara the opportunity to at least threaten to distance itself from the West and move closer toward Moscow. The Trump Administration placing less emphasis than the Obama Administration on democracy and human rights in other nations may not only serve to improve U.S. ties with Russia, but also with Turkey. While concerned about human rights in Turkey, European states may now be more concerned about preserving Turkey's cooperation in stemming the refugee flow from Syria to Europe. If Russian-Western relations deteriorate, the West may actually be better off if Russian-Turkish relations are good than if they become hostile again to the point of raising the question whether NATO might be called upon to defend Turkey against Russia.

Iran

The Obama Administration's hopes that achieving a nuclear accord with Iran would lead to a broader Iranian-American rapprochement as well as more moderate Iranian behavior in general were not fulfilled. Iran is heavily engaged in supporting the Assad regime in Syria. America's allies in Israel and most of the Gulf Cooperation Council states continue to see Iran as an existential threat. During the 2016 U.S. presidential election campaign, candidate Donald Trump regularly denounced the Joint Comprehensive Plan of Action (or JCPOA, as the Iranian nuclear accord is usually referred to) as being a "bad deal" which he would "tear up." But America's EU/NATO partners, Russia, and many other governments all support the JCPOA. Any effort by the Trump Administration to dismantle the Iranian nuclear accord would put the U.S. at odds with its EU/NATO partners, Russia, and many other states on this issue. There have even been warnings from knowledgeable voices in Israel and the GCC states about how dismantling the JCPOA could well result in Iran acquiring nuclear weapons.

Yet after comparing the costs and benefits of retaining vs. abandoning the JCPOA, the Trump Administration now appears to agree with the EU/NATO allies, Russia, and others that retaining it is the better option for ensuring that Iran does not acquire nuclear weapons. One of the costs of not adopting this approach, the Trump Administration may understand, is that this would put increased strains on U.S. ties with its EU/NATO partners—and that this is something that Russia could be expected to exploit.

Yet even if America, Europe, and Russia all work together in upholding the JCPOA, this still leaves the question of whether a common approach can be achieved regarding Iran's regional behavior, which includes involvement in conflict situations as well as hostile relations with Israel and most GCC states. America, Europe, and Russia acting in concert might be able to persuade Iran on the one hand and the GCC and Israel on the other to ratchet down their hostility, if not actually normalize relations. Even under the best of circumstances, however, this will not be easy. Still, it should be recognized that much of Israeli and GCC opposition to the Obama Administration's efforts to achieve an Iranian nuclear accord were motivated by fears that this would (as Obama hoped) lead to improved Iranian-American ties, and that this would further lead to a reduced American commitment to Israel and the GCC. The Trump Administration appears to be in a better position to allay such fears while at the same time upholding the JCPOA.

On the other hand, a lack of cooperation among America, Europe, and Russia will contribute to continued Iranian-Israeli as well as Iranian-GCC hostility. The Trump Administration would definitely express strong support for Israel and the GCC. Russia would continue with its current policy of cooperating with Iran, but also pursuing good relations with Israel and the GCC. Some European states (notably Britain and France) would pursue security relations with the GCC, but most EU/NATO partners would probably focus on promoting their economic ties with all states of the region. While none of these outside parties would encourage either Iranian-Israeli or Iranian-GCC hostility, their lack of effort to ameliorate these relationships increases the probability of a crisis occurring that negatively affects them all.

Yemen, Libya, Iraq, and Afghanistan

The ongoing conflicts in these four countries are different from each other in many ways, but they have two common features: 1) governmental authority has not been, and does not seem likely to be, secured throughout each of them due to severe internal divisions; and 2) the U.S., EU/NATO partners, and Russia seek to avoid becoming heavily involved militarily in any of them even (indeed, especially) if they had been so in the past.

The West and Russia would prefer to see governmental authority re-established in each of them. At least in Iraq and Afghanistan there are governments that have authority in some parts of the country. In Libya and Yemen, however, the internationally recognized governments are extremely weak.

Cooperation among the United States, EU/NATO partners, and Russia on these regional conflicts could help focus efforts on containing and even reducing the jihadist elements operating in each of them as well as the search for federal political solutions that seek to accommodate ethnic, sectarian, or just tribal differences within them. In Iraq, this might mean seeking a solution that recognizes the Shi'a-dominated government, but also accommodates both the Kurdish Regional Government as well as a similar, non-jihadist, Sunni Arab regional government in the western part of the country. In Afghanistan, some sort of federal solution recognizing Pushtun control of the south and non-Pushtun control over other parts of the country could be explored. In Libya, this would mean building autonomous regional governments in the west (Tripolitania) and the east (Cyrenaica) under the umbrella of a unified whole. In Yemen, groups in various parts of the country would need to be accommodated, including the Houthis in the north, non-Houthi northerners, southerners in Aden and surrounding areas, and perhaps Hadhramis and others in the far eastern section of the country.

Because none of them wishes to become over-committed in any of these four countries, even a cooperative approach on the part of the United States, EU/NATO partners, and Russia may have difficulty in achieving much where local and regional actors are determined to fight. Their working together, though, could help promote conflict resolution efforts if and when local and regional actors become more amenable to them (as can happen if a conflict goes on long enough to convince all participants that none can actually win militarily). If the West and Russia work at cross purposes, though, local and regional rivals will be encouraged to seek support from rival external powers.

The Israeli-Palestinian Conflict

It is difficult to see how this conflict, which has defied all previous attempts to end it, can be resolved under current circumstances even if the West and Russia cooperate on this. American support for Israel, and the lack of any substantial external support for the Palestinians, means that Israel cannot be forced to make concessions to the Palestinians. And the Netanyahu government has demonstrated that it will not be persuaded to do so. Still, the problem will not go away either. And with the Palestinian population growing relatively faster than the Jewish population, the continued lack of an Israeli-Palestinian peace settlement will mean continued Israeli suppression of Palestinian nationalism that will be costly for both the Israeli and the Palestinian communities.

Trump administration figures have expressed confidence that they can succeed where others have failed in bringing about a solution to this long-running conflict. But if Trump goes through with his campaign pledge to move the U.S. Embassy in Israel to Jerusalem (which the U.S. as well as other countries have avoided doing up to now in order not to offend Arabs and Muslims generally), then the Palestinians are not going to see Washington as a reliable mediator. Interestingly, Russia seems to have suggested a compromise solution on this issue by recognizing West Jerusalem as the capital of Israel. Neither Russia nor the EU, though, appears willing to take up the thankless task of attempting to achieve an Israeli-Palestinian settlement. The continuation of the current state of relations between Israel and the Palestinians is the most likely scenario whether the U.S., its EU/NATO partners, and Russia cooperate with one another or not.

Concluding Thoughts

The lack of cooperation between Russia and the West will only serve to exacerbate the ongoing problems of the Middle East. Yet even if the United States, its EU/NATO partners, and Russia can cooperate with one another, it will still be difficult for them to ameliorate any, much less most or all, of this fractious region's problems. And despite the common interests they may appear to have in cooperating in the Middle East, significant differences between them elsewhere (whether over Ukraine, the Baltics, or Russian interference in Western elections) may prevent the West and Russia from working together in the Middle East. The recent deterioration in the Trump-Putin relationship, though, does not bode well for this possibility. But even if there were good personal relations between Putin on the one hand and Trump as well as various European leaders on the other, this would not necessarily increase the prospects for conflict resolution in the Middle East. Indeed, the sheer difficulty of ameliorating any of the Middle East's many problems might only serve to undermine the initial hopes that Putin and Trump may initially have for cooperating with each other.

On the other hand, if Western policymakers can convey to Moscow that they are willing to work with Russia on common American/European/Western interests in the Middle East despite differences elsewhere, there may be some hope not only for achieving some of their common aims in the Middle East, but that working together to achieve them in this region could serve as an example for Russian-Western cooperation elsewhere.

Chapter 9
Sino-Russian Relations and Transatlantic Ties
Richard Weitz

The improved relations between the Russian Federation and the People's Republic of China (PRC) since the Cold War's end have global implications, including on the transatlantic relationship. In recent years the two countries' bilateral ties have increased in many arenas—politically, economically, and militarily. Moreover, both governments have carefully avoided taking provocative actions against each other. China has become Russia's main trading partner, and the two sides have increased the frequency and number of their defense exchanges. Russian President Vladimir Putin now denotes the relationship as a "comprehensive partnership and strategic collaboration. 'Comprehensive' means that we work virtually on all major avenues; 'strategic' means that we attach enormous intergovernmental importance to this work."[1]

Leaders of both countries engage via more than 20 joint intergovernmental mechanisms, though the importance and activism of these bodies is unclear.[2] It is hard to argue with the regular assertions of Russian and Chinese leaders that their bilateral relations are the best they have ever been.

Several drivers are responsible for this growing partnership, which began in the early 1990s: economic incentives, similar world views, mutual security concerns, and shared interests in claiming sovereignty over nearby regions.[3] The sanctions imposed by the United States and the European Union (EU) after the 2014 annexation of Crimea have accelerated—rather than caused—Russia's pivot to China.

---

[1] Marc Bennetts, "Shunned by West, Putin Seeks Friend, Financier on China Visit," *The Washington Times*, June 23, 2016, http://www.washingtontimes.com/news/2016/jun/23/putin-seeks-friend-financier-on-china-visit/ (accessed February 7, 2017).

[2] Xinhua, "Putin Eyes Closer Partnership with China," *China Daily*, June 24, 2016, http://www.chinadaily.com.cn/china/2016-06/24/content_25830253.htm (accessed February 7, 2017).

[3] "Putin Seeks 'More Productive' China Ties," *The Straits Times*, June 23, 2016, http://www.straitstimes.com/world/europe/putin-seeks-more-productive-china-ties (accessed February 7, 2017).

Despite these connections, Moscow's relations with Beijing have never been as strong as the post-World War II transatlantic ties between Western Europe and the United States. Sino-Russian interactions are still mostly marked by harmonious rhetoric, with few concrete projects outside of arms sales, diplomatic consultations, and intermittent energy deals. Despite improved relations, Russia and China have not formed a mutual defensive alliance and still tend to pursue parallel, but distinct, policies regarding many issues. The PRC's indigenous industry has improved enough that Beijing has lost interest in buying Soviet-era defense and manufacturing technologies. For example, the People's Liberation Army (PLA) is now interested in obtaining only Russia's most advanced weapons, which Russians hesitate to sell these without extensive safeguards against the Chinese again copying their sophisticated military technologies and illegally introducing them into other PRC-made weapons systems.

Moreover, the quadrilateral relationship between Russia, China, Europe, and the United States is uniquely cross-cutting and highly complex. Russia seeks to overturn the Western-led global order with a new one, where Moscow would exert greater influence, and where universal values are lacking beyond those agreed by nation states in international law and within the UN Security Council. China also seeks to reform the existing order to give Beijing more influence, but is not yet prepared to try to create an alternative order due to doubts that it will have the capacity, skill, and luck to make a better world in its place. Europeans favor the existing world order, but lack the means to maintain it without U.S. help. Finally, U.S. President Donald Trump is a wild card, in that it is unclear the extent to which he will uphold or abandon traditional Western international liberal principles, norms, and institutions. Thus far, Russia and China have regularly blocked U.S. and European-backed initiatives in the UN Security Council and other multinational bodies, but have also partnered with Western countries on important measures.

China's relations with Russia and the EU are more stable and strong than Beijing's or Moscow's ties with Washington. Until recently, PRC-U.S. relations have been seriously strained. Yet, these ties are still better than the more comprehensively unhealthy Russian-U.S relationship. Russia's pivot toward Asia has focused almost entirely on China, whereas the U.S. pivot to Asia has been more widely targeted but less successful regarding Beijing. Europe's trade-focused approach toward China is also imbalanced. While Russian-U.S. exchanges remain dominated by Cold War-era issues such as arms control and regional security, the Russian-

EU, Russia-China, and Russia-U.S. dialogues extend to encompass many more non-military issues. The China-U.S. and China-EU relationships are sustained by the large number of commercial and academic exchanges, which are almost entirely lacking in the Russian-U.S. and Russian-Chinese relationships.

Moscow's main source of influence remains its military power, as well as its arms and energy exports, despite Russian efforts to diversify assets by advancing its economic, diplomatic, and soft persuasive power. China, the United States, and Europe enjoy a much more robust power portfolio. Yet, China and Europe as well as Russia face major demographic (and therefore socioeconomic) challenges, due to their aging workforce and low birth rates. While Russia's demographic challenges are unprecedented for an advanced and educated society, and China's low-cost working-age population is shrinking due to its aging population and the migration of low-skilled rural workers moving to cities for higher education, the United States is in better shape due to immigration and other favorable conditions.[4]

These complexities are replicated on specific geographic and functional issues—there are not always two opposing dyads (Russia-China vs. Europe-U.S.) in a renewed bipolar confrontation. In some instances, Russia and China do align against Europe and the United States, but in other cases their alignments differ. For example, while Beijing and Moscow denounce U.S. missile defense initiatives in Korea, Chinese government officials have not expressed much concern about U.S. and NATO missile defenses in Europe. Moreover, Moscow wants Beijing to participate in the hitherto exclusively Russian-U.S. strategic arms reductions process, which China refuses even to consider until the two other countries make major nuclear weapons first. Russian representatives repeatedly state that their Chinese counterparts share their views regarding the flaws of the Western-led global order, Western military unilateralism, and other transatlantic-related issues. Yet, Chinese government representatives are cautious in their public statements about the West, citing both benefits and costs to China from the system.[5]

---

[4] Linette Lopez, "What is China's Demographic Challenge?" World Economic Forum, October 22, 2015 https://www.weforum.org/agenda/2015/10/what-is-chinas-demographics-challenge/ (accessed March 12, 2017).

The Socioeconomic Dimension

China's trade and investment ties with Russia are visibly small compared with the PRC's economic relations with Western states. China has been Russia's largest trading partner since 2010, displacing Germany and other European countries. Russia also regularly vies with Saudi Arabia and Angola as the PRC's largest single national supplier of imported oil.[6] Chinese investors have also taken advantage of the new development mechanisms created by Russian authorities—the Far East Development Fund, Advanced Development Territories, the Vladivostok free port area, and targeted infrastructural project support funds—to secure greater PRC direct investment in Russian projects, particularly in the Russian Far East.[7] Meanwhile, Russian-European economic ties are fraying. Their arms trade has collapsed, European direct investment in Russia has fallen considerably since its 2013 peak, and Europeans are striving to reduce their dependence on Russian energy imports.[8] Likewise, Russian-U.S. economic ties remain insignificant. For example, in 2015, China's two-way trade with the United States and with Europe each approached $600 billion, whereas its bilateral commerce with Russia was about one-tenth of that level. The PRC is the second largest foreign holder of U.S. Treasury securities, the second-largest U.S. trading partner, and the leading source of U.S. imports. China has surpassed Russia as the EU's second largest trade partner, with Russia falling to fourth place behind Switzerland, whose imports from the EU are twice as large.[9] The EU is China's biggest trading partner and the PRC has also become an increasingly important investor in Europe.[10]

---

[5] Fu Ying, "Major Countries Need to Build Trust," Valdai Discussion Club, October 25, 2016, http://valdaiclub.com/a/highlights/major-countries-need-to-build-trust/ (accessed February 7, 2017).

[6] "Saudi Regains Top Oil Supplier Spot to China in Jan—Customs," Reuters, February 24, 2017, http://af.reuters.com/article/angolaNews/idAFB9N1FY02I?feedType=RSS&feedName=angolaNews&utm_source=feedburner&utm_medium=feed&utm_campaign=Feed:+reuters/AfricaAngolaNews+(News+/+Africa+/+Angola+News)&&rpc=401 (accessed March 13, 2017).

[7] "China Invests Over $2.4Bln in Russian Far East," Sputnik, July 5, 2016, https://sputniknews.com/russia/201607051042440286-china-far-east-investments/ (accessed February 7, 2017).

[8] European Commission, "Trade Policy: Countries and Regions: Russia," http://ec.europa.eu/trade/policy/countries-and-regions/countries/russia/ (accessed March 13, 2017).

[9] European Commission Directorate General for Trade, "Client and Supplier Countries of the EU28 in Merchandise Trade (value %, 2015, including Intra-EU trade), http://trade.ec.europa.eu/doclib/docs/2006/september/tradoc_122530.pdf (accessed March 13, 2017).

[10] European Commission, "Trade Policy: Countries and Regions: China," http://ec.europa.eu/trade/policy/countries-and-regions/countries/china/ (accessed March 13, 2017).

Sino-Russian ties offer Europe more economic opportunities than the United States. Both Russian and European leaders view China's rising economic prosperity as primarily benign, whereas Trump sees the PRC mostly as an economic competitor. Europe's economic importance to Russia and the United States is declining, whereas it is rising for China, whose "One Belt, One Road" initiative has a major prong directed toward Europe.

Of greatest importance, Russian policy makers have hoped that China might provide an alternative to Western energy and capital markets whose access has been severely limited by EU and U.S. sanctions. European governments have renewed sanctions on several occasions despite suffering greater economic losses than the United States from the foregone investment and trade. Europeans worry that Russians' commercial reorientation toward China could challenge European sales of electronic machinery, equipment, and nuclear energy technologies to Russia.[11] Russian advocates of pursuing deeper ties with Asia and Eurasia argue that building such relations would eventually make Russia a more attractive partner for Europeans.[12] Yet, Russian aspirations of China filling the Western sanctions gap have not panned out. Russian-Chinese trade plunged by almost percent in 2015 due the lower value of Russian commodity exports, slowing Russian and Chinese economic growth, and a massive devaluation of the Russian ruble. Trade stabilized at this lower level in 2016, at around $70 billion, but only due to growing Chinese exports to Russia.[13]

Both Russian and Chinese analysts have expressed enthusiasm for the British vote to leave the EU, which they see as making it easier for their countries to cultivate favorable ties with individual EU members (which they have already done successfully with Switzerland and other European states) as well as collectively enhancing their leverage with a weakened EU. Still, while there are plausible suspicions that Moscow encouraged Brexit by rendering propaganda and other support to its advocates, Beijing initially viewed the withdrawal as a threat to economic and financial stability, even if PRC analysts have since seen opportunities in the British decision as

---

[11] Alicia García-Herrero & Jianwei Xu, "The China-Russia Trade Relationship and Its Impact on Europe," *Bruegel Working Paper*, Issue 4, July 14, 2016, http://bruegel.org/wp-content/uploads/2016/07/WP-2016_04-180716.pdf (accessed February 7, 2017).

[12] Sergey Karaganov, "С Востока на Запад, или Большая Евразия (From East to West, or Greater Eurasia)," *Rosiiskaya Gazeta*, October 24, 2016, https://rg.ru/2016/10/24/politolog-karaganov-povorot-rossii-k-rynkam-azii-uzhe-sostoialsia.html (accessed February 7, 2017).

[13] "Chinese-Russian Trade Grows 2.2% in 2016—Customs Data," Sputnik, January 13, 2017, https://sputniknews.com/business/201701131049547358-china-russia-trade/ (accessed March 13, 2017).

well.[14] In any case, Russian and Chinese analysts have cited political developments in Europe and the United States as well as the decrease in the number of political democracies globally as evidence of a decline in worldwide support for globalization, liberal interventionism, and Western efforts to export what they see as universal political principles.[15]

Security Ties

The Sino-Russian partnership poses more of a military challenge to the United States than to Europe. Neither Russia nor Europe perceives China as a near-term defense threat, while Pentagon planners are very worried about the PLA's military might. Russian and Chinese leaders both see the United States as their main and sole equal strategic rival. Russians view China as an emerging great power partner, while PRC analysts assess Russia as a declining great power. Elites in all three countries see Europe's strategic and economic role in the world as in secular decline, with Asia becoming the most crucial global region in terms of share of the world economy and potential for great power war.

Russian and Chinese analysts denounce U.S.-led military alliances as anachronistic legacies of the Cold War and reflections of an outdated bloc mentality of containing Beijing and Moscow.[16] In the current atmosphere of Russia-U.S. tensions, Russian analysts have depicted U.S. defensive military cooperation in Asia (with South Korea and Japan) warily, expressing concern that Washington is trying to construct the same kind of regional defensive military alliance that the U.S. leads in Europe in northeast Asia in a Pacific version of the NATO alliance.[17] Yet, while Russia has

---

[14] Mansur Mirovalev and Eric Baculinao, "Russia, China See Silver Linings After U.K.'s Brexit Vote," NBC, http://www.nbcnews.com/storyline/brexit-referendum/russia-china-see-silver-linings-after-u-k-s-brexit-n602451?mc_cid=9d77718c87&mc_eid=2529d84389 (accessed February 7, 2017); and François Godement and Angela Stanzel, "China and Brexit: What's In It for Us?," European Council on Foreign Relations, September 9,2016, http://www.ecfr.eu/publications/summary/china_and_brexit_whats_in_it_for_us7112 (accessed March 12, 2017).

[15] Speeches at the 2015 and 2016 sessions of the Valdai Discussion Club, author's notes, October 2015 and October 2016.

[16] See for example Admiral Sun Jianguo, Deputy Chief, Joint Staff Department, Central Military Commission, China, IISS Shangri-La Dialogue 2016 Fourth Plenary Session," June 5, 2016, http://www.iiss.org/en/events/shangri%20la%20dialogue/archive/shangri-la-dialogue-2016-4a4b/plenary4-6c15/jianguo 6391 (accessed February 7, 2017).

[17] Alexander Zhebin, remarks at "Russia and the Korean Peninsula: Policy and Investment Implications," Center for Strategic and International Studies, Washington, DC, May 14, 2015, https://www.youtube.com/watch?v=w2ZCGZBVVrc (accessed February 7, 2017).

vigorously opposed NATO's preeminent role in European security and sought to limit its expansion and weaken transatlantic ties in general, China has simply shunned NATO despite its growing aversion in recent years to the U.S. alliances with Japan and South Korea. Only a stunted China-NATO dialogue has developed to address Afghanistan and other regional issues. However, Russia has traditionally been open to more partnership activities with NATO as an institution than China, which has distrusted the organization since the accidental NATO airstrike against the Chinese Embassy in Belgrade during the Kosovo War. Conversely, Russia has sought to circumvent the EU as an institution and cultivate good relations with key European leaders of various left- and right-wing movements in Europe, whereas the Chinese government has been more comfortable dealing with the EU as an organization as well as dealing with its member governments bilaterally.

The Russian-China arms trade has strengthened China's military capacity directly through the PLA's incorporation of advanced Russian military technologies and Russia's military power indirectly through the revenue provided Russian defense firms, which they reinvest into Russian defense research and development, and by forcing the Pentagon to pay greater attention to Asian military contingencies rather than concentrate more on confronting Russian military power in Europe. U.S.-European defense industrial partnerships have boosted both parties' military capabilities but remain constrained by limited pooling and sharing, a reluctance of European governments to abandon some unprofitable national defense enterprises for economic and political reasons, and barriers to greater U.S. imports of European defense products. Both Russian-Chinese and the European-U.S. defense industrial ties look likely to diminish in importance in future years, albeit for different reasons. In the former case, China's need for Russian military imports is declining due to the improving capacity of the Chinese military-industrial complex. Indeed, PRC arms exports are emerging as more serious competitors to Russian weapons exporters on third markets. Meanwhile, the Trump administration's "buy and hire American" stance threatens to inflict collateral damage on transnational defense industrial ties.

Russia and China have directly affected the U.S. defense budget and the U.S. military commitment to NATO, though this impact is due to the Pentagon's perceptions of growing threats from the two countries independently rather than from their bilateral defense ties. During the two decades after the Cold War, the United States substantially cut its military deployments in Europe due to a determination that the new Russian Federation, whose armed forces were in disarray after the collapse of the Warsaw Pact and integrated Soviet military-industrial complex, did not represent a near-term military threat. Following the U.S.-led military interventions in Afghanistan and Iraq, the Pentagon used Europe primarily as a staging point to project power into Central Asia and the Middle East. U.S. officials pressed European states to deemphasize territorial defense and instead focus on developing power-projection and counterinsurgency assets suitable for fighting insurgents in Afghanistan and dealing with Middle Eastern instability, such as the wars in Iraq and Libya. Meanwhile, during the past decade, U.S. military planners have seen China as a rising defense challenge. A major component of the Obama administration's Pacific Pivot was to rebalance U.S. military power from Europe to Asia. The Russian military intervention in Georgia in 2008 did not appreciably change this approach. It was only Moscow's coercion in Ukraine that led to a reversal of U.S. policy. The last defense budget submitted by the Obama administration was marked by a major increase in spending allocated to countering "higher-end" threats from China but mostly Russia. Of note, the budget supported a major increase in funding for U.S. forces in Europe, which resulted in more American soldiers deployed in NATO countries, a quantitative and quality growth in U.S. military equipment based in Europe, and an improvement in the infrastructure required to reinforce U.S. military power in Europe in a Russia-NATO conflict. The increased capabilities for countering China were mostly in terms of developing new military technologies and defense innovations rather than expanding the current U.S. maritime and other conventional forces in the Pacific.[18] Some NATO and EU members have increased their own military capabilities for such contingencies.

Yet, the advent of the Trump administration could see heightened transatlantic tensions over defense spending increase. One of the first acts of the new administration was to announce that it wanted to greatly increase U.S. defense capabilities. Trump has berated NATO allies for not paying sufficiently for defense and threatened not to protect NATO countries that do not meet their spending obligations. He does not value NATO, the EU, or other transnational institutions in the abstract and only meas-

---

[18] Missy Ryan, "Pentagon Unveils Budget Priority for Next Year: Countering Russia and China," *Washington Post*, February 2, 2016, https://www.washingtonpost.com/news/checkpoint/wp/2016/02/01/pentagon-unveils-budget-priorities-for-next-fiscal-year-countering-russia-and-china/?utm_term=.2a62feec11b8 (accessed February 7, 2017).

ures their worth in terms of their perceived concrete contributions to U.S. security. Potentially divisive to transatlantic ties, Trump has downplayed Russia as a military threat to the United States while describing China as a long-term problem that will persist beyond the defeat of Islamic terrorism. Insofar as this perception shapes U.S. defense spending, the Pentagon will likely return to the early Obama approach of rebalancing U.S. military resources toward the Pacific, especially by building air and naval capabilities to counter China. Current U.S. policy makers also seem more interested in meeting commanders' demand for near-term force size increases (such as more warships) than did Ash Carter's Pentagon. Conversely, the new U.S. policy makers have expressed much less concern about sub-conventional political-military hybrid (also called "grey area") threats than have U.S. allies in Europe and Asia, except for the special case of cyber threats. Under Trump, Europeans could see harsher U.S. demands to increase their own defense spending, renewed calls to prioritize counterterrorism rather than conventional defense forces, less U.S. interest in addressing Russian hybrid threats through preemptively fortifying European societies against such subversion, and a White House that will focus on preparing for possible future fights with China while downgrading near-term Russian-related contingencies.

Implications and Recommendations

The ties between Russia and China do not appear to have given them any appreciable leverage over Europe or even the United States. U.S. officials have tended to downplay the partnership while European officials generally ignored it. However, Trump has faulted U.S. policy for driving Russia and China into aligning against the United States. Some of Trump's team has justified his plans to improve ties with Russia as a means of enhancing U.S. leverage with China, which they see as the more serious long-term economic and security threat. Meanwhile, several recent developments have begun to reduce the negotiating asymmetry between Russia and China, decreasing the advantages Beijing has obtained from the Western sanctions on Russia, the collapse of the cost of Russian commodity exports, and other trends adverse to Moscow since 2014. These include China's need for Russian support to build its Silk Road to Europe, the recent success of pro-Russian political candidates in key Western countries, and Trump's wanting to improve relations with Russia while viewing China as the more serious competitor to U.S. economic and military primacy.

In some cases, Sino-Russian collaboration could arguably benefit Western countries. Having genuine Russian-Chinese cooperation against terrorism, even if only in Eurasia, might prove useful. Greater Russian and Chinese security assistance to the Afghan government and military could allow NATO to redirect its counterterrorism resources to other areas. In recent years, NATO has trained, advised, and equipped the Afghan armed forces with minimal Russian and Chinese help. NATO and the United States may wish to reconsider their stance of shunning direct contacts with the Moscow-led Collective Security Treaty Organization (CSTO), Eurasian Economic Union (EEU), and the Shanghai Cooperation Organization (SCO), where Moscow shares control with China, since these bodies could provide frameworks for securing greater collective burden sharing with Russia and China in Afghanistan and Central Asia.

The proposed merger of the EEU and Beijing's One Belt One Road (OBOR) could increase Sino-European trade and investment (such as for transportation infrastructure), strengthen their regional security cooperation (to preserve stability in the transit countries), and expand people-to-people exchanges between China and Europe.[19] Even without the merger, the OBOR offers Europeans potential economic opportunities, including increased mutual trade and investment with China and other Asian countries as well as Chinese-funded rail, road, and other transportation networks.[20] Yet, European involvement with OBOR could be divisive given Trump's economic nationalism and hostility to China, so will need to be managed carefully.

Strong transatlantic ties give Europeans and Americans an unparalleled comparative advantage over Russians and Chinese. Despite the importance of the Sino-Russian alignment, the greatest near-term impact on transatlantic ties will likely come from the political transformations in the United States and Europe. Obama's Asia pivot made Europeans worry that the United States would neglect their interests. U.S. policy makers had to engage in extensive efforts to reassure them. Now Trump's criticism of NATO, his admiration of Putin, and his confrontationist stance with foreign leaders have reawakened and probably deepened these anxieties.

---

[19] Shaohua Yan, "Why the 'One Belt One Road' Initiative Matters for the EU," *The Diplomat*, April 9, 2015, https://thediplomat.com/2015/04/why-the-one-belt-one-road-initiative-matters-for-the-eu/.

[20] Julie Makinen and Violet Law, "China's Bold Gambit to Cement Trade with Europe—Along the Ancient Silk Road," *Los Angeles Times*, May 1, 2016, http://www.latimes.com/world/asia/la-fg-china-silk-road-20160501-story.html (accessed February 7, 2017).

Americans and Europeans share more political values and human ties than do Russians and Chinese, but the new U.S. president appears to diverge from the liberal democratic principles of the Western community and to share more of the overtly nationalist and illiberal values of the Eurasian autocracies. Trump has blown hot and cold on NATO—describing the alliance as "obsolescent" but still having the potential to make a greater counterterrorism contribution. He has more consistently welcomed the EU's weakening and does not stress special relationship with privileged foreign partners.

Europeans could win favor with Trump by continuing to deny Beijing defense technologies. If Europeans offered to sell arms to China, such sales could increase U.S. anxieties about Beijing's growing military capabilities, furthering perceptions that ungrateful Europeans were sacrificing joint transatlantic security interests in pursuit of commercial opportunities. A repeal could also communicate the wrong signal to China. For example, Beijing could plausibly see the embargo's repeal as Europe being unconcerned about China's human rights practices, its growing military potential, expansive territorial claims, or its self-claimed right to employ military force to recover Taiwan. In return for maintaining the EU embargo on China, Europeans should insist that Washington engage in a robust transatlantic dialogue regarding U.S security policies in Asia that could affect critical European interests.

Despite years of sustained efforts by both governments to promote humanitarian exchanges and the study of the other country's language, popular ties between Chinese and Russians remain minimal. Their political and commercial elites send their children to schools in Europe and the United States rather than to Beijing and Moscow. Western policy makers should promote such societal linkages with emerging Russian and Chinese leaders by making it easier for students, scholars, and tourists from both countries to come to the West and for Europeans and Americans to travel and study in Russia and China.

Chapter 10

Russia–China Relations and the West

Marcin Kaczmarski

U.S. domination in global politics provided a powerful incentive for the post-Cold War rapprochement between Russia and China. The worsening of Russia's relations with the West since 2014 has made Moscow even more willing to offer significant concessions to Beijing. However, closer Russian–Chinese cooperation predates the Russian–Western crisis over Ukraine and reaches back to the 2008–2009 global economic crisis. Even the growing power asymmetry has not dissuaded Moscow from deepening its cooperation with China. This has challenged widespread Western expectations that Russia would be eager to cooperate with the West in order to compensate for China's increasing advantage. Hence, a potential improvement of Russian–Western relations is highly unlikely to result in the weakening of Russian–Chinese ties.

Two long-term factors facilitate close Russia–China cooperation. First, their shared opposition to political values and norms promoted by the West creates a strong bond. Both reject the U.S. claim to primacy and Western domination in the world. Both jealously guard their sovereignty (which both understand as noninterference in domestic affairs) and suspect the West of plotting regime change under the banner of spreading democracy and/or human rights. Second, Moscow and Beijing feel certain that the other side in their duo would not subvert the ruling regime nor criticize the other's domestic political system.

There are three key obstacles to a long-term stable Russian–Chinese alliance. First, Russia and China avoid supporting each other in pursuing territorial claims (Crimea, South China Sea, East China Sea), even though they did lend support to one another regarding territorial integrity in the 1990s and 2000s. Second, Russia and China have differing approaches to economic globalization and diverging assessments when it comes to anti-globalization trends. Third, as a consequence, both states see their contribution to global security and economic governance differently.

The Trump administration's opening towards Russia may, paradoxically, strengthen Russian–Chinese relations rather than weaken them. Better relations with the United States would partially compensate for the increasing power gap between Russia and China. Beijing, in turn, may be more willing to offer concessions to Moscow in order to maintain close cooperation.

The West–Russia–China Strategic Triangle and Its Limitations

U.S. domination in global politics has been a strong incentive for the post-Cold War rapprochement between Moscow and Beijing. U.S. policies pushed both states towards closer cooperation to the extent that pundits came to assume that the dyad was overly reliant on interactions each state had with the U.S. Yet, while the relevance of the American factor for Russia–China relations cannot be underestimated, developments taking place between Moscow and Beijing are not a mere reaction to the United States power and policies. The Ukrainian crisis and the related worsening of Russian–Western relations made Moscow more dependent on China's support and thus more willing to offer concessions to Beijing. However, Russia and China strengthened their cooperation in energy, security and defense, and arms trade prior to the Ukrainian crisis. Shared opposition to Western domination in international politics and fears of "color revolutions" sponsored from abroad provides a long-term foundation for Russian–Chinese cooperation, regardless of the state of their current relations with the West. As a result, potential changes in U.S. or European policies toward either Russia or China can influence the Sino–Russian relationship only to a limited extent.

Russia aims to maintain a diversified foreign policy and wants to avoid dependence on either the West or China (this is a policy direction that has changed little since it was first proposed under the label of a "multi-vector" foreign policy by Yevgeny Primakov in the mid-1990s). Russian rhetoric of seeking an alternative should be regarded as a way of pressuring partners for concessions rather than genuine willingness to reorient its foreign policy to one side (be it the West or Asia/China). Similarly, China aspires to pursue a balanced foreign policy, with the United States, the EU, and Russia treated as key partners (the EU is seen as the major economic partner, Russia the major strategic/political partner).

The role of Europe in West–Russia–China triangle is limited. China sees Europe as the key *economic* partner, and cooperation with Europe is necessary for Beijing to improve its position in the international economic and financial system, and in the realm of global governance. China, does not, however, recognize Europe as a strategic/geopolitical actor of significant relevance. Russia attempts to portray its cooperation with China as leverage it has over the European Union, especially in the energy sphere, but this policy has brought no tangible results.

This chapter examines aspects of Russia–China relations most relevant to the strategic triangle comprising the West, Russia, and China. I first discuss the intensification of Russian–Chinese cooperation, which took place against the backdrop of increasing power asymmetry. I then analyze long-term drivers of Russian–Chinese cooperation and contrast them with what I identify as key obstacles to a stable long-term Russia–China alliance. Finally, I present possible changes in the West–Russia–China strategic triangle and offer recommendations for the West.

Close Russian–Chinese Cooperation Amidst Increasing Power Asymmetry

The most characteristic feature in the Russian–Chinese relationship is the deepening of cooperation between the two states despite the growing asymmetry of power between them. Not only has Russia decided not to balance against China, it has opted for ever-closer cooperation. This has been particularly visible in the energy realm as well as in security and defense spheres.

The Growing Gap in Material Power

Prior to the 2008 financial crisis and ensuing Great Recession, China's GDP was more than two and half times bigger than that of Russia, but both economies grew at an impressive pace, 5–6% and over 10% respectively.[1] Global financial turmoil wreaked havoc on the Russian economy and increased the gap between the two states. Russia suffered a recession from which it has yet to recover; its economy rose around 2% per annum until 2014 when another recession hit. China has managed to maintain high-level growth, even if its pace of growth has decreased. As a result, prior to the Ukrainian crisis, in 2013, China's economy was four times bigger than that of Russia.[2] The fall in oil prices, coupled with Western

---

[1] In 2008 Russia's GDP was $1.6 trillion and China's GDP $4.5 trillion.
[2] Russia's GDP reached the level of $2.1 trillion, while China's skyrocketed to $9.1 trillion.

sanctions following the annexation of Crimea, led the Russian economy into recession. China, meanwhile, maintained its growth level at around 7%. Consequently, by 2016, China's GDP had become 8 times larger than that of Russia.[3] In terms of GDP measured according to purchasing power parity, China's GDP was more than five times bigger than that of Russia.[4]

These differences in economic performance have translated into a growing asymmetry between the two states' military expenditures. In terms of military budgets, China used to spend twice more than Russia on its armed forces (which to some extent can be justified by the fact that the Chinese armed forces are twice the size of their Russian counterparts). In 2008 Russia's military expenditure amounted to $61 billion; China's was $106 billion. In 2013 Russia spent $84 billion on defense, while China spent $171 billion. In 2015, Russia spent $66 billion and China $214 billion, three times as much. Even more important, China's military expenditures increased in absolute numbers but remained below 2% of GDP. In the case of Russia, the increase in the military budget has come at the cost of its rising share in GDP, from 3.3 percent in 2008 to 5.4% in 2015 and 6% in 2016.

These two indicators do not reveal the whole complexity of both states' material power, but they do reflect the key trend: the growing gap in material capabilities. Closer cooperation between Russia and China should be expected to further increase this gap.

Energy Cooperation—The Economic Pillar of Russia–China Relations

Energy cooperation has emerged as the economic pillar of the Russian–Chinese relationship. The combination of infrastructure ties and long-term contracts have made China a major recipient of Russian crude oil. While China maintains a diversified portfolio of oil imports, in 2016 Russia emerged as its number one provider, taking over from Saudi Arabia. Currently Russia sells only minimal amounts of natural gas to China, but the construction of the Power of Siberia gas pipeline will make Russia an important exporter. The pipeline can be expected to go online around 2020 and achieve full capacity 2–3 years later. The existence of a direct

---

[3] Russia's GDP fell to the level of $1.3 trillion, while China's skyrocketed to $11.3 trillion.
[4] In terms of purchasing power parity in 2016, China's GDP was estimated at $21.2 trillion and Russia's GDP at $3.7 trillion (5.72:1 ratio).

overland connection between Russia and China gives a strategic dimension to Russian deliveries of natural resources.

The most important delivery route is the ESPO oil pipeline's branch Skovorodino-Daqing, agreed to in 2008 and initiated in 2011. It binds both states into a long-term commitment. Russia agreed to supply China with oil in return for loans, enduring security of demand and prospects for entering a promising downstream market. At the same time, the ESPO branch to the Pacific coast was intended to guarantee that Russian exports to the Asian market would remain diversified. It was projected that Chinese companies would collect only half of the pipeline's oil in the first stage of its functioning and a little more than one-third following the pipeline's completion in 2018.

However, this formula of energy cooperation evolved further during the early part of this decade. China managed to convince Russia to renegotiate lower prices and to increase the volume of deliveries. In 2013 Russia's Rosneft agreed to a series of new multi-billion dollar contracts with Chinese companies. The Russian company affirmed its readiness to send an additional 10 million tons of oil to China via the Kazakhstani pipeline and agreed to double the amount of oil to be sent to China via the ESPO by 2018. Rosneft signed a contract with a leading Chinese energy company, CNPC, to deliver 15 million tons (300,000 barrels per day) of oil for 25 years, worth up to $270 billion. In addition, both states agreed to build an additional pipeline along the existing Skovorodino-Daqing route, thus doubling the capacity of the pipeline (from 15 to 30 million tons). The pipeline is facing delays on the part of CNPC and its opening will probably be postponed beyond initially planned date of early 2018.

The combination of new contracts and the rise in demand of small Chinese refineries made Russia China's biggest oil supplier. Russia delivered 50 million tons of crude oil, or 1.05 million barrels per day. China purchased—in addition to all of the oil sent via the ESPO branch to Daqing—70% from the ESPO Pacific coast terminal, effectively dominating Russian oil sales to the Asian market.[5]

---

[5] "Russia Emerged as China's Biggest Oil Supplier in 2016, Overtaking Saudi Arabia," Reuters, http://www.reuters.com/article/us-china-economy-trade-crude-idUSKBN1570VJ; "Analysis: China buys 70% of Russian ESPO Cargoes from Kozmino in 2016," Platts, http://www.platts.com/latest-news/oil/moscow/analysis-china-buys-70-of-russian-espo-cargoes-27753440.

Russian–Chinese cooperation in the gas realm has failed thus far to produce as impressive results as those obtained in the oil sphere. In 2013, CNPC joined the Yamal-LNG project, operated by the Russian independent gas producer Novatek, along with the French energy company Total. CNPC acquired a 20% stake in the project, which equates to the production of 3 million tons of LNG, and signed a contract on additional gas deliveries from Yamal-LNG at a level of 3 million tons of LNG. In 2016, Chinese banks provided a $10 billion loan for the project's development.[6] In 2014 Gazprom and CNPC agreed on the construction of the Power of Siberia gas pipeline and signed a 30-year contract on deliveries of 38 billion cubic meters of gas per annum, worth in total $400 billion.

Both the gas pipeline and LNG export from the Yamal project will not be complete before 2020.[7] Nonetheless, the contract binds Gazprom in a long-term perspective to the Chinese market, even more so because the Russian company in practice abandoned its planned LNG project in Vladivostok, which would have given it access to other Asian customers. Given China's soaring gas imports, it is difficult to forecast Russia's share in the Chinese gas market. It will probably remain lower than China's imports from Central Asian states, but it provides China with a direct overland pipeline. Another proposed gas pipeline, Altai, remains Russia's political tool towards Europe and will probably remain on paper.[8]

The major weakness of energy cooperation is the absence of mutual investment in the oil and gas sectors. Chinese companies have not received major shares in Russia's upstream. Russian companies, in turn, do not have access to China's downstream, even though joint projects, such as the refinery in Tianjin, have been discussed over the course of the last decade. This illustrates both states' unwillingness to open up their markets for potential competition and, especially in the case of Russia, makes visible the fears of becoming too dependent on the other side.

---

[6] "Russia LNG Plant Gets $12 Billion From China Amid Sanctions," Bloomberg, https://www.bloomberg.com/news/articles/2016-04-29/russian-lng-project-gets-12-billion-china-loans-amid-sanctions.

[7] "Power of Siberia Gas Pipeline to Start Delivering Russian Gas to China in 2020," Sputnik, https://sputniknews.com/business/201610041045980213-pipeline-siberia-china-gas/; "Gazprom's Power of Siberia Pipeline Set for 2019 Launch," RBTH Asia, http://rbth.com/news/2016/06/14/gazproms-power-of-siberia-pipeline_set-for-2019-launch_602753.

[8] The Altai pipeline would link Russian gas fields with the western parts of China, where it would have to compete with the Central Asian gas. Moreover, delivering Russian gas to eastern parts of China would require additional investment in cross-country pipelines.

The Deepening of Security and Defense Cooperation, and the Revival of Arms Trade

Russian–Chinese cooperation in the realm of security and defense rests on two pillars: joint military exercises and Russian arms sales. Both states started organizing joint land exercises, codenamed *Peace Mission*, in the mid-2000s, but only for the last five years they have been conducted on an annual basis. The exercises are conducted in two formats, either as bilateral Russian–Chinese drills or in a multilateral format under the Shanghai Cooperation Organization framework. Since 2012, Russia and China have begun conducting annual naval drills code-named *Joint Sea/Naval Co-operation*. These exercises took place mostly in the Asian seas, with the exception of one extra drill held in the Mediterranean in 2014. The latest edition, *Joint Sea 2016*, was staged in the South China Sea.

While the exercises have practical purposes, such as practicing joint operations or increasing interoperability, their primary goal is to send a political signal to the West. Joint exercises imply the possibility of both states being able to forge a genuine political-military alliance and help reinforce each state's great-power credentials. The switch in the center of gravity of Russian–Chinese security and defense cooperation from land to sea has met Beijing's strategic needs primarily, and reflected China's increased self-confidence in its security and defense relationship with Russia. China started playing the Russian 'military card' against the United States and American allies in East Asia.

Russian arms sales revived in the early-2010s, following a sharp drop in the mid-2000s. That drop reflected Moscow's disappointment with the scope of Chinese illegal copying of Russian equipment, relative saturation of the Chinese market, as well as overall Russian distrust. The revival resulted partially from technical deficiencies of the Chinese military-industrial complex, which, among other things, turned out to be unable to produce reliable jet engines. Sales reached around $2 billion per annum. Only in 2016, however, did Russia decide to sell China complex weapon systems: the four-plus generation Su-35 fighter jets and S-400 anti-missile systems. Russia reversed its usual pattern of arms sales in Asia, according to which India always obtained slightly better equipment than China. Now, Russia will provide the same class of arms to the two strategic rivals, as India became the second customer for Su-35 and S-400.

This element of Russian–Chinese cooperation can be expected to diminish, however. The Chinese military-industrial complex is becoming self-sufficient, and there are relatively few types of Russian weapons in which China is interested. There is a growing unwillingness on the part of China to maintain its dependence on Russia in terms of military imports. Chinese media boast of the new fifth-generation fighter jet, which is expected to make imports from Russia redundant.[9] It can be expected that servicing of existing Russian equipment in China will replace arms sales in the near future. In order to maintain a high level of cooperation in this sector, Russia and China would have to embark on joint production of weapon systems.

Meanwhile, a common response to U.S. missile defense could emerge as a new element of Russian–Chinese security and defense cooperation. Russia and China have consistently criticized U.S. plans and subsequent deployment of missile defense systems in South Korea. They declared their readiness to coordinate responses, even though still fell short of implementing any practical steps.

Russia's Failure to Implement its Eastern Pivot

Russia's failure to establish itself as an autonomous player in East Asia (mirroring Chinese advancements in Central Asia) limits Russia's possibilities to exert pressure and gain leverage over China. This failure, especially when coupled with China's advances in Central Asia (see the next section), adds to the existing power asymmetry between the two states.

By declaring and implementing a turn to Asia, Moscow wanted to achieve two interrelated goals. First, it sought to make Russia a fully-fledged player in East Asian politics, a *sui generis* third party for the smaller states squeezed between the United States and China. Second it sought to avoid dependence on China in East Asian politics. Behind the pivot was the Kremlin's assumption that Russia was able to become a relevant actor in the East Asian region, in terms of politics, inter-state relations, economic ties, energy deliveries, trade, and investment. By becoming attractive to East Asian states, Russia could also revive its own Far East. There was also an implicit assumption that Russia had tools at its disposal that would make such a shift towards the East possible.

The implementation of Russian ideas in East Asia has, however, lagged behind, and Moscow's policy towards the region has remained Sinocentric.

---

[9] "Air Force Receives Four of Russia's Latest Fighters," *China Daily*, January 6, 2017, http://china.org.cn/china/2017-01/06/content_40049996.htm.

China has maintained its position as Russia's most important trade partner among East Asian states. In 2015 Russian–Chinese trade reached $64 billion, three times as much as Russia's trade with Japan ($20 billion) and four times as with South Korea ($16 billion). The existing infrastructure is mostly bound for China, and China has increased its position as the number one customer for Russian crude oil. China purchases increasing amounts of Russian crude oil, using not only the pipeline to Daqing but also the Pacific terminal, which Russia assumed would serve as a tool of diversification, providing the resources for customers other than China.

Russia's close cooperation with China has seriously limited Moscow's ability to act as an independent player in the East Asian regional order. Sinocentrism has become a major structural obstacle to Russia's turn to the East. Instead of playing a third party role of balancer in the region dominated by China and the United States, Moscow is increasingly supporting Beijing. Russia failed to do in East Asia what China managed to do in Central Asia: become an equal participant in regional politics. As a result, Russia's turn to the East has not transformed the Russian–Chinese relationship in any meaningful way. Moscow has not won leverage over China. On the contrary, one can expect reinforcement of the Sinocentric orientation in Russia's Asia policy, in the form of further support for China in the territorial disputes in the South China Sea.

Reconciliation of Russia and China's Conflicting Interests in Central Asia

Observers of Russian–Chinese relations tend to regard Central Asia as the most probable point of future tensions between Russia and China. Political and economic interests of the two states intersect in this region. Moreover, both are pursuing conflicting regional initiatives: the Eurasian Economic Union (Russia) and the Silk Road Economic Belt (China). Despite far-reaching power shifts in the region, Russia and China have so far demonstrated their ability to reconcile differences over Central Asia. This in turn has reduced the potential for conflict. The two states actively sought to avoid competition and even the U.S. partial withdrawal from Afghanistan—which implies a fading challenge to both states from U.S. political and military presence—has not led to any increase in Russian–Chinese rivalry.

China began to extend its influence in Central Asia after the end of the Cold War, and in the early part of this decade it gained the upper hand, mostly at Russia's expense. The new configuration has been far from optimal for either Moscow or Beijing, but has nevertheless been satisfactory enough to remove Central Asia from China's list of pressing concerns. China has shown strategic restraint and expanded its presence mostly in energy and economic realms. Russia has remained dominant in the sphere of regional security.

China emerged as Central Asia's top economic partner in the late 2000s. It became the region's largest trading partner, the key provider of commercial loans and development aid, and a major investor in Central Asian states' infrastructure. China also gained pre-eminence in the energy sphere. It built a network of gas pipelines and signed a number of long-term contracts on the delivery of gas. The new pipelines deprived Russia of its monopoly on the transit of Central Asian gas. Three states—Turkmenistan, Uzbekistan, and Kazakhstan—could export their production bypassing Russian territory. Second, China locked in Central Asian gas supplies for its own needs, replacing Russia in this role.

Russia and China's influence in the security and defense realm differs significantly. Russian influence rests on four pillars: the presence of troops, the formal alliance in the form of the Collective Security Treaty Organization (CSTO), military-to-military cooperation and military equipment supplies. China, in turn, has no military presence on the ground and it cooperates with Central Asian states within multilateral (SCO) rather than bilateral frameworks. China has shown tangible restraint with regard to the security realm and maintained its practical engagement in security issues at low levels. Bilateral security and defense ties have remained limited and China has not expressed ambitions to deploy its troops in the region or to lease any military facilities. In addition, concern about the possible destabilization of the Central Asian regimes, shared by Russia and China, pushed both states towards cooperation rather than competition. The Central Asian states themselves have facilitated Russia–China relations in the region.

It must be noted that this *sui generis* division of influence takes place in an informal way. Although the creation of Shanghai Cooperation Organization (SCO) reflected the willingness to limit competition, different visions of the organization's future development held by Moscow and Beijing led to a stalemate as early as the mid-2000s. SCO turned out to be incapable of fostering closer economic or political collaboration in Central Asia, except in the internal security sphere, where cooperation is driven by a shared fear of 'color revolutions.' SCO's enlargement to include India and

Pakistan will probably deepen the deadlock rather than generate any genuine cooperation.

Against this backdrop, Russia and China can be expected to reconcile their key regional initiatives, the Eurasian Economic Union and the New Silk Road. Not only do Moscow and Beijing appear to be aware of possible tensions, they undertake steps aimed at lowering this risk. Russia turns out to be unable to prevent China's project from being implemented in Central Asia. China's focus on tangible economic goals, coupled with limited political aims, helps avoid a direct confrontation or open competition. Despite close economic ties, Beijing has not embarked upon political domination of Central Asia. China has framed its project in such terms to prevent Russia's resistance by making it a stakeholder in the New Silk Road. In addition, the implementation and the final shape of Russia's project are far from certain. The Russian project does not offer any explicit concession to China, although it could facilitate China's trade with the bulk of the post-Soviet area by removing trade barriers between the EEU's member states. Moreover, Russia's focus on the symbolic impact of its project can be reconciled with China's economy-focused approach.

Russian and Chinese leaders have recognized the potential for competition. They have been undertaking intentional attempts to reconcile their projects since the Shanghai summit in May 2014, when the two states openly declared their willingness to accommodate the two initiatives. A year later, at the May 2015 summit in Moscow, Russia and China adopted a separate document on the two projects, entitled *Joint Statement on Co-operation in the Construction of the Eurasian Economic Union and the Silk Road Economic Belt*. The two sides declaratively supported one another's projects and China proclaimed its readiness to conclude an agreement on economic co-operation with the EEU. Moscow and Beijing both expressed willingness to co-ordinate their regional efforts and named several priorities, such as trade and investment collaboration, investment facilitation and cooperation on transport infrastructure. The two sides also announced the establishment of a working group, tasked with coordination of the two projects. Although Russia and China recognized the SCO as one of key platforms for coordinating the two projects, the subsequent SCO summit in Ufa in July 2015 brought no further developments in this regard. The working group talks at the level of deputy ministers took place only in late 2015. Still, Russian and Chinese representatives continue to assure that the two projects are not in direct competition with one another.

Long-Term Drivers of Russian–Chinese Cooperation

Regardless of the growing power asymmetry between Russia and China, the two countries are finding greater common ground with regard to opposition towards political norms propagated by the West, and their mutual concern for domestic regime survival.

Shared Opposition towards Western Primacy and Western Political Norms

Russia and China share opposition towards Western primacy in the global order. Both awaited the dusk of U.S. preponderance, and regarded unipolarity as a temporary aberration of international politics. The global economic crisis validated their claims that Western domination of the international order was fading away. Russia and China oppose political values and norms promoted by the West. They guard their sovereignty and suspect the West of plotting regime change under the banner of spreading democracy and human rights. They remain skeptical of the idea of humanitarian intervention, regarding it as a pretext for Western interference. Russia and China stress their special roles and special responsibilities in international politics. Both states believe strongly that the international order is undergoing transformation from Western dominance to multipolarity. They both depict international security as indivisible, which in practice means granting them a veto over the West's decisions, with regard to any potential enlargement of existing military alliances. They defend the central role of the UN Security Council and the UN as a whole.

This similarity of views on global politics has been reflected in Russia and China's cooperation in international fora, in particular the UN Security Council and the UN Human Rights Council. Both states tended to coordinate their positions. They often jointly veto resolutions proposed by the West, especially when such projects envision diplomatic and political pressure, sanctions against regimes violating human rights, or allow for the use of force.

Given the similarity of their views on international politics, Russia and China need each other's support, which cannot be offered by other states. Both states share a great-power identity. Their partners in BRICS—India, Brazil, or South Africa—or among non-Western states cannot offer either Russia or China substantial political support on the international stage. These states fall behind in terms of material (military potential) and institutional (a permanent seat in the UN Security Council) capabilities. Moreover, they often lack determination to challenge or resist U.S. primacy.

Mutual Concern for Regime Survival

The political systems of Russia and China evolved in different ways. Russia's political regime has transformed into a personalized system, while China's has taken on an institutionalized form. What links them is their increasingly non-democratic nature. Vladimir Putin's third presidential term is marked by authoritarian and conservative tendencies. Xi Jinping's first years led to the reversal of certain political reforms in China and to increasing crackdown on any opposition. The similarity of views on international politics presented above is embedded in the non-democratic nature of political systems and reflects underlying fears of regime survival.

Domestic politics is conducive to close Russian–Chinese cooperation in two basic ways. First, the ruling political-economic coalitions in both states support close cooperation and do not regard their counterparts as threatening to their interests. Thus Moscow and Beijing lack domestic incentives to portray the other side as threatening. China's rise undermined neither the Russian domestic balance of power nor the position of the incumbent regime. For most of the key actors able to influence domestic politics, China's rise presented an opportunity rather than a threat. Members of the winning coalition preferred engagement and regarded deeper cooperation with China as favorable to their political and economic interests. Similar process took place in China. Second, neither state threatens the survival of another's political regime. The West, on the contrary, is regarded both in Russia and China as a potential threat to the regime survival.

Key Obstacles to a Russian–Chinese Alliance

Obstacles to long-term stable cooperation between Russia and China include the lack of mutual support for territorial claims, differing responses to economic globalization and anti-globalist movements, and distinct approaches to global governance. These obstacles prevent both states from concluding a fully-fledged alliance.

Lack of Mutual Support for Territorial Claims

In the 1990s, mutual support for sovereignty and territorial integrity was fundamental to forging the post-Cold War relationship between Russia and China. Domestically, China and Russia encountered strong separatist movements fueled by the collapse of the communism and the break-up of the Soviet Union. Internationally, China and Russia felt threatened by Western liberal ideology. Towards the late 2000s, the importance of the territorial integrity issue for the mutual relationship faded away.

In this decade, issues of sovereignty and territorial integrity have taken on a new form. Russia and China began to pursue offensive territorial claims, attempting to secure new territories and redefine the scope of their sovereignty. Russia annexed Crimea from Ukraine and included it into the Russian Federation as two new federal subjects. China has been incrementally increasing effective control over the islands in the South China Sea and embarked upon a program of mass land reclamation. In the East China Sea, Beijing has intensified political and military pressure on Japan over the contested Senkaku (Diaoyu in Chinese) islands. In all of these cases, Russia and China have not supported each other's territorial claims, maintaining what could be termed as "benign neutrality."

China reacted in a reserved way to the annexation of Crimea and Russia's undeclared intervention in Ukraine. Beijing carefully avoided a for-or-against choice, and preferred not to air its opinions. It neither supported Russia openly, nor condemned its actions. Chinese representatives abstained in the UN Security Council and the General Assembly. Beijing explained its neutral position concerning Crimea with reference to specific historic circumstances, but declared support for Ukraine's territorial integrity. In addition, China opposed Western sanctions against Russia. China recognized that Russia's behavior may fuel separatism and rejected the form of Russia's support for Crimean separatism, a declaration by its inhabitants expressed in a referendum. At the same time China considered the Maidan revolution to be a Western-led conspiracy that overthrew the legal government (in a similar way to the "color revolutions" of the mid-2000s). China perceived the protests in Tibet in 2008 and in Xinjiang in 2009, as well as in Hong Kong in 2014, as having been inspired from abroad. From this perspective, Russia's intervention in Crimea was interpreted as a proper response to Western subversion.

In case of the South China Sea, Russia maintained strict neutrality with regard to the territorial disputes. Moscow's position did, however, evolve over the last two years. In terms of rhetoric, Russia declared at several occasions that outside powers should not interfere with the disputes, thus repeating and reaffirming the Chinese position. The *Joint Sea-2016* naval drills took place in the South China Sea. Their scenario envisioned amphibious landing and taking over the islands. As such, Russia's participation in the exercise was a way of subtle support for China's claims. Russia's policy is incrementally moving from strict neutrality to tacit, or even unintentional, support for China's position. Still, in the East China Sea Moscow has managed to stay away from the ongoing Sino–Japanese dispute.

Differing Responses to Economic Globalization and Anti-globalist Movements

Reluctance and resistance towards the West's domination of global politics has fueled Russian–Chinese relations for the past two decades. Yet the responses of Russia and China to anti-globalist movements and global populism differ significantly, as do their long-term expectations related to the future of globalization.

Russia appears to relish the West's internal difficulties, embracing and propping up the populist, anti-globalization turn. The Russian president has depicted globalization as a project in crisis, led by a selfish elite who left the majority impoverished and frustrated. The Russian elite did not hide its satisfaction in Trump's victory in the U.S. election. Russia also cheered the Brexit result and the United Kingdom's decision to leave the European Union, seeing it as the first step to a further unraveling of Europe's post-war political and economic project. Over the years Russia has established a network of contacts with Europe's far right and, to a lesser extent, far left political parties.

China, on the other hand, is emerging as a staunch supporter of globalization, viewing the turmoil in Western political landscape with a mixture of *schadenfreude* and genuine concern. Chinese leaders argued that globalization cannot be blamed for all the world's problems, and warned that a reversal of globalization is unachievable. China has opted for stability and incremental change. Beijing was in favor of the UK remaining in the EU. Having repeatedly declared its support for European unity, China denounced the rise of populist forces throughout Europe. Regarding the US presidential election, voices in China remain divided. State media presented Trump's controversial campaign and his subsequent victory as the ultimate proof of democracy's inherent weaknesses. Although Hillary Clinton was not particularly liked in Beijing due to her contribution to the U.S. "pivot to Asia" policy, her election victory would have brought much more predictability to Sino–American relations.

China needs international stability more than Russia does. China's economic growth—which is the ultimate means of legitimizing the power of the Chinese Communist Party—relies on open trade and stable markets, as well as on the wealth of Western consumers. China needs an external environment conducive to selling its whole range of goods, from low- to high-end, such as high-speed trains, to export the overcapacity of its industry, and to invest its currency reserves. Russia counts on potential chaos beyond its borders as a way of relatively upgrading its position in the international realm. The instability inside the West not only makes it easier to blame the outside world for Russia's own failures, but also helps Russia divide the Western community by cherry-picking potential partners.

This varied attitude towards globalization is also reflected in Russia and China's regional initiatives. For China, the creation of the Silk Road Economic Belt is a way to increase China's ties with a broader world and deepen mutual interdependence. China aspires to reinforce openness generated by globalization and to prevent other powers from building closed regional blocs. China's goal behind the New Silk Road is to foster greater extra-regional integration and offer a new version of globalization. For Russia, the Eurasian Economic Union is a way to fence off the post-Soviet space from global influences and to introduce protectionist measures.

Different Approaches to Global Governance

The differences presented above lead to Russia and China pursuing divergent approaches to global governance. China appears to be genuinely interested in contributing to political and economic stability. Russia aims first and foremost at the symbolic confirmation of its great-power status and does not mind the role of an occasional spoiler.

In the realm of global economic governance, China pursues a dual policy of reinforcing its position in existing institutions and establishing its own parallel institutions. China's share increased both in the IMF and the World Bank. The IMF included the yuan as a reserve currency. At the same time, China established the Asian Infrastructure Investment Bank (AIIB), despite the open opposition of the United States, and convinced a number of American allies from Europe and Asia to join (it is worth noting that Russia and India are among the founding members of the Bank). In the BRICS framework, China supported the establishment of the New Development Bank and the Contingent Reserve Arrangement, which duplicate the functions of the IMF and the World Bank. Making Shanghai the seat of the new bank symbolically confirmed China's leadership within the BRICS.

Russia's role in global economic governance remains marginal. Moscow usually follows China in this realm. China has a sufficient economic basis to upgrade its position within international financial institutions, while Russia is forced to defend its status quo position.

Russian and Chinese approaches to global security governance vary. Russia continues to stand out as the West's major interlocutor and a challenger in the global strategic realm. Moscow compensates for its economic weakness with intensified political activity, particularly with regard to international crises. Russia played the key role in the Iranian nuclear crisis, especially giving support to the 2010 sanctions adopted by the UN Security Council, and in the civil war in Syria. Not only did it prevent the U.S. military intervention in 2013, it was also able to intervene militarily on its own and uphold the regime of Bashar Assad.

China maintains a low profile with regard to international crises, in spite of its growing material capabilities and increasing global ambitions. China's limited engagement in the Syrian civil war illustrates that Beijing tends to acquiesce to Russia's engagement in particular crises, but refrains from active support. China joined Russia several times in vetoing UN Security Council resolutions proposed by the Western states. The Chinese state media presented Russia's military intervention in Syria in a positive way, as a fight against terrorism, but China did not join Russia in the intervention.

At the same time, China has significantly increased its role in multilateral crisis management. Chinese armed forces regularly participate in UN peacekeeping missions, such as Mali or South Sudan. In 2013 Chinese combat troops were deployed in a peacekeeping role for the first time ever. This policy serves the dual purpose of securing economic interests in areas in which Beijing has become engaged and creating the image of a responsible stakeholder. In 2015 China promised to establish a 10-year, $1 billion China–UN peace and development fund, offered $100 million to the African Union for the purpose of establishing a rapid reaction force, and committed itself to the creation of a special police unit of up to 8,000 troops for UN peacekeeping operations.

The fundamental difference in Russia and China's approaches towards global governance illustrates that both states agree on which norms, promoted by the West, they reject (liberal democracy, rule of law, or human rights.) Russia and China do not, however, agree what alternative norms they would like to promote instead. China aims to support globalization and the openness of global markets, as it has been a major beneficiary.

The West's Possibilities to Influence the Relationship

Russia's cooperation with China remained an important element of Moscow's policy towards the West. Close ties with Beijing prevented Russia's isolation by the West after the Ukraine crisis and helped partially offset economic losses. Russia's conflict with the West strengthened its relations with China as well as weakened Moscow's bargaining position toward Beijing, and made it even more willing to grant concessions to Beijing. The underlying trends, however, had been in place well before the sanctions; the key oil contract was signed in 2013. This implies that even if Russian–Western relations improve, the intensity of Russia's cooperation with China will not necessarily decrease.

Russia attempted to switch sides after the terrorist attacks against the United States in 2001. After 9/11 Moscow put aside its previous cooperation with China and embraced the prospects of a strategic partnership with the United States. The subsequent failure made Russia more cautious towards Washington. The Russian–American reset (2009–2011) included a new nuclear disarmament treaty, redrawing of U.S. missile defense plans, and the reduction of political support for post-Soviet states. But during that period Russian–Chinese relations did not deteriorate—on the contrary, Russia intensified its cooperation with China.

Following the annexation of Crimea, Russia needed to demonstrate its good relations with China to the United States. This weakened Moscow's bargaining position towards Beijing and prompted Moscow to make concessions.

The scenario in which the United States reaches out to Russia, trying to appease it, while it is confronting China, is probable. But the Trump administration's opening towards Russia may paradoxically strengthen the Russian–Chinese relationship by balancing China's upper hand over Russia and strengthening Moscow in its dialogue with Beijing. Fearing Russia's defection, China may turn out to be more eager to offer some concessions. Thus the improvement of Russian–American ties may strengthen Moscow's position vis-à-vis Beijing. There are, however, scarce indications that the United States would be able to seriously undermine the Russian–Chinese relationship.

The potential influence of Europe on the Russian–Chinese relations remains limited. In case the European sanctions against Russia are lifted, Moscow's position vis-à-vis Beijing will improve. But, similarly to potential alterations in U.S. policy, this does not need to result in a weakening of Russian–Chinese ties. It can rather be expected to diminish the scope of the Russian–Chinese power gap. At the same time, numerous factors prevent Russia and China from transforming their relationship into a fully-fledged alliance.

Common Recommendations for the United States and the EU

It will be difficult, if not impossible, for either the United States or the EU to weaken the long-term foundations of Russian–Chinese cooperation. As the two states reject Western political norms and suspect the West of interference in what they deem to be their domestic affairs, even cooperative policies can be insufficient. At the same time, the United States and the EU should exploit existing differences between Russia and China with regard to global governance and economic globalization.

From the Western perspective, China is a more cooperative partner in global governance, both in terms of economy and security. Given China's pragmatic interest in global and regional stability as well as its support for the existing economic order, China's upper hand in its relationship with Russia is potentially beneficial for the West. China may turn out to have more influence than Western states have over Russia, and thus mitigate to some extent Moscow's assertive behavior. The United States and the EU should avoid efforts to balance the Russian–Chinese relationship by strengthening their relations with Russia. Instead, the West should take advantage of China's interest in international stability and direct economic gains it receives from open global economy, and reinforce their cooperation with China on these issues. Engaging with China's international initiatives, such as the Belt and Road Initiative, offers the West an opportunity to genuinely influence Beijing's foreign and economic policies.

Consistent Western opposition to the annexation of Crimea and support for Ukraine's territorial integrity correspond to China's unwillingness to recognize Crimea as part of the Russian Federation. A change in Western policy towards accommodating the Kremlin's demands could lead China to reconsider its policy and to openly support Russia's aggressive policy in the post-Soviet space. This, in turn, could push Russia to support China's territorial demands in the East and South China Seas. Thus, it seems of particular relevance that the United States and the EU maintain the policy of not recognizing territorial annexations and territorial claims, either of Russia or of China.

Recommendations for the United States

Russia's foreign policy remains diversified—the Kremlin aims to avoid dependence on *any one* external partner, be it the United States, Europe, or China. It is thus highly unlikely that Russia would seriously limit its engagement with China, even if the United States improved its relations with Russia. On the contrary, a Russian–American grand bargain is more likely to strengthen Russia's hand in dealings with Beijing and thus reinforce, rather than weaken, Russian–Chinese relations. Similarly, the worsening of American–Chinese relations would also strengthen Russia, making it a more relevant partner from China's perspective.

Recommendations for the EU

While China does not regard the EU as a relevant strategic actor, it is nonetheless interested in close economic cooperation with Europe. In particular, China has a stake in the success of the New Silk Road initiative and in the smooth functioning of the land corridors linking its economy with the EU. As the shortest route goes through Russia, stable and cooperative Russian–European relations are of value for Beijing. The EU could use China's interest in the stability of trade and transit in order to mitigate Russia's assertiveness.

Russia has limited options to switch its gas sales from Europe to China, especially given China's lack of interest in the implementation of the *Altai* gas pipeline project. Thus there is little reason for the EU to bend down under Russia's threats to redirect its gas export away from Europe, even if Russia increases its gas exports to China.

Chapter 11

The Struggle for the Hearts and Minds of Russians

András Simonyi

In the 25 years since the collapse of communism, Russia has not changed as much as the perception of Russia in the West as a whole has changed. It is a country that shows traces of modernity, for those favored few wealthy enough to afford it, but as a whole Russia remains feudal in its social and economic system, and keeps most of its population stuck in the past. Americans and Europeans alike must also understand that Russia will never be a friend or an ally that shares strategic interests with the West as long as this feudal autocratic-kleptocratic system prevails. The Western value-based democratic system of checks and balances poses the same threat to the present Russian autocratic system as it posed to the communist system. But what have we done to build a different kind of a relationship?

It is timely and useful to dust off the books about Stalinism, about Brezhnev's Soviet Union, the many studies about how the KGB operates, and about Mikhail Andreyevich Suslov, the chief ideologue of the Communist Party of the Soviet Union. Consult those still-living experts from the former Communist bloc who endured almost five decades of Soviet rule. Otherwise, we will never understand the subtleties of Russian power, Russian social and intellectual diversity, and the ever-more complicated relationship between the people and their rulers.

Some simplistically choose to explain the difficulties of understanding Russia by over-emphasizing the Russian soul, *russkaya dusha*. It is often stated that the Russian soul is impossible to understand, it is something esoteric. There isn't anything esoteric about the Russian soul. What they call the "Russian soul" is just the reflection of centuries of socio-political and cultural developments. But we should not deceive ourselves by suggesting that the Russian people are not ripe for Western-style democracy and freedom. That is the wrong question. The right question is: why did Russia miss the opportunity of a millennium to catch up with lost time, to leapfrog to fast track development and modernization? Why is it that they still yearn for the strong leader without checks and balances? Why is it that we should all just accept the fact that illiberal democracy is the right kind of system for Russia? Explaining this all away because of the Russian soul is much too easy and much too shallow.

In the Soviet Union people yearned for the West. America was the beacon on the hill for Russian elites and the general public alike. The West was admired, copied and emulated. How have we, in a matter of just 25 years, arrived at a situation where the West is despised and hated? Or is it really? Maybe it's just that we have a lot less access to Russian society than we had during the dark days of the Soviet Union. Maybe it is because we have lost touch with Russian society. Maybe it is because we have allowed hundreds of thousands of personal contacts and relationships wither. Maybe it is because the West, in its greed and complacency, focused so much on the peace dividend of the 1990s that it took for granted the transformation of the dictatorial Soviet Union into a market-based democracy. And perhaps we thought that the Russia box had been checked, and that we needed no further investments in its people.

When we contemplate the future of Russian-Western relations, it is an enormous task to understand the reasons we got to this place, to find points of access to penetrate this seemingly impenetrable new Russia, to design strategies and build a not-so-soft-soft-power toolbox to work with. But it is not impossible, and it is also absolutely necessary in order to complement our strategic and economic baskets.

The Current Non-influence of Western Soft Power in Russia

After the fall of communism the West made the same mistake the Russians made during communism: they imposed an ideology rather than values and good practices. Free market liberalism was introduced to a country whose elites and general population were totally unprepared for it. Imposing a liberal market economy on a country with zero experience in democracy had catastrophic results. The West missed an opportunity by not launching a magnanimous Marshall plan for defeated Russia, which would have tied it to our world in the same way it tied the Western part of (defeated) Nazi Germany to the democratic West.

The West wasted the incredible goodwill and potential it had at the outset of the 1990s, a mistake and deficit from which we will never in our lifetime be able to recover. Establishing a fast track liberal democracy in Russia was doomed to fail from the start. The world, including Russia, had a unique historic chance to turn an enemy into a partner, to change its perception of itself. There was a window for Russia to modernize, to give itself a chance to be something it had rejected time and again throughout history. But the change Russians were yearning for came as an alien force imposed from abroad. It came too fast, hit Russia too hard, with pressures too big, with an air of superior arrogance. Russians were hurt where the hurt would hit the hardest—their self-esteem. This led to the loss of confidence in the West. Our goodwill capital was squandered.

Transition is hard, and the West did not make it easier. The new era had few positive consequences for the average Russian. Unknowingly, the West destroyed every valuable asset created during the Cold War. In the 1950s, 1960s, 1970s, and all the way up to 1989, the West, the United States, Western Europe, and other prosperous Western democracies, were the envy and standard bearer for a better life for Russians. The way of life, the freedoms, the quality of life, personal and community security, and the perspective of life lived well attracted millions and millions of Russians to the West.

Famously in the 1960s, when Beatlemania hit the world, the West gained an incredibly powerful tool of unintentional influence in Eastern Europe, including the Soviet Union. It was Western soft power at its best, because hundreds and hundreds of rock and roll bands would gain the respect and adoration of young Soviet citizens. They saw the West through the lens of rock. John Lennon and Paul McCartney did not look like the bureaucrats in the Kremlin, or the caricature of the ugly capitalist with a cigar hanging from his mouth that they knew from Soviet-Russian propaganda. Listening to Western rock and roll bands was a way of protesting the dull life in communist Russia. Soviet youth would emulate their peers in the West, would illegally fabricate electric guitars, and their devotion and eagerness to join the ranks of the West by playing rock and roll music could not be stopped by the KGB, the Komsomol, or the Party. In spite of the communist regime meting out the most serious of punishments, including imprisonment and years in the Gulag, the onslaught of Western soft power could not be stopped.

Filmmakers from Andrei Tarkovsky to Mikhail Kalatozov and Sergej Bondarchuk were looking for appreciation and acknowledgement from their peers in Hollywood, Rome or Paris. Hollywood was the standard bearer. Scientists seized any chance to communicate with their colleagues in Western universities. Artists wanted to be exhibited in the MoMa, the Centre Pompidou, or the Louisiana.

Then there were the products from the West. Western products were never just products. They were the symbols of a different world, a better life. Levi's jeans lived their own lives behind the Iron Curtain. Unbeknownst to its producers in San Francisco, in Russia they were worn not only as a reflection of style but as a sign of ideological discontent. It was a statement of where one belonged, or rather where one was longing to belong. Even party bureaucrats would want to own a pair. The same was true with other western products: a bar of quality soap, a nice perfume, a silk scarf or tie were all reflections of a desire for a better life, a sense of belonging. When VCRs and satellite television were invented, they became a drug, and the onslaught of Western movies was unstoppable even if, for an individual, it meant taking risks and surmounting major obstacles to obtain them.

The West helped distribute samizdat, indigenous and Western forbidden literature, thus making its support credible and sincere. The credibility of media outlets like Radio Free Europe, the Voice of America, the BBC, and other Western radio stations, transmitting in Russian, was strengthened by everything else Western. Without these unintentional tools of Western soft power, Western media would have just been considered propaganda.

Yes, this was a war, and it was a cutthroat competition for hearts and minds, which the Soviets were losing in stunning fashion. On one side there was credibility. On the other there was an army of Russian propagandists, censors, political police, and harsh sentencing with the goal of stopping people from listening to western radio stations, and most importantly, to stop emulating the West. Of course nothing could stop these millions of Soviet citizens. BBC, VOA, and RFE were considered credible, not just about the world but also about their own internal situation. No one believed what was written in *Pravda*. They all asked: what did the BBC, Radio Free Europe or Voice of America say about this or that? When the Chernobyl catastrophe occurred, Russians did not go to Russian sources to find out what really went on at the meeting of the Politburo. They never believed the state-run television or the radio stations or Pravda. Instead they were huddled around their small transistor radios to find out the truth. The West commanded respect.

When the West took sides with the political opposition in Eastern Europe, in Poland, Czechoslovakia, or Hungary, or indeed the Soviet Union, the citizens of these countries never doubted that the West was on their side and that it was the right side. There was no credibility issue.

Russia's Soft Power: Weapons of Mass Disruption!

Russia, including those tedious years when it went as the Soviet Union, always viewed power differently than the West. Western soft power was deployed not just by governments, but by non-governmental, independent platforms as well: social organizations, NGOs, individuals acting on their own, artists, writers, and the private sector, among others. Soviet communist propaganda was centralized, the content determined by the aforementioned Comrade Suslov and his predecessors and petty bureaucrats under him. There was always a huge bureaucratic infrastructure employed since the bloody birth of Communism in 1917, during 70 years of communism, and all the way up to Gorbachev's perestroika. With only a short respite in the late 1980s and the messy Yeltsin era, propaganda resumed with a vengeance. Vladimir Putin understood the force, he also understood that soft power is a misnomer: it is certainly hard on impact. But once he was done with occupying the centers of power, airwaves, pushing down unfriendly oligarchs and replacing them with his own friends, lining his own pockets with money, he turned on the West. And by portraying the West as the world's worst bogeyman, he managed to enshrine himself as the great savior.

Lessons learned from the last ten years are many. First, the West—if indeed it ever was a common entity in this century—never took the Russian threat seriously until the invasion of Ukraine. Even then, many Western governments deluded themselves into thinking that this was a one-off and that other countries would be insulated. How wrong they were!

Second, Western capitals, including Washington, Berlin, Paris, and Rome, did not understand the underlying Russian strategy: to reverse the fragile transitions to democracy in eastern Europe, to drive a wedge between East and West, and to disrupt the U.S.-Europe relationship.

In many ways, the hard power and the so-called soft power aspects weighed equally. The efforts to disrupt the democratic institutions of individual countries, including the United States, is nothing new. It is taken from an old playbook. But now Russia has embraced and retooled new technologies to fit its own narrative of the world, and this is a game changer. They got smarter. The internet, Facebook, Twitter, etc., once heralded as the ultimate medium of democratization (see the Western naïveté of the Facebook revolutions of the Arab Spring), has been turned against us. In the hands of Russian agencies, all these amazing gadgets have turned into formidable weapons of mass disruption. Russia Today

(RT) has only a relatively small Western audience, but the disturbing fact is that it is broadcast side by side with ABC, FOX, CNN, or NBC on many university campuses, 24/7. The untrained and very naïve eye will be confused. It is Russia that invented fake news: news based on real events, false facts. They have also learned their lesson from the past. Even a trace of Russian accent will spoil the whole message. Americans and British nationals employed by RT (yes, please call them traitors) give the fake, distorted news, aka, propaganda a totally different level of credibility.

Russia can count on anti-American sentiment in Europe, where significant parts of the cultural and political establishment and huge numbers of a disoriented population see America as the bigger danger to democracy. That is not new. The launch of super-weapon Snowden was a stroke of a genius on behalf of Vladimir Putin, on a par with Hitler's communication evil genius Goebbels, which not only damaged the immune system of the West, but also, cleverly, managed to divide Europe and America. One wonders why Americans and Europeans are now surprised at the efforts by Russia to influence democratic elections in America, Germany, and in defenseless Hungary, Macedonia, and Montenegro.

Speaking of not-so-soft Russian soft power, communications is certainly not the only tool. Economics, in particular energy, is as worrying, if not a lot more worrying, in the long run. While Russian communications soft power is annoying, economic influence, and in its wake corruption in the institutionally weaker and vulnerable parts of the West, can turn democracies into illiberal regimes and benign or not-so-benign dictatorships. Hungary's disastrous turnaround from being a cheerleader to a sad little autocracy is a case in point. Nothing has done more to keep the onslaught of Viktor Orban's illiberal regime than his cozy relationship with Russia, cementing his reign and Hungary's energy dependence on Russia for decades to come. And all of this was accomplished with a great degree of cynicism on the part of the European Union. But Hungary is not alone: infiltrating corporations, going on a buying spree to obtain Western assets, real estate, even influencing whole banking systems has become a powerful tool for Russia, an investment in the future.

Reinventing Not-So-Soft Soft Power: What Is To Be Done?

The pushback starts at home. Declaring how angry we are, drawing red lines, but doing nothing when they are crossed, will not suffice. The West needs to build its defenses and fight back against the Russians and

Russian active measures, rather than fight each other. A common Western approach is needed. As long as the Russians are only a pretext, a proxy in the war between Democrats and Republicans, the Europeans and Americans, Putin will have the upper hand.

The West has sheepishly shut down or scaled back its institutions of influence: Radio Free Europe, Voice of America, and BBC have left the field to one player in Russia. We told human rights activists to fight, and when things got bad, we just left, leaving them not just exposed but helpless. Never do that again! Americans have their share of responsibility for these failures, but Europeans are a lot worse. There is today almost nothing on the ground to help deploy thoughts, to help disseminate proper information about ourselves, our realities. We have not given serious thought, and certainly no serious financial support, to using 21st century technology to get our own message through. We have ceded control of our narrative to Putin, who has created his own image of the West as a bunch of depraved people with no moral code intent on wrecking the very fabric of Russian society. We never cared much about our image in Russia in the last 25 years. We were distracted by the adoration of soft power as if it was the secret potion, which will do its magic on its own. Don't blame it on the theory, blame it on complacent politics.

Once our own defenses are in place, we should move to push back on Putin at home. Almost nothing has been done in the last 25 years to regain some influence on the mindset of Russian elites, Russian society at large and the Russian people themselves. During the last 25 years we have never engaged in a serious and strategic exercise to rethink and launch a war of thoughts. We have been terrible at explaining to Russians (let alone to our own people) that democracies do better economically, socially, in the quality of life and global influence in general. We never engaged in a serious intellectual exercise to define the 21st century message of democracies.

We have two major targets. First we must seek opportunities to engage with Russian political, scientific, and cultural elites. The thousands of Russians spending time in the most wealthy neighborhoods of Europe, on the French Riviera in the Swiss Alps, and the most expensive neighborhoods of London, New York, Berlin, Budapest, or Vienna do not make up for real and deep contacts with Russia's elite. They are just the extended arm of the regime. We have been blinded by surrogates for Vladimir Putin. We need to find ways to reverse the trends and broaden our concept of the elite, to include much more than the super wealthy and Putin's willing servants. We need to reconnect with artists, scientists, inventors, engineers, city planners, architects, university professors, students in a big way; the ones who yearn to be appreciated by the West, the next generation of the Yuriy Gagarins and Sergey Magnitskys.

New means of communication are at our disposal, which need to be selective and diversified. Russia is a strange construction of world-class elites, a cosmopolitan Moscow and St. Petersburg, and a few other big cities. The rest, the majority of the country's population, live in poverty and in isolation, both physically and mentally. A striking number have never had internet access. These people's thoughts focus on survival, nothing else, and at this point we have not the slightest idea how to address them. Russia is not the Soviet Union, however 70 years of communist domination over the minds of people has left its mark, has become part of their genetic code. But then, we have no clue what their true issues are. We don't even know the extent of their disdain for Putin. We must assume, that in the confines of their small kitchens, behind closed doors, they curse Putin as much as they cursed Brezhnev. And they too need to be reached.

What rock and roll music did to promote ideals of freedom and democracy to the Russians during the Cold War cannot be repeated. Rock and roll in this case is only a metaphor. We need to invent new tools and content that touch the imagination of the Russian people. It is time to make them understand that we, the West, are not part of the problem causing their crushing poverty and less-than-developed country status. We are part of the solution.

We need to put our best minds in foreign affairs to find new attractive ways to get our message through that the individual citizen matters for the future of society. Bring our best practices to the Russian people. Learn from the enormous success of America's fight against cancer, a disease decimating Russians. Bring the American Race for the Cure to Moscow. And be stubborn in letting Russians know that Sergey Magnitsky was a hero who tried to cure another form of cancer killing Russia: corruption. We must reach the young and smart, let them know that their future lies in embracing modernity. And communicate, communicate and communicate. This must be a truly transatlantic endeavor: Europe and America needs to hold hands in pursuing the goal of getting our message through to Russians.

We ourselves have allowed a bottleneck to be created. Presently the West communicates only through Putin and his surrogates. One wonders where all those networks of the past have gone. Where are the myriad contacts which were so enthusiastically established during the good times of perestroika, during the early days after the fall of the Soviet Union?

It is time for a fresh start. It is time to understand that it is all about the *hearts and minds* of people.

About the Authors

Daniel S. Hamilton is the Austrian Marshall Plan Foundation Professor and Founding Director of the Center for Transatlantic Relations at Johns Hopkins University's Paul H. Nitze School of Advanced International Studies (SAIS). From 2002-2010 he served as the Richard von Weizsäcker Professor at SAIS. From 2001-2015 he also served as Executive Director of the American Consortium for EU Studies. He has held a variety of senior positions in the U.S. Department of State, including Deputy Assistant Secretary for European Affairs; U.S. Special Coordinator for Southeast European Stabilization; Associate Director of the Policy Planning Staff for two U.S. Secretaries of State; and Director for Policy in the Bureau of European Affairs. In 2008 he served as the first Robert Bosch Foundation Senior Diplomatic Fellow in the German Foreign Office. He is or has been an advisory board member for a dozen U.S. and European foundations and think tanks. He has authored over 100 articles, books and other commentary on international affairs, and has also taught at the Hertie School of Governance in Berlin, the University of Innsbruck and the Free University of Berlin. From 1990–1993 he was Senior Associate at the Carnegie Endowment for International Peace and from 1982–1990 Deputy Director of the Aspen Institute Berlin. He has a Ph.D and MA with distinction from Johns Hopkins University SAIS. Recent publications include (with Stefan Meister, eds.) *The Eastern Question: Russia, the West, and Europe's Grey Zone* (2016), and *Eastern Voices: Europe's East Faces an Unsettled West* (2017).

Stefan Meister directs the Robert Bosch Program Center for Central and Eastern Europe, Russia, and Central Asia at the Robert Bosch Center of the German Council on Foreign Relations (DGAP). Previously he worked as a senior policy fellow on the European Council on Foreign Relations' Wider Europe Team and as a senior research fellow at the DGAP (2008–13). He has been engaged in research and work on Russia and the post-Soviet countries for nearly 20 years. He is a member of the Valdai Club, the Yalta European Strategy and the Astana Club and was Fellow at the Transatlantic Academy on Russia in 2015/16. His areas of focus include Russian domestic, foreign, and energy policy; Ukraine and Belarus; EU-Russia relations; and Russia's policy toward post-Soviet countries. He has served several times as an election observer for the OSCE in post-Soviet countries and was responsible for educational projects in Russia. In 2003–04 he was researcher-in-residence at the Center for International Relations in Warsaw, analyzing Polish Eastern policy. He earned his doctorate at the University of Jena and holds an MA in political science and East European history. His Ph.D thesis was on the "Transformation of the Russian Higher Education System." He recently edited a volume on Russia's policy towards post-Soviet countries (with Nomos Verlag), and he writes extensively on Germany's Russia policy, conflicts in the post-Soviet region (especially the South Caucasus), the interrelationship between Russian domestic and foreign policy, as well as on the EU's Eastern Partnership. In 2014 he was part of the steering committee that drafted a new German Russia policy for the planning staff of the German Foreign Office. Recent publications include (with Daniel S. Hamilton, eds.) *The Eastern Question: Russia, the West, and Europe's Grey Zone* (2016) and *Eastern Voices: Europe's East Faces an Unsettled West* (2017).

Vladislav Inozemtsev is a Russian economist and director and founder of the Center for Post-Industrial Studies in Moscow, a nonprofit institution that specializes in organizing conferences on global economic issues and publishing books. He is a professor and the chair at the Department of World Economy, Faculty of Public Governance, Moscow State Lomonosov University. He served as the 2016-2017 Austrian Marshall Plan Foundation Fellow at the Center for Transatlantic Relations at Johns Hopkins SAIS. He has also served as a senior visiting fellow at the Institute for Human Sciences in Vienna, the Center for Strategic and International Studies and the Atlantic Council in Washington, DC, and the German Council on Foreign Relations DGAP in Berlin. He has taught at various universities, including MGIMO (the University of International Relations) and at the Higher School of Economics in Moscow. From 2002 to 2009, he was head of the Scientific Advisory Board of the journal *Russia in Global Affairs*. In 2011, he was managing director of the Global Political Forum, organized in Yaroslavl under the authority of then-President Dmitry Medvedev. He is the author of over 600 printed works on contemporary issues.

Marcin Kaczmarski is the Head of the China-EU Program at the Center for Eastern Studies (OSW) in Warsaw, and Lecturer at the Institute of International Relations at the University of Warsaw. He was a Visiting Researcher at the Slavic-Eurasian Research Center, Hokkaido University in 2017 and a Taiwan Fellow at Chengchi University in 2016. In 2012-2013 he was a visiting scholar at Aberystwyth University and between 2006-2012 served as an analyst in the Russian Department at the Centre for Eastern Studies. He is the author of many published works, including *Russia-China Relations in the Post-Crisis International Order* (2015).

Mark N. Katz is Professor of Government and Politics at George Mason University. Before starting to teach at George Mason University in 1988, he was a research fellow at the Brookings Institution (1980-81), held a temporary appointment as a Soviet affairs analyst at the U.S. Department of State (1982), was a Rockefeller Foundation international relations fellow (1982-84), and was both a Kennan Institute/Wilson Center research scholar (1985) and research associate (1985-87). He has also received a U.S. Institute of Peace fellowship (1989-90) and grant (1994-95), and several Earhart Foundation fellowship research grants. He has been a visiting scholar at the King Faisal Center for Research and Islamic Studies (Riyadh, May 2001), the Hokkaido University Slavic Research Center (Sapporo, June-July 2007), the Higher School of Economics (Moscow, March 2010), the Middle East Policy Council (Washington, DC, September 2010-January 2011), the Arab Gulf States Institute in Washington (January-March 2017), and the Finnish Institute of International Affairs (April-September 2017). He is the author of many books, including *Leaving without Losing: The War on Terror after Iraq and Afghanistan*.

Andrey Kortunov has been Director General of the Russian International Affairs Council (RIAC) since 2011. He has led several public organizations involved in higher education, social sciences and social development, such as the Moscow Public Science Foundation (1993–2001); the Information, Scholarship, Education Center (2002–2017); and the New Eurasia Foundation (2004–2017). He has been the President of the New Development Technologies Autonomous Non-profit Organization since 2015. In 1982–1995, he held various positions in the Institute for U.S. and Canada Studies, including Deputy Director. He has taught at universities around the world, including the University of Miami, Lewis and Clark College in Portland, Oregon, and the University of California, Berkeley. He is the author of over 120 publications dedicated to the analysis of Soviet/Russian-American relations, global security, and the foreign and domestic policy of the USSR and Russia. He graduated from the Moscow State Institute of International Relations (MGIMO) in 1979 and completed his postgraduate studies at the Institute for U.S. and Canada Studies of the USSR Academy of Sciences in 1982. He holds a Ph.D in History.

Nikolay Kozhanov is a Senior Lecturer in Political Economy of the Middle East at the School of Economics of St. Petersburg State University. He also works as an expert at the Institute of the Middle East in Moscow. He has served as a visiting fellow with The Washington Institute for Near East Policy and Academy Associate at Chatham House in London. During

2006-2009 he worked as an attaché at the Political and Economic Section of the Russian Embassy in Tehran, where his responsibilities included the analysis of socio-economic developments in Iran. He holds a Ph.D in international economics and economic security from St. Petersburg State University.

Mikhail Krutikhin is a partner of RusEnergy, a Moscow-based independent consulting agency. He holds a Ph.D in modern history and since 1993 has been analyzing the oil and gas industry in the former USSR, providing advisory services to investors.

Fyodor Lukyanov is editor of *Russia in Global Affairs* and a research professor at Russia's national research university, the Higher School of Economics, in Moscow. He is chairman of the Presidium of the Council on Foreign and Defense Policy, research director of the Valdai International Discussion Club, and member of the presidium of the Russian International Affairs Council. He has an extensive background in different Russian and international media as a commentator on international affairs. He was senior editor of the Department for Broadcasting to Northern Europe of International Radio Moscow (now Radio Sputnik), correspondent at the international desk of *Segodnya* newspaper, editor of the international desk of *Vremya MN* newspaper and deputy editor-in-chief of *Vremya Novostei* newspaper.

Andrey Movchan is a senior fellow and director of the Economic Policy Program at the Carnegie Moscow Center. His research focuses on Russia's economy, the Eurasian Economic Union, and the future of Russia's economic relations with the EU. He has been a top executive for Russian and international financial institutions since 1993. He was an executive director of the Troika Dialog for six years. From 2003 to 2009, he headed the Renaissance Investment Management Group, which he founded, and from 2006 to 2008, he was the CEO of Renaissance Credit Bank. He also founded the Third Rome investment company, and was its CEO and managing partner from 2009 until the end of 2013. He is one of Russia's best known financial managers. He was named "the most successful CEO of an asset management company in Russia" by *Forbes* in 2006 and "the best CEO of an asset management company" by the Russian magazine *Finance* in 2008. His op-eds and commentary regularly appear in the media. He won two PRESSzvanie business journalism awards in 2011 and 2013.

Lyubov Shishelina is Head of the Section of Central and Eastern Europe Studies at the Institute of Europe of the Russian Academy of Sciences. In 2006 she also established the Visegrad Research Center – the only Russian analytical center specializing in the studies of the region. For 10 years she served as Professor at the Chair of Foreign Policy and International Relations at the Russian State University of Humanities and at the Chair for Social Sciences at Hungarian János Kodolányi University College. Currently she is Honorary Professor at this University and since 2015 a member of the Foreign Corps of the Hungarian Academy of Sciences. In 2010 she was awarded the Knight's Cross of the State Order of Hungary. Since 1994 she is a permanent chair of the International scientific conference "Russia and Central Europe in the new Geopolitical Realities," the author of seven monographs and more than 200 articles, and the editor-in-chief of a series of books on relations between Russia and Central Europe, as well as the editor of the annual Visegrad issue of the Russian Academy of Science's scholarly magazine *Modern Europe*. She holds a doctorate in history.

András Simonyi is the Managing Director of the Center for Transatlantic Relations at the School of Advanced International Studies at Johns Hopkins University in Washington D.C. He served as Hungary's Ambassador to NATO and to the United States. He was a key player on behalf of his country in preparing for the Dayton agreement and for the stationing of US/SFOR and US/IFOR troops in Hungary. His focus is on transatlantic security and business, democratic transition, and human rights. He is a contributor to the *Huffington Post*, *The Hill* and is a commentator on *Newsmax* on Russia, Ukraine, the EU and human rights. He holds a Ph.D in Political Science.

Richard Weitz is Senior Fellow and Director of the Center for Political Military Analysis at the Hudson Institute, a nonpartisan research organization based in Washington, DC. Before joining Hudson in 2005, he worked for shorter terms at the Institute for Foreign Policy Analysis, Center for Strategic and International Studies, Defense Science Board, Harvard University, and the U.S. Department of Defense. He has authored or edited several books and monographs, including *Promoting U.S.-Indian Defense Cooperation* (2017); *Enhancing the Georgia-US Security Partnership* (2016); *Parsing Chinese-Russian Military Exercises* (2015); and *China and Afghanistan After the NATO Withdrawal* (2015). He holds a Ph.D in political science from Harvard University.